# 15 Great Austrian Economists

Edited with an Introduction
by Randall G. Holcombe

Ludwig von Mises Institute
Auburn, Alabama

**COVER PHOTOGRAPHS**

1. Murray N. Rothbard
2. Frank A. Fetter
3. Frédéric Bastiat
4. F.A. Hayek
5. Murray Rothbard and Henry Hazlitt
6. Ludwig von Mises
7. F.A. Hayek and Ludwig von Mises
8. Philip Wicksteed
9. Henry Hazlitt
10. Diego de Covarrubias
11. Eugen von Böhm-Bawerk
12. Jean-Baptiste Say
13. A.R.J. Turgot
14. Carl Menger
15. Böhm-Bawerk as Austrian Finance Minister
16. Wilhelm Röpke
17. William Hutt
18. Carl Menger

(No known picture of Richard Cantillon exists.)

For photographs on the cover and throughout the book, many thanks to the Austrian National Library, The Bartley Institute, Cambridge University Library, Henry Hazlitt, The Carl Menger Papers in the Special Collections Library at Duke University, Margit von Mises, Princeton University, Jesús Huerta de Soto, JoAnn Rothbard, and the University of Vienna. The painting of Covarrubias is by El Greco.

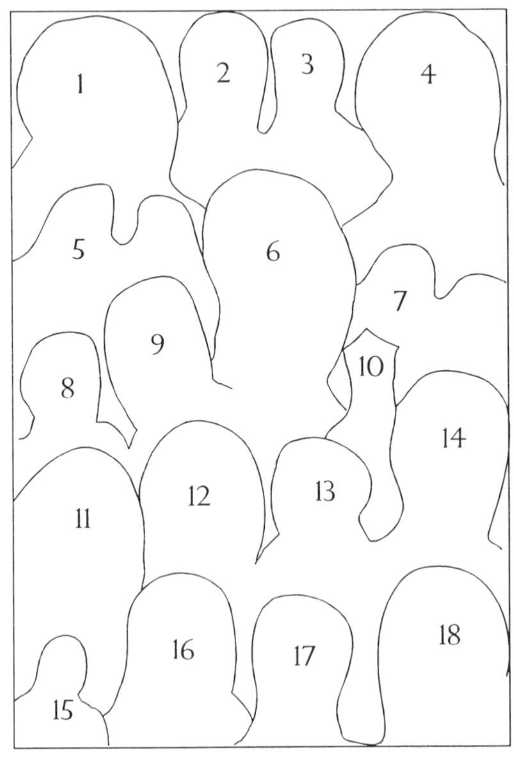




ISBN: 0-945466-04-8

## CONTENTS

Introduction: The Austrian School Past and Present
*Randall G. Holcombe* . . . . . v

1. Juan de Mariana: The Influence of the Spanish Scholastics
*Jesús Huerta de Soto* . . . . . 1

2. Richard Cantillon: The Origin of Economic Theory
*Mark Thornton* . . . . . 13

3. A.R.J. Turgot: Brief, Lucid, and Brilliant
*Murray N. Rothbard* . . . . . 29

4. Jean-Baptiste Say: Neglected Champion of Laissez-Faire
*Larry J. Sechrest* . . . . . 45

5. Frédéric Bastiat: Between the French and Marginalist Revolutions
*Thomas J. DiLorenzo* . . . . . 59

6. Carl Menger: The Founding of the Austrian School
*Joseph T. Salerno* . . . . . 71

7. Philip Wicksteed: The British Austrian
*Israel M. Kirzner* . . . . . 101

8. Eugen von Böhm-Bawerk: Capital, Interest, and Time
*Roger W. Garrison* . . . . . 113

9. Frank A. Fetter: A Forgotten Giant
*Jeffrey M. Herbener* . . . . . 123

10. Ludwig von Mises: The Dean of the Austrian School
*Murray N. Rothbard* . . . . . 143

11. Henry Hazlitt: The People's Austrian
*Jeffrey Tucker* . . . . . 167

12. F.A. Hayek: Austrian Economist and Social Theorist
*Peter G. Klein* . . . . . 181

13. William H. Hutt: The "Classical" Austrian
*John B. Egger* . . . . . 195

14. Wilhelm Röpke: A Humane Economist
*Shawn Ritenour* . . . . . 205

15. Murray N. Rothbard: Economics, Science, and Liberty
*Hans-Hermann Hoppe* . . . . . 223

Index . . . . . 245

About the Contributors . . . . . 259

The Ludwig von Mises Institute acknowledges with gratitude the generosity of all the donors who contributed to making *Fifteen Great Austrian Economists* possible, and thanks in particular:

James M. Rodney
Romill Foundation
Reed W. Mower

---

Arthur Cinader
R.E. Fox†
Robert M. Hansen, M.D.
Edward W. Rehak

---

Mark M. Adamo
Dr. Larry J. Eshelman
James W. Frevert
In Memory of John and Erlene Hendrickson
Russel A. Hoelscher
Mr. and Mrs. W.R. Hogan, Jr.
James Kuden
Joe R. Lee
Arthur L. Loeb
Mr. and Mrs. William Lowndes, III
Roland Manarin
Mr. and Mrs. William W. Massey, Jr.
Joseph Edward Paul Melville
Victor Pankey
Don Printz, M.D.
Betty P. Ramsay
James A. Reichert
Mr. and Mrs. John Salvador
Conrad Schneiker
Josephine H. Spidell
William V. Stephens
Lawrence Van Someren, Sr.

# INTRODUCTION: THE AUSTRIAN SCHOOL PAST AND PRESENT

RANDALL G. HOLCOMBE

AT THE END of the twentieth century, the Austrian School of economics is exerting a significant influence both on the development of academic economics and on the application of economic theory to public policy. An increasing number of economics professors are sympathetic with the fundamental ideas of Austrian economics, and academic journals are taking more account of the Austrian School.[1] A half century ago, few academic economists would even have been familiar with the Austrian School, except superficially, and among those who were, most would have disagreed with its methods and conclusions. Today, the ideas of Austrian economics are closer to the mainstream of economic thought, not because Austrian economics has changed, but because mainstream economics has moved toward the Austrian point of view. A similar shift has occurred in the public-policy arena. The policy implications of Austrian economics, once rejected as extreme, are now embraced as true. In the process, the Austrian School has become increasingly visible as an intellectual force.

Despite the significant advances that Austrian economics has made, it still plays a minor role in academic economics, and only a small minority of academic economists consider themselves members of the Austrian School. The Austrian School of economics is growing, but is not yet a part of the mainstream of academic economics. Its impact on public policy is more difficult to judge, because in many policy areas, other schools of thought arrive at similar conclusions. For example, the Chicago School, led by the ideas of Milton Friedman, often supports public policies consistent with Austrian economics, so the ideas of these schools can reinforce each other.

[1] Two recent examples are the review article by Israel M. Kirzner, "Entrepreneurial Discovery and the Competitive Market Process: An Austrian Approach," *Journal of Economic Literature* 35, no. 1 (March 1997): 60–85; and Sherwin Rosen, "Austrian and Neoclassical Economics: Any Gains From Trade?" *Journal of Economic Perspectives* 11, no 4. (Fall 1997): 139–52. Both of these journals are publications of the American Economic Association, indicating the degree to which Austrian ideas are at least recognized, if not embraced, by the profession's mainstream.

Policy initiatives may find their intellectual foundations in many different schools of thought, but it should be apparent that the laissez-faire approach to public policy so often promoted by the Austrian School is much more accepted at the end of the twentieth century than it was in the middle. Ideas do have consequences, and an appreciation for the workings of the market system, always a hallmark of the Austrian School, has found its way into the public-policy debate.

If the ideas of Austrian economics have made such inroads, one might wonder why, in the academic arena, Austrian economics does not play a bigger role. Part of the answer has to do with academic institutions themselves. Most university faculty teach at state institutions, which by itself may bias them toward supporting the state and being suspicious of laissez-faire ideas. Most university faculty have tenure, which slows the turnover of personnel, and perhaps of ideas. Furthermore, academic ideas find their outlets largely in academic journals, and the editorial boards of those journals tend to be controlled by the academic mainstream, further promoting mainstream ideas over alternative schools of thought.[2] Because publication in academic journals is often a prerequisite for promotion and tenure in a university environment, academic survival often pushes young scholars in the direction of the mainstream methods and ideas in their discipline.

Austrian economics has fought an uphill battle for acceptance for several reasons, but at the same time, the Austrian School has been gaining in strength, and is becoming more accepted in academia. A growing number of economics professors align themselves with the Austrian School, and even among those who do not, Austrian ideas are becoming more recognized and respected. Interestingly enough, the late-twentieth-century resurgence of interest in the Austrian School has been concentrated in the United States. This is largely due to Ludwig von Mises's migration, and his Austrian economics seminar at New York University. One might go so far as to argue that the modern Austrian School would not exist were it not for the influence of Ludwig von Mises on his American students.[3]

Of course, economists before Mises developed the foundation on which he built his ideas, and he had like-minded contemporaries who also influenced the direction of Austrian economics. By the late 1940s, the Austrian School was scarcely wider than Mises and those who studied directly under him at New

---

[2]See Leland B. Yeager, "Austrian Economics, Neoclassicism, and the Market Test," *Journal of Economic Perspectives* 11, no. 4 (Fall 1997): 153–65, for an insightful discussion on the challenges that an alternative to mainstream ideas faces in the academic marketplace.

[3]See Karen I. Vaughn, *Austrian Economics in America: The Migration of a Tradition* (New York: Cambridge University Press, 1994), for a good discussion of the development of the modern Austrian School. Also see Murray N. Rothbard, "The Present State of Austrian Economics," *Money, Method, and the Austrian School*, vol. 1, *The Logic of Action* (Cheltenham, U.K.: Edward Elgar, 1997).

York University. From there, the students of Mises found their own students, and by the 1970s the Austrian School had begun to blossom.

## AUSTRIAN ECONOMICS BEFORE 1950

Carl Menger is generally regarded as the founder of the Austrian School, but prior to about 1920, Austrian economics was not very different from economics in general. Economic theory had taken a great leap forward in the 1870s when the concept of marginal utility was independently discovered by Léon Walras, William Stanley Jevons, and Carl Menger.[4] Each of these three individuals pushed the concept in different directions, but the integration of the marginal theory of value into economics was a major leap for all of economics. Eugen von Böhm-Bawerk's capital theory, now seen as Austrian, was viewed more generally as a part of economics when it was published in the 1880s and 1890s, and Ludwig von Mises's *Theory of Money and Credit,* published in 1912, established him as a leading authority on monetary economics.[5]

Although there was a recognizable Austrian School at the time with its own distinct identity, the Austrian School was a part of mainstream economics in the same way that the Keynesians and monetarists were two mainstream schools in the 1970s. The characterization of the *Theory of Money and Credit* as a mainstream work stands in stark contrast to the profession's assessment of *Human Action,* which was published in 1949. The 1947 appearance of Paul Samuelson's *Foundations of Economic Analysis* defined the cutting edge of the mainstream at that time, and a comparison of the two books shows how different Mises's conception of economics was from mainstream economics at the middle of the twentieth century.

There are two main factors that served to separate Austrian economics from the mainstream in the first half of the twentieth century. The first had to do with the development of economics as an academic discipline. Economists and policymakers wanted to extend concepts of scientific management, introduced around the turn of the century, to management of the economy as a whole. This led economists to adopt more sophisticated mathematical and statistical techniques. Following models developed by physicists, economic models increasingly became focused on the mathematical properties of equilibrium, neglecting the analysis of market processes that has always been a core part of Austrian economics. By focusing on equilibrium, the role of economic profits became secondary, and entrepreneurial activities were

---

[4]The first edition of Menger's *Principles of Economics* was published in German in 1871. While it was generally recognized as a landmark contribution in economics, an English translation was not published until 1950.

[5]Murray N. Rothbard, in *Ludwig von Mises: Scholar, Creator, Hero* (Auburn, Ala.: Ludwig von Mises Institute, 1988), p. 13, notes that Mises's early work on monetary theory, while controversial, was published in the *Economic Journal,* one of the leading mainstream economic journals of the time.

completely neglected. In short, as economic theory developed, the issues it addressed became narrower and excluded facets of the economy that were central to the Austrian School.

The development of macroeconomics following the publication of John Maynard Keynes's *The General Theory of Employment, Interest, and Money* in 1936, further pushed mainstream economics away from the fundamental tenets of Austrian economics. Austrian economics always begins with individuals as the unit of analysis, while Keynesian macroeconomics was built on economic aggregates that could not easily be traced to individual behavior. In addition, the Austrian business-cycle theory developed by Mises and F.A. Hayek emphasizes malinvestment as an underlying cause of business cycles, whereas most macroeconomic models, even today, make the simplifying assumption that capital is homogeneous, ruling out the kind of malinvestment that occurs in Austrian macroeconomic models. In the 1930s, Mises and Hayek were among the leading macroeconomic theorists in the world (although the term macroeconomics was not yet in use). By the 1940s, their ideas had been swept aside by the Keynesian revolution.

The divergence of mainstream economic science from Austrian economics was in part a matter of government policy. The idea that the economy could be managed more scientifically brought with it the support of government policymakers who believed that with better economic models, government policy could engineer the economy to perform better. Advances in economic theory were envisioned as tools for creating a more potent government that would better be able to control the nation's economy.

In order to be applied, advanced models required better economic data to measure the performance of the economy and the impacts of policy. In the early 1920s, the National Bureau of Economic Research was created with the support of government, academic institutions, and the private sector, to make economic theories more scientific, and to develop economic data to aid in applying economic theory. National income accounting was developed in the 1920s and implemented in the 1930s, using better data and more precise models developed with the encouragement of the federal government. Thus, government policy pulled mainstream economics away from the core Austrian ideas by promising economists more power to control public policy, and by providing financing for economic research aimed at devising better methods for controlling the economy through government intervention. Economists who cooperated with the government's agenda were rewarded with money, power, and prestige, but the government's agenda was quite at odds with the ideas of Mises and Hayek, the leading Austrian economists of the time.

Herbert Hoover, an engineer by training, served as Secretary of Commerce from 1921 to 1929, throughout the entire administrations of Harding and Coolidge, before ascending to the presidency himself. Hoover was one of the key individuals pushing economics to become more like engineering, to use mathematical modeling, and to develop better data for analysis. With the onset of the Great Depression, the desire to use economics to engineer the economy back to prosperity was even stronger, and was encouraged even more by government policymakers. The lure to economists was powerful, for economists were offered the opportunity to move from being passive observers of economic activity to being active policymakers, and the temptation pulled the economics profession ever toward developing models of optimal government intervention. Meanwhile, Austrian economics, emphasizing the perils of government intervention, was left by the wayside.

Thus, the main factor that pushed mainstream economics away from Austrian ideas was the increased emphasis on mathematical and statistical techniques. The theoretical focus was on the mathematical properties of equilibrium, and the policy focus was on designing interventionist policies to produce prosperity. The Austrian emphasis on the market process was inconsequential to mainstream analysis, and the policy implications of Austrian economics suggested less intervention rather than more, putting Austrian economics at odds with the mainstream.

An additional factor that pushed Austrian economics from the mainstream was the socialist calculation debate. In 1919, shortly after the Soviet Union was formed, Ludwig von Mises presented an article to a professional meeting making the claim that centrally planned economies were doomed to failure. Mises followed up on this idea in later works and continued to defend his claim until his death in 1973. Hayek conspicuously joined Mises's side of the debate, but most other economists weighed in on the other side, creating what was referred to as the socialist calculation debate. The consensus of the economics profession was that Mises was wrong, and that not only was central planning viable, it was superior to the market as a method of allocating economic resources. Mises, the preeminent spokesman for the Austrian School, was so closely identified with his stance in the socialist calculation debate that it cast a shadow on all of Austrian economics. By 1950, any economist expressing allegiance to the Austrian School was implicitly taking what was generally viewed as the losing side on the debate. Few academic economists were willing to do so.

By the middle of the twentieth century, economic theory focused on the mathematical conditions for economic equilibrium, and economic policy focused on the ways that government intervention in the economy could foster prosperity. Austrian economics, with its emphasis on the market process rather than equilibrium conditions, with its focus on entrepreneurship rather than zero-profit competitive equilibrium in markets, and with its focus on market allocation rather than government planning, had moved from a major force at the center of economic thought to the fringes of economics.

## AUSTRIAN ECONOMICS AFTER 1950

By 1950, all that was left of the Austrian School was Ludwig von Mises and his students at New York University. Mises and Hayek, the two most visible Austrians, were always identified with their insistence that socialist economies were doomed to failure, discrediting them in the eyes of most academic economists. Hayek migrated to the University of Chicago, and might well be identified as a Chicago economist today were it not for the modern revival of the Austrian School. Mises had prominent supporters like W.H. Hutt and Henry Hazlitt, both profiled in this volume, but none of his supporters were teaching Austrian economics as an alternative to the academic mainstream. Meanwhile, Mises promoted the ideas of Austrian economics to a handful of followers at New York University. Had he not done so, Austrian economics as an identifiable school of thought probably would have vanished. It is not much of a stretch to argue that by 1950, the Austrian School had only one academic economist actively promoting its ideas as a consistent body of thought.

While Ludwig von Mises is not the founder of the Austrian School, he is beyond a doubt solely responsible for its survival to the end of the twentieth century. Mises did two things to ensure the survival of the school. First, he wrote *Human Action,* which clearly laid out the intellectual foundations of Austrian economics. Through *Human Action,* readers could see that Austrian economics consisted of a comprehensive and consistent body of ideas, and they could also see how Austrian economics differed from the mainstream economic ideas of the day. *Human Action* provided a ready reference to the fundamental ideas of Austrian economics in much the same way that Paul Samuelson's *Foundations of Economic Analysis* provided a ready reference to fundamental concepts of mainstream economic theory. Second, through his seminars at New York University, Mises attracted a group of students who recruited other students, giving Austrian economics an academic rebirth. Two of Mises's American students stand out for their academic achievements and for their impact on the modern Austrian School: Israel M. Kirzner, an author of one of this volume's chapters, and Murray N. Rothbard, an author of two chapters and is profiled in a third chapter. Both established reputations as insightful economists, prolific authors and—more to the point for present purposes—strong proponents of the Austrian School. They influenced students, not only at their own universities, but at other universities as well, by giving seminars and speaking at conferences, and of course through the impact of their writing. While Austrian economists are still rare in academic institutions, many of those students influenced by Kirzner and Rothbard now hold academic positions, and are in turn influencing a new generation of students.

From its low point in the middle of the twentieth century, Austrian economics has continued to gain visibility both inside academia and out. F.A. Hayek won the Nobel prize in economics in 1974, giving the Austrian School attention and respectability. By then, a small Austrian revival was already underway, led by Kirzner and Rothbard, and Hayek's Nobel prize gave the revival additional momentum. Still, the Austrian School was branded by being on the losing side of the socialist calculation debate. In 1973, the year Mises died, Paul Samuelson, another Nobel laureate in economics and among the most prominent of mainstream academic economists, argued in his introductory textbook that even though the Soviet Union had roughly half the per capita income of the United States, their superior economic system based on central planning gave them faster growth. Based on this, Samuelson projected that per capita income in the Soviet Union could catch up to that of the United States as early as 1990, and almost surely by 2015.[6] Keep in mind that Samuelson's projection was in his best-selling introductory college textbook, and was the standard line taught in college classrooms at the time. Clearly, the mainstream had not accepted the ideas of Austrian economics.

Ironically, the socialist calculation debate that so tarnished Austrian economics because Mises and Hayek refused to concede became one of the crowning achievements of Austrian economics once the Berlin Wall came down in 1989, followed by the collapse of the Soviet Union in 1991. Mises was right, it turned out, and critics of the Austrian School who had once dismissed its outlandish claims were converted to, if not fans, at least curiosity seekers. Economists who at one time dismissed the Austrian School wanted to discover what insights had led Mises and only a handful of others to have been so certain of their ideas, despite the almost unanimous disapproval of academic and professional economists.

As the twentieth century draws to a close, many of the ideas that at one time differentiated Austrian economics from the mainstream are now being explored by mainstream economists. Decades ago, macroeconomists recognized that they needed to disaggregate their theories to the level of individual behavior, and economists are increasingly recognizing the importance of uncertainty and imperfect information to the way that individuals make decisions and the way that markets operate. Still, there remains a wide gulf in many areas, perhaps the most obvious is the mainstream's continuing focus on the mathematical properties of equilibrium, in contrast to the Austrian focus on the market process.

---

[6]Paul A. Samuelson, *Economics*, 9th ed. (New York: McGraw-Hill, 1973), p. 883.

Much could be written comparing and contrasting the Austrian School of economics with other schools of economic thought, but the purpose of this volume is to focus on some of the people who have made the Austrian School what it is today. All of the individuals here have steered the development of the Austrian School in ways that go beyond just their expositions of economic theory.

In many cases, seeing the context in which they developed their ideas helps to clarify why they chose to promote the ideas of the Austrian School, and also helps to illustrate the personal and intellectual integrity shown by so many of these great minds. The individuals profiled in this volume have contributed to the development of Austrian economics in vastly different ways. Some predated Carl Menger's founding of the Austrian School, but laid the foundations upon which Menger and later Austrians built. Mariana, Turgot, Bastiat, Say, and Cantillon fall into this category. The insights of these economists laid a solid foundation for the understanding of the functioning of markets that led to the founding of the Austrian School. With the development of modern neoclassical economics, the contributions of these individuals have been largely ignored. Many of the fallacies that have found their way into mainstream economic thought were long ago dealt with and refuted by these economists, and it is worthwhile to profile these predecessors to the Austrian School both to celebrate their contributions and to show how their ideas remain relevant today.

Some featured here, such as Wicksteed and Fetter, were contemporaries of Menger, Böhm-Bawerk, and Mises, and developed ideas consistent with the Austrian School even as Austrian economics was developing its own identity as a school of economic thought. Some were won over by the power of the ideas of a more mature Austrian School, and went on to make their own contributions to the development of Austrian economics. Hutt, Hazlitt, Röpke, and Rothbard are in this group. Of course, there have been many other prominent Austrian economists who are not profiled here, and the choice of these fifteen economists in no way should be taken as an indication that these are the fifteen most important Austrian economists. Rather, they are an interesting cross-section of individuals who have contributed to the Austrian School in a variety of ways.

The individuals profiled in this volume make up a diverse group, but they share a deep insight into the fundamental concepts of economics, and the ability to effectively communicate those concepts in writing. Each of them has had a substantial and lasting influence on the development of economic ideas.

# 1
# JUAN DE MARIANA: THE INFLUENCE OF THE SPANISH SCHOLASTICS

JESÚS HUERTA DE SOTO

THE PREHISTORY OF the Austrian School of economics can be found in the works of the Spanish scholastics written in what is known as the "Spanish Golden Century," which ran from the mid-sixteenth century through the seventeenth century.[1]

*Diego de Covarrubias (1512–1577), one of the Spanish Scholastics*

Who were these Spanish intellectual forerunners of the Austrian School of economics? Most of them were scholastics teaching morals and theology at the University of Salamanca, in the medieval Spanish city located 150 miles northwest of Madrid, close to the border of Spain with Portugal. These scholastics, mainly Dominicans and Jesuits, articulated the subjectivist, dynamic,

---

[1]Murray N. Rothbard first developed this thesis in 1974, in the paper entitled "New Light on the Prehistory of the Austrian School," which he presented at the conference held in South Royalton, Vermont, and which marked the beginning of the notable re-emergence of the Austrian School. That paper was published two years later in *The Foundations of Modern Austrian Economics*, Edwin Dolan, ed. (Kansas City: Sheed and Ward, 1976), pp. 52–74. He then developed it more fully in his monumental *Economic Thought Before Adam Smith*, vol. 1, *An Austrian Perspective on the History of Economic Thought* (Cheltenham, U.K.: Edward Elgar, 1995), chap. 4, "The Late Spanish Scholastics," pp. 97–133.

Rothbard was not the only Austrian economist to show the Spanish origins of the Austrian School. F.A. Hayek held the same view, especially after meeting Bruno Leoni, the great Italian scholar, and author of *Freedom and the Law* (Indianapolis, Ind.: Liberty Fund, 1991). Leoni met Hayek in the 1950s, and convinced him that the intellectual roots of classical economic liberalism were continental and Catholic,

and libertarian tradition on which, two-hundred-and-fifty years later, Carl Menger and his followers would place so much importance.[2] Perhaps the most libertarian of all the scholastics, particularly in his later works, was the Jesuit Father Juan de Mariana.

Mariana was born in the city of Talavera de la Reina, near Toledo. He appears to have been the illegitimate son of a canon of Talavera, and when he was sixteen, joined the Society of Jesus, which had just been created. At the age of twenty-four, he was summoned to Rome to teach theology, then transferred to the school the Jesuits ran in Sicily, and from there to the University of Paris. In 1574, he returned to Spain, living and studying in Toledo until his death at the age of eighty-seven.

Although Father Mariana wrote many books, the first one with a libertarian content was *De rege et regis institutione* (On the king and the royal institution), published in 1598, in which he set forth his famous defense of tyrannicide. According to Mariana, any individual citizen can justly assassinate a king who imposes taxes without the consent of the people, seizes the property of individuals and squanders it, or prevents a meeting of a democratic parliament.[3] The doctrines contained in this

---

and should be sought in Mediterranean Europe, not in Scotland. One of Hayek's best pupils, Marjorie Grice-Hutchinson, specialized in Spanish literature and translated the main texts of the Spanish scholastics into English in what is now considered a short classic, *The School of Salamanca: Readings in Spanish Monetary Theory, 1544–1605* (Oxford: Clarendon Press, 1952). In addition, an excellent resource is *Economic Thought in Spain: Selected Essays of Marjorie Grice-Hutchinson*, Laurence Moss and Christopher Ryan, eds. (Cheltenham, U.K.: Edward Elgar, 1993). I even have a letter from Hayek, dated January 7, 1979, in which he asked me to read Murray Rothbard's article on "The Prehistory of the Austrian School" because he and Grice-Hutchinson "demonstrate that the basic principles of the theory of the competitive market were worked out by the Spanish Scholastics of the sixteenth century and that economic liberalism was not designed by the Calvinists but by the Spanish Jesuits." Hayek concludes his letter saying that "I can assure you from my personal knowledge of the sources that Rothbard's case is extremely strong."

[2]The most up-to-date work on the Spanish scholastics is the book by Alejandro Chafuen, *Christians for Freedom: Late Scholastic Economics* (San Francisco: Ignatius Press, 1986).

[3]Mariana describes the tyrant as follows:

> He seizes the property of individuals and squanders it, impelled as he is by the unkingly vices of lust, avarice, cruelty, and fraud. . . . Tyrants, indeed, try to injure and ruin everybody, but they direct their attack especially against rich and upright men throughout the realm. They consider the good more suspect than the evil; and the virtue which they themselves lack is most formidable to them. . . . They expel the better men from the commonwealth on the principle that whatever is exalted in the kingdom should be laid low. . . . They exhaust all the rest so that they cannot unite by demanding new

book were apparently used to justify the assassination of the French tyrant kings Henry III and Henry IV, and the book was burned in Paris by the executioner as a result of a decree issued by the Parliament of Paris on July 4, 1610.[4]

In Spain, although the authorities were not enthusiastic about it, the book was respected. In fact, all Mariana did was to take an idea—that natural law is morally superior to the might of the state—to its logical conclusion. This idea had previously been developed in detail by the great founder of international law, the Dominican Francisco de Vitoria (1485–1546), who began the Spanish scholastic tradition of denouncing the conquest and particularly the enslavement of the Indians by the Spaniards in the New World.

But perhaps Mariana's most important book was the work published in 1605 with the title *De monetae mutatione* (On the alteration of money).[5] In this book, Mariana began to question whether the king was the owner of the private property of his vassals or citizens and reached the clear conclusion that he was not. The author then applied his distinction between a king and a tyrant and concluded that "the tyrant is he who tramples everything underfoot and believes everything to belong to him; the king restricts or limits his covetousness within the terms of reason and justice."

From this, Mariana deduced that the king cannot demand tax without the consent of the people, since taxes are simply an appropriation of part of the subjects' wealth. In order for such an appropriation to be legitimate, the subjects must be in agreement. Neither may the king

---

> tributes from them daily, by stirring up quarrels among the citizens, and by joining war to war. They build huge works at the expense and the suffering of the citizens. Whence the pyramids of Egypt were born. . . . The tyrant necessarily fears that those whom he terrorizes and holds as slaves will attempt to overthrow him. . . . Thus he forbids the citizens to congregate together, to meet in assemblies, and to discuss the commonwealth altogether, taking from them by secret-police methods the opportunity of free speaking and freely listening so that they are not even allowed to complain freely.

Cited in Rothbard, *Economic Thought Before Adam Smith*, pp. 118–19.

[4]See Juan de Mariana, *Discurso de las enfermedades de la Compañía* (Madrid: Don Gabriel Ramírez, 1768), p. 53, "Dissertation on the author, and the legitimacy of this discourse."

[5]I will be quoting *in extenso* from the latest Spanish edition of this book, which was published with the title of *Tratado y discurso sobre la moneda de vellón*, with an Introduction by Lucas Beltrán (Madrid: Instituto de Estudios Fiscales, 1987).

create state monopolies, since they would simply be a disguised means of collecting taxes.

And neither may the king—this is the most important part of the book—obtain fiscal revenue by lowering the metal content of the coins. Mariana realized that the reduction of the precious metal content in the coins, and the increase in the number of coins in circulation, is simply a form of inflation (although he does not use this word, which was unknown at the time), and that inflation inevitably leads to an increase in prices because "if money falls from the legal value, all goods increase unavoidably, in the same proportion as the money fell, and all the accounts break down."

Mariana describes the serious economic consequences to which the debasement and government tampering with the market value of money lead as follows:

> Only a fool would try to separate these values in such a way that the legal price should differ from the natural. Foolish, nay, wicked the ruler who orders that a thing the common people value, let us say, at five should be sold from ten. Men are guided in this matter by common estimation founded on considerations of the quality of things, and of their abundance or scarcity. It would be vain for a Prince to seek to undermine these principles of commerce. 'Tis best to leave them intact instead of assailing them by force to the public detriment.[6]

We should note how Mariana refers to the fact that the "common estimation" of men is the origin of the value of things, thus following the traditional subjectivist doctrine of the scholastics, which was initially proposed by Diego de Covarrubias y Leyva. Covarrubias (1512–1577), the son of a famous architect, became bishop of the city of Segovia and a minister to King Philip II. In 1554, he set forth better than anyone before the subjectivist theory of value, stating that "the value of an article does not depend on its essential nature but on the subjective estimation of men, even if that estimation is foolish," illustrating his thesis with the example that "in the Indies wheat is dearer than in Spain because men esteem it more highly, though the nature of the wheat is the same in both places."[7]

Covarrubias's subjectivist conception was completed by another of his scholastic contemporaries, Luis Saravia de la Calle, who was the first to demonstrate that prices determine costs, not vice versa. Saravia de la Calle also had the special distinction of writing in Spanish, not in Latin.

---

[6]Quoted in Rothbard, *Economic Thought Before Adam Smith*, p. 120.

[7]Diego de Covarrubias y Leyva, *Omnia Opera* (Venice, 1604), vol. 2, chap. 4, p. 131.

Its title was *Instrucción de mercaderes* (Instruction to merchants), and there we can read that "those who measure the just price by the labor, costs and risk incurred by the person who deals in the merchandise are greatly in error. The just price is found not by counting the cost but by common estimation."[8]

The subjectivist conception initiated by Covarrubias also allowed other Spanish scholastics to get a clear insight of the true nature of market prices, and of the impossibility of attaining an economic equilibrium. Thus, the Jesuit Cardinal Juan de Lugo, wondering what the price of equilibrium was, as early as 1643 reached the conclusion that the equilibrium depended on such a large number of specific circumstances that only God was able to know it ("*Pretium iustum mathematicum licet soli Deo notum*").[9] Another Jesuit, Juan de Salas, referring to the possibilities of knowing specific market information, reached the very Hayekian conclusion that it was so complex that "*quas exacte comprehendere et ponderare Dei est non hominum*" (only God, not men, can understand it exactly).[10]

Furthermore, the Spanish scholastics were the first ones to introduce the dynamic concept of competition (in Latin *concurrentium*), which is best understood as a process of rivalry among entrepreneurs. For instance, Jerónimo Castillo de Bovadilla (1547–?) wrote that "prices will go down as a result of the abundance, rivalry (*emulación*), and competition (*concurrencia*) among the sellers."[11]

This same idea is closely followed by Luis de Molina.[12] Covarrubias also anticipated many of the conclusions of Father Mariana in his empirical

---

[8]Luis Saravia de la Calle, *Instrucción de mercaderes* (1544); republished in *Colección de Joyas Bibliográficas* (Madrid, 1949), p. 53. Saravia's book addresses the business entrepreneur (in Spanish *mercaderes*) following a continental Catholic tradition that can be traced back to San Bernardino de Siena (1380–1444). See Rothbard, *Economic Thought Before Adam Smith*, pp. 81–85.

[9]Juan de Lugo (1583–1660), *Disputationes de iustitia et iure* (Lyon, 1642), vol. 2, d. 26, s. 4, n. 40, p. 312.

[10]Juan de Salas, *Commentarii in secundam secundae D. Thomae de contractibus* (Lyon, 1617), vol. 4, no. 6, p. 9.

[11]Jerónimo Castillo de Bovadilla, *Práctica para corregidores* (Salamanca, 1585), vol. 2, chap. 4, no. 49. See also the important comments on the scholastics and their dynamic concept of competition written by Oreste Popescu, *Estudios en la historia del pensamiento económico latinoamericano* (Buenos Aires: Plaza and Janés, 1987), pp. 141–59.

[12]Luis de Molina, *De iustitia et iure* (Cuenca, 1597), vol. 2, disp. 348, no. 4, and *La teoría del justo precio*, Francisco Gómez Camacho, ed. (Madrid: Editora Nacional, 1981), p. 169. Raymond de Roover, ignoring the work of Castillo de Bovadilla, acknowledges how "Molina even introduces the concept of competition by stating

study on the history of the devaluation of the main coin of that time, the Castilian Maravedí. This study contained a compilation of a large number of statistics on the evolution of prices in the previous century and was published in Latin in his book *Veterum collatio numismatum* (Compilation on old moneys).[13] This book was highly praised in Italy by Davanzaty and Galiani and was also quoted by Carl Menger in his *Principles of Economics*.[14]

We should also note how Father Mariana, when explaining the effects of inflation, listed the basic elements of the quantity theory of money, which had previously been explained in full detail by another notable scholastic, Martín Azpilcueta Navarro (also known as Dr. Navarro), who was born in Navarra (northeast Spain, near France) in 1493. Azpilcueta lived ninety-four years and is famous especially for explaining, in 1556, the quantity theory of money in his book *Resolutory Commentary on Exchanges*. Observing the effects on Spanish prices of the massive inflow of precious metals coming from America, Azpilcueta declared that

> as can be seen from experience, in France, where there is less money than in Spain, bread, wine, clothing, labor, and work cost much less; and even in Spain, at the time when there was less money, the things which could be sold and the labor and work of men were given for much less than after the Indies were discovered and covered her with gold and silver. The cause of which is that money is worth more where and when it is lacking than where and when it is in abundance.[15]

Returning to Father Mariana, it is clear that his most important contribution was to see that inflation was a tax that "taxes those who had money before and, as a consequence thereof, are forced to buy things more dearly." Furthermore, Mariana argues that the effects of inflation cannot be solved by fixing maximum rates or prices, since experience shows that these have always been ineffective. In addition, given that inflation is a tax, according to his theory of tyranny, the people's consent would, in any event, be required but, even if such consent existed, it would always be a very damaging tax that disorganized economic life: "this new levy

---

that concurrence or rivalry among buyers will enhance prices." See his article "Scholastic Economics: Survival and Lasting Influence from the Sixteenth Century to Adam Smith," *Quarterly Journal of Economics* 69, no. 2 (May 1955): 169.

[13]Included in Covarrubias, *Omnia Opera*, vol. 1, pp. 669–710.

[14]Carl Menger, *Principles of Economics* (New York: New York University Press, 1981), p. 317.

[15]Martín Azpilcueta Navarro, *Comentario resolutorio de cambios* (Madrid: Consejo Superior de Investigaciones Científicas, 1965), pp. 74–75.

or tax of the alloyed metal, which is illicit and bad if it is done without the agreement of the kingdom, and if it is done therewith, I take it as erroneous and harmful in many ways."

How could resorting to the comfortable expedient of inflation be avoided? By balancing the budget, for which purpose Mariana basically proposed spending less on the royal family because "a moderate amount, spent with order, glitters more and represents greater majesty than a superfluous amount without order."

Second, Mariana proposed that "the king should reduce his favors," in other words, he should not reward the real or supposed services of his vassals so generously:

> there is no kingdom in the world with so many prizes, commissions, pensions, benefits, and posts; if they were well distributed in an orderly fashion, less would need to be taken from the public treasury or from other taxes from which money contributions can be got.

As we can see, the lack of control over public spending and the purchase of political support with subsidies dates from a very long time ago. Mariana also proposed that "the king should avoid and excuse unnecessary undertakings and wars, cut off the cancerous limbs that cannot be healed." In short, he set forth a whole program for a reduction in public spending and keeping the budget balanced which would, even today, serve as a model.

It is obvious that if Father Mariana had known the economic mechanisms that lead to the credit expansion process generated by banks and the effects of this process, he would have condemned these as robbery. He would have condemned not only the government debasement of coins but also the even more disturbing credit inflation created by banks. However, other Spanish scholastics were able to analyze the credit expansion of banks. Thus, de la Calle was very critical of fractional-reserve banking. He maintained that receiving interest was incompatible with the nature of a demand deposit, and that, in any case, a fee should be paid to the banker for keeping the money under his custody. A similar conclusion is reached by the more famous Navarro.[16]

Molina was sympathetic to fractional-reserve banking and confused the nature of two different contracts, loans and deposits, which Azpilcueta and Saravia de la Calle had clearly differentiated from each other previously. A more relevant aspect is that Molina was the first theorist to discover, in 1597 (therefore much earlier than Pennington in 1826), that

---

[16]See Jesús Huerta de Soto, "New Light on the Prehistory of the Theory of Banking and the School of Salamanca," *Review of Austrian Economics* 9, no. 2 (1996): 59–81.

bank deposits are part of the monetary supply. He even proposed the name "*chirographis pecuniarium*" (written money) to refer to the written documents that were accepted in trade as bank money.[17] Our scholastics included, therefore, two incipient schools. The first is a kind of "Currency School," formed by Saravia de la Calle, Azpilcueta Navarro, and Tomás de Mercado, who were very distrustful of banking activities, for which they implicitly demanded a one-hundred-percent reserve should be held. The second was a kind of "Banking School," headed by the Jesuits Luis de Molina and Juan de Lugo, who were much more tolerant toward fractional-reserve banking.[18] Both groups were to a certain extent the forerunners of the theoretical developments which were to arise three centuries later in England as a result of the debate between the Currency School and the Banking School.

Murray Rothbard stresses how another important contribution of the Spanish scholastics, especially of Azpilcueta, was to revive the vital concept of time preference, originally developed by one of the most brilliant pupils of Thomas Aquinas, Giles Lessines, who, as early as 1285, wrote

> that future goods are not valued so highly as the same goods available at an immediate moment of time, nor do they allow their owners to achieve the same utility. For this reason, it must be considered that they have a more reduced value in accordance with justice.[19]

Father Mariana also wrote another important book, *Discurso de las enfermedades de la Compañía* (A discourse on the sicknesses of the Jesuit order), which was published posthumously. In that book, Mariana criticized the military hierarchy established in the Jesuit order, but also developed the pure Austrian insight that it is impossible to endow state commands with a coordinating content due to lack of information. In Mariana's words:

---

[17]Luis de Molina, *Tratado sobre los cambios*, Introduction by Francisco Gómez Camacho (Madrid: Instituto de Estudios Fiscales, 1990), p. 146. Also James Pennington's memo dated February 13, 1826, "On the Private Banking Establishments of the Metropolis," included as an Appendix in Thomas Tooke, *A Letter to Lord Grenville; On the Effects Ascribed to the Resumption of Cash Payments on the Value of the Currency* (London: John Murray, 1826).

[18]However, according to Father Bernard W. Dempsey, if the members of this second group of the School of Salamanca had had a detailed theoretical knowledge of the functioning and implications of the economic process to which fractional-reserve banking gives rise, it would have been described as a perverse, vast and illegitimate process of institutional usury, even by Molina, Lessius, and Lugo themselves. See Father Bernard W. Dempsey, *Interest and Usury* (Washington, D.C.: American Council of Public Affairs, 1943), p. 210.

[19]Quoted in ibid., p. 214, n. 31.

> power and command is mad. . . . Rome is far away, the general does not know the people or the facts, at least, with all the circumstances that surround them, on which success depends. . . . It is unavoidable that many serious errors will be committed and the people are displeased thereby and despise such a blind government. . . . It is a great mistake for the blind to wish to guide the sighted.

Mariana concludes that, when there are many laws, "as not all of them may be kept or known, respect for all of them is lost."[20]

In summary, Father Mariana and the Spanish scholastics were capable of developing the essential elements of what would later be the theoretical basis of the Austrian School of economics, specifically the following: first, the subjective theory of value (Diego de Covarrubias y Leyva); second, the proper relationship between prices and costs (Luis Saravia de la Calle); third, the dynamic nature of the market and the impossibility of the model of equilibrium (Juan de Lugo and Juan de Salas); fourth, the dynamic concept of competition understood as a process of rivalry among sellers (Castillo de Bovadilla and Luis de Molina); fifth, the rediscovery of the time-preference principle (Martin Azpilcueta Navarro); sixth, the distorting influence of the inflationary growth of money on prices (Juan de Mariana, Diego de Covarrubias, and Martin Azpilcueta Navarro); seventh, the negative economic effects of fractional-reserve banking (Luis Saravia de la Calle and Martin Azpilcueta Navarro); eighth, that bank deposits form part of the monetary supply (Luis de Molina and Juan de Lugo); ninth, the impossibility of organizing society by coercive commands, due to lack of information (Juan de Mariana); and tenth, the libertarian tradition that any unjustified intervention on the market by the state violates natural law (Juan de Mariana).

In order to understand the influence of the Spanish scholastics on the later development of the Austrian School of economics we should remember that in the sixteenth century Emperor Charles V, who was the King of Spain, sent his brother Ferdinand I to be King of Austria. "Austria" means, etymologically, "eastern part of the Empire," and the Empire in those days comprised almost all of continental Europe, with the sole exception of France, which remained an isolated island surrounded by Spanish forces. So it is easy to understand the origin of the intellectual influence of the Spanish scholastics on the Austrian School, which was not purely coincidental or a mere whim of history, but originated from the intimate historical, political, and cultural relations which existed between Spain and Austria from the sixteenth century onwards. In addition, Italy

---

[20]Mariana, *Discurso de las enfermedades de la Compañía*, pp. 151–55, 216.

also played an important role in these relations, acting as an authentic cultural, economic, and financial bridge over which the relations between the two farthest points of the Empire in Europe (Spain and Vienna) flowed. So there are very important arguments to defend the thesis that, at least at its roots, the Austrian School is truly a Spanish School.

Indeed, we could say that the greatest merit of Carl Menger was to rediscover and take up this continental Catholic tradition of Spanish scholastic thought that was almost forgotten and cut short as a consequence of the black legend against Spain and the very negative influence on the history of economic thought of Adam Smith and his followers of the British Classical School.[21]

Fortunately, and despite the overwhelming intellectual imperialism of the British Classical School, the continental tradition was never totally forgotten. Economists like Cantillon, Turgot, and Say kept the torch of subjectivism burning. Even in Spain, in the years of decadence in the eighteenth and nineteenth centuries, the old scholastic tradition survived in spite of the inferiority complex toward the British intellectual world that was so typical of those years.

Proof of this is how another Spanish Catholic writer solved the "paradox of value" and clearly set forth the theory of marginal utility twenty-seven years earlier than Carl Menger. This was the Catalonian Jaime Balmes (1810–1848). During his short life, he became the most important Spanish Thomistic philosopher of his time. In 1844, he published an article entitled "True idea of value or thoughts on the origin, nature, and variety of prices," in which he solved the paradox of value and clearly sets forth the idea of marginal utility. Balmes wondered, "Why is a precious stone worth more than a piece of bread?" And he answered,

> It is not difficult to explain. Being the value of a thing its utility . . . if the number of units of this means increases, the need of any one of them in particular decreases; because being possible to choose among many

[21]See Leland B. Yeager, "Book Review," *Review of Austrian Economics* 9, no. 1 (1996): 183, where he says:

> Adam Smith dropped earlier contributions about subjective value, entrepreneurship and emphasis on real-world markets and pricing and replaced it all with a labor theory of value and a dominant focus on the long run "natural price" equilibrium, a world where entrepreneurship was assumed out of existence. He mixed up Calvinism with economics, as in supporting usury prohibition and distinguishing between productive and unproductive occupations. He lapsed from the laissez-faire of several eighteenth-century French and Italian economists, introducing many waffles and qualifications. His work was unsystematic and plagued by contradictions.

units, none of them is indispensable. For this reason there is a necessary relation between the increase or decrease in value, and the shortage or abundance of a thing.[22]

In this way Balmes was able to close the circle of the continental tradition, which was ready to be taken up, completed, and enhanced a few years later by Carl Menger and his followers from the Austrian School of economics.

### SELECTED READINGS

Azpilcueta Navarro, Martín. 1965. *Comentario resolutorio de cambios*. Madrid: Consejo Superior de Investigaciones Científicas.

Chafuen, Alejandro. 1986. *Christians for Freedom: Late Scholastic Economics*. San Francisco: Ignatius Press.

Grice-Hutchinson, Marjorie. 1952. *The School of Salamanca: Readings in Spanish Monetary Theory, 1544–1605*. Oxford: Clarendon Press.

Leoni, Bruno. 1991. *Freedom and the Law*. Indianapolis, Ind.: Liberty Fund.

Mariana, Juan de. 1768. *Discurso de las enfermedades de la Compañía*. Madrid: Don Gabriel Ramírez.

Moss, Laurence, and Christopher Ryan, eds. 1993. *Economic Thought in Spain*. Cheltenham, U.K.: Edward Elgar.

Roover, Raymond de. 1955. "Scholastic Economics: Survival and Lasting Influence from the Sixteenth Century to Adam Smith." *Quarterly Journal of Economics* 69, no. 2 (May).

Rothbard, Murray N. 1995. *Economic Thought Before Adam Smith*. Vol. 1. *An Austrian Perspective on the History of Economic Thought*. Cheltenham, U.K.: Edward Elgar.

---

[22]Jaime Balmes, "Verdadera idea del valor o reflexiones sobre el origen, naturaleza y variedad de los precios," en *Obras Completas* (Madrid: B.A.C., 1949), vol. 5, pp. 615–24. Balmes also described the personality of Juan de Mariana with the following graphic words:

> The overall impression that Mariana offers is unique: an accomplished theologist, a perfect Latin scholar, a deep knowledge of Greek and the eastern languages, a brilliant man of letters, an estimable economist, a politician with great foresight; that is his head; add an irreproachable life, strict morality, a heart which does not know untruth, incapable of flattery, which beats strongly at the mere name of freedom, like that of the fierce republicans of Greece and Rome; a firm, intrepid voice, that is raised against all types of abuse, with no consideration for the great, without trembling when it addressed kings, and consider that all this has come together in a man who lives in a small cell of the Jesuits of Toledo, and you will certainly find a set of virtues and circumstances that seldom coincide in a single person.

See the article "Mariana," in *Obras Completas*, vol. 12, pp. 78–79.

——. 1976. "New Light on the Prehistory of the Austrian School." In Edwin Dolan, ed., *The Foundations of Modern Austrian Economics.* Kansas City: Sheed and Ward.

Soto, Jesús Huerta de. 1996. "New Light on the Prehistory of the Theory of Banking and the School of Salamanca." *Review of Austrian Economics* 9, no. 2.

# 2
# RICHARD CANTILLON[1]: THE ORIGIN OF ECONOMIC THEORY

MARK THORNTON

MANY CRUCIAL AUSTRIAN insights have been found in the economics of Irish banker Richard Cantillon (1680[2]–1734) and his lone surviving publication, *Essai sur la Nature du Commerce en Général*.[3] It seems clear that Cantillon was an important influence on the development of Austrian economics, and that he can be considered a member of the Austrian School. Carl Menger had a copy of the *Essai* in his library prior to the publication of *The Principles of Economics*.

Indeed, the origins of economic theory itself can be traced to Cantillon. William Stanley Jevons, one of the cofounders of the marginalist revolution, and the economist who is generally credited with rediscovering Cantillon, called the *Essai* "a systematic and connected treatise, going over in a concise manner nearly the whole field of economics. . . . It is thus the *first treatise on economics*." He dubbed the work the "Cradle of Political Economy."[4] Joseph Schumpeter, the great historian of economic thought and student of Eugen von Böhm-Bawerk, described the *Essai* as

The author would like to thank Robert F. Hébert, Robert Ekelund, Jeffrey Tucker, and Audrey Davidson for helpful comments and suggestions.

[1]No known picture of Cantillon exists.

[2]The date of Cantillon's birth, like many things about his life, remains a mystery.

[3]See for example, Robert F. Hébert, "Was Richard Cantillon an Austrian Economist?" *Journal of Libertarian Studies* 7, no. 2 (Fall 1985): 269–80; Murray N. Rothbard, *Economic Thought Before Adam Smith*, vol. 1, *An Austrian Perspective on the History of Economic Thought* (Cheltenham, U.K.: Edward Elgar, 1995); Jörg Guido Hülsmann, "Cantillon as a Proto-Austrian: Further Evidence," working paper, September 1997.

[4]William Stanley Jevons, "Richard Cantillon and the Nationality of Political Economy," *Contemporary Review* (January 1881), reprinted in *Essai sur la Nature du Commerce en Général, by Richard Cantillon* [and other essays], Henry Higgs, ed. and trans. (London: Frank Cass, [1931] 1959), p. 342, with emphasis in the original.

"the first systematic penetration of the field of economics."[5] In his treatise on the history of economic thought, Murray N. Rothbard named Cantillon "the founding father of modern economics."[6]

The key episode in Cantillon's life was his involvement with John Law and his monetary schemes. Cantillon was opposed to the inflationist theories of Law, but he understood how the schemes worked and what their fatal flaws were. Thus, he was able to create a large fortune from the Mississippi System and South Sea Bubble. In the aftermath of these financial debacles, Cantillon wrote his famous *Essai*, breaking out of the muddleheaded Mercantilist thinking of his day to make a pathbreaking contribution to our knowledge of method, theory, and policy. Shortly after writing the *Essai*, Cantillon was murdered under mysterious conditions, and his *Essai* remained unpublished for more than twenty years.

The *Essai* is considered influential for the development of both the Physiocrats and the classical economists and Cantillon was one of the very few people mentioned by Adam Smith in the *Wealth of Nations*. Unfortunately, Smith misrepresented Cantillon's work. Both Cantillon and his *Essai* were largely forgotten during the period of classical economics. The true significance of the *Essai* was gleaned by the French economists A.R.J. Turgot and J.B. Say, who were important precursors to the modern Austrian School.[7] Since his rediscovery during the marginalist revolution,

---

Jevons went on to say that "Richard Cantillon had a sound and pretty complete comprehension of many questions about which pamphleteers are still wrangling and blundering, and perplexing themselves and other people," and that "the third part especially is almost beyond praise."

[5]Schumpeter goes on:

> Individual problems are presented in the light of unified explanatory principles and form part of a boldly designed comprehensive analysis. The narrowness of earlier trains of thought is transcended. Primitive mistakes are avoided, those arising from deficient analytic training no less than those for which the influence of philosophy must shoulder the blame.

Joseph Schumpeter, *Epochen der Dogmen-und Methodengeschichte, Grundriz der Sozialökonomik,* 1st ed. (Tübingen: J.C.B. Mohr, 1914), vol. 1, pt. 1, p. 143, as quoted in F.A. Hayek, [1931] "Richard Cantillon (c.1680–1734),"Introduction to Richard Cantillon, *Essai sur la Nature du Commerce en Général*, Grete Heinz, trans., reprinted in F.A. Hayek, *Economic History*, vol. 3, *The Collected Works of F.A. Hayek*, W.W. Bartley, III, and Stephen Kresge, eds. (Chicago: University of Chicago Press, 1991), p. 258–59.

[6]Rothbard, *Economic Thought Before Adam Smith*, chap. 12, pp. 343–62.

[7]See Anthony Brewer, "Cantillon and the Land Theory of Value," *History of Political Economy* 20, no. 1 (Spring 1988): 1–14; Leonard P. Liggio, "Richard Cantillon and the French Economists: Distinctive French Contributions to J.B. Say," *Journal of Libertarian Studies* 7, no. 2 (Fall 1985): 295–304; Joseph T. Salerno, "Comment on the French Liberal School," *Journal of Libertarian Studies* 2, no. 3 (Winter 1978): 65–68; and

a substantial body of literature has grown up in appreciation of Cantillon and a number of mysteries surrounding him and the *Essai* have been solved. Most importantly, the Scottish philosopher and tax collector Adam Smith should no longer be considered the father of economics. That title now belongs to the Irish entrepreneur and Austrian economist, Richard Cantillon.

## CANTILLON AND THE *ESSAI*

The mystery of Richard Cantillon begins with his birth, which is now placed during the 1680s in southwest Ireland.[8] He was born into a family of Catholic landlords who had fought for the Stuart cause, and thus were dispossessed of their lands by Cromwell. His origins in the landed gentry shines through in the *Essai* where the landlord, the truly independent person in the economy, plays the crucial decisionmaking role in both production and consumption.

The *Essai* follows a progressive arrangement of ideas appropriate for the elucidation of economic theory (like Menger's *Principles*), and also shows many links to Cantillon's own life. Part one is an analysis of the real economy of the isolated state loosely based on the pre-capitalist economy of his family's heritage. Here the prince in the capital city rules over the landlords of the cities, market towns, and villages. Landlords collect rents from farmers who in turn hire labor to work the fields. Cantillon acknowledges that the large estates were taken by force, reflecting the fact that his ancestors took ownership of the land from the Irish and that these estates were in turn taken from them by force.[9]

The second half of part one is where Cantillon becomes the first economist to develop the key Austrian insights concerning the entrepreneur and the role entrepreneurship plays in the economy.[10] The entrepreneur is the bearer of risks inflicted by the changes in market demand. This is a direct reflection of Cantillon's own early career as an assistant to British

---

idem, "The Influence of Cantillon's *Essai* on the Methodology of J.B. Say," *Journal of Libertarian Studies* 7, no. 2 (Fall 1985): 305–16.

[8]Antoin E. Murphy, *Richard Cantillon: Entrepreneur and Economist* (New York: Oxford University Press, 1986), p. 10. My article relies heavily on this biography.

[9]The isolated state allows Cantillon to ignore the two great forces that otherwise permeate the *Essai*. The first force is the economic ebb-and-flow of foreign trade and the balance of payments between nations. The second is the relative military power between nations. Cantillon is concerned with the public good of national defense (the duty of the Prince) throughout the *Essai*, and his concessions from laissez-faire are made in this light.

[10]See for example, Rothbard, *Economic Thought Before Adam Smith*, p. 351; and Hébert, "Was Richard Cantillon an Austrian Economist?" p. 273.

Paymaster James Brydges during the War of Spanish Succession. There he learned and excelled in the role of accountant and contract negotiator, and learned the basics of banking and international finance. This experience also exposed Cantillon to gross government inefficiency and corruption. His travels through Europe during the War may have sparked his interest and insights into his subjectivist theory that population was based on the decisions of the landlord concerning how resources are used and on differences in cultural choice.

In part two of the *Essai*, Cantillon laid out his pathbreaking Austrian analysis of the monetary economy, exposing the great error of mercantilism (that money is wealth). This parallels Cantillon's second career as a Parisian banker that began in the service of his elder cousin's bank.[11] After the War of Spanish Succession, there was a great deal of economic instability, and this made the business of banking particularly dangerous. His cousin eventually had to sign over his bank to Cantillon and declare bankruptcy in 1716. In a lost manuscript, "Observations on the Trade and Luxury of Both Nations," Cantillon blamed conditions on the opulence and heavy war debts of Britain and France.[12]

Two historically important people were influential at this stage in Cantillon's life. Matthew Decker, a director of the East India Company and a prominent banker, was important because he helped Cantillon get established in banking. Another important influence was Lord Bolingbroke, a leader of the Jacobite cause who fled to France and became Cantillon's friend through the banking business. He introduced Cantillon to many of the leading thinkers of the day, including Montesquieu and Voltaire. Bolingbroke, as a leading opponent of the new financial system, was the important intellectual influence, having solidified Cantillon's "innate conservatism" on issues like monetary policy and the national debt.[13]

In part three of the *Essai*, Cantillon addresses the issues of foreign trade, exchange rates, and the role of banks. Here, Cantillon makes some

---

[11]Cantillon's secondary business was as a wine merchant, which no doubt sharpened his understanding of entrepreneurship, risk taking, and interest and price formation.

[12]See Murphy, *Richard Cantillon*, p. 50. Cantillon thought that the superfluities of life were part of wealth, but he often wrote as if he opposed excessive luxury. In particular, Cantillon opposed the opulence of the King and his court in terms of imported luxury items, which required too great a sacrifice from the provinces in terms of the productive capacity of the land, and thus hurt the peasants and landlords, and weakened the state.

[13]Ibid., pp. 48–49. Murphy considers Bolingbroke's strong Aristotelian views on society to be a major influence in chapter 12 of part 1 of Cantillon's *Essai*.

of his most important contributions to economic understanding. This section is a critique of mercantilist policies and the financial innovations of John Law during the Mississippi System and South Sea Bubble. This is a reflection of the third period in Cantillon's career, during which he made a fortune by understanding Law's system and its inevitable consequences.

From 1721 to his death in 1734, Cantillon was embroiled in legal disputes. He was involved with several lawsuits involving his banking business and the South Sea Bubble. He was also accused of attempted murder and was briefly imprisoned twice. The *Essai* was written at this time and there is good reason to suspect that Cantillon developed economic theory as part of his legal defense against charges of usury.[14]

## THE ORIGINS OF ECONOMIC THEORY

Cantillon was involved in the crucial events of his day, and he knew many great intellectuals of his age, including several important mercantilist writers. He did not completely escape the mercantile mindset and vernacular, but it is truly amazing how cleanly he broke with the past and struck out on his own to produce the first coherent and comprehensive work of economic theory.[15]

Cantillon's contributions to the method of economics, while unappreciated in his time and largely forgotten, are truly remarkable when placed in historical context. What impressed important economists such as Jevons, Schumpeter, Hayek, and Rothbard was Cantillon's scientific approach and the logical-deductive theorizing that is so characteristic of the Austrian School and the marginal revolution. Throughout the *Essai*, Cantillon is concerned with providing a scientific explanation for economic phenomena. His investigations are concerned with establishing cause and effect. Cantillon often expressed the causal relation with the term "natural," which he used thirty times in the *Essai*.[16]

---

[14]Ibid., p. 247, shows that sections of the *Essai* are very similar to sections of the legal defense testimony of his lawyers.

[15]As Hayek observed, "this gifted independent observer, enjoying an unsurpassed vantage point in the midst of the action, coordinated what he saw with the eyes of the born theoretician and was the first person who succeeded in penetrating and presenting to us almost the entire field which we now call economics." See F.A. Hayek, [1931] "Richard Cantillon," Micheál Ó. Súilleabháin, trans., *Journal of Libertarian Studies* 7, no. 2 (Fall 1985): 227. Or, as Anthony Brewer observed, the *Essai* "was the first systematic treatment of economic principles, of a sort modern economists would recognize" it as "a work of genius." See Brewer, "Cantillon and the Land Theory of Value," p. 10.

[16]Hayek, "Richard Cantillon," p. 260. Cantillon writes that the natural way to bring about or cause an increase in population is to have employment for the people and to make the land produce the means of their support. See Cantillon, *Essai*, p. 85.

Another hallmark of his Austrian analysis is his intention to limit himself to the positive economics of his subject, an attribute that Hayek considered especially remarkable for a writer of his time.[17] In several chapters, Cantillon halts his commentary and declines to offer value judgments concerning the subject matter at hand. For example, Cantillon writes that the issue of whether it is better to have a large but poor population or a small, wealthy population is a question outside of his subject.[18] He does likewise concerning the motives of a French Minister who debased the currency.[19]

Cantillon also employs the method of abstraction or imaginary construction to theorize about the economy. He uses the *ceteris paribus* assumption, for example, when discussing the productivity of labor. "The more labor is expended on it (land), *other things being equal*, the more it produces."[20] He uses the theoretical tool of the small isolated state as the modern theorist does to eliminate complicating factors such as monetary disturbances and international trade. More importantly, he used this construction or model to deduce the core Austrian point that production depends on demand, in this case the demand of the landowner of the great estate. Furthermore, as the landlord contracts out the production of his lands to farmers, he creates entrepreneurs, and an economy develops with exchange, prices, money, and competition.[21]

---

[17]Hayek, "Richard Cantillon," p. 260.

[18]Cantillon, *Essai*, p. 85.

[19]Henry Higgs, "Richard Cantillon," *Economic Journal* 1 (1891): 279. Of course, Cantillon uses these limits both to refrain from unnecessary value judgments and to prevent diverting himself from the main objects of his task. For example, in one case, he does make a brief value judgment concerning taxes, but quickly ends the subject as not essential to his purpose. See Cantillon, *Essai*, p. 159. In reading the *Essai*, you will find Cantillon making many value-laden statements but many of these can be explained with reference to the theoretical development of the *Essai* and his previous findings. This is, therefore, a likely source of confusion when interpreting Cantillon's work.

[20]Ibid., p. 47. The fact that he used the phrase "all things being equal" in the rather obvious case of more labor resulting in more production is evidence of clear intent.

[21]Cantillon clarifies this at the end of chapter 14 in the *Essai* with the statement:

> I do not consider here the variation in Market prices which may arise from the good or bad harvest of the year, or the extraordinary consumption which may occur from foreign troops or other accidents, so as not to complicate my subject, considering only a State in its natural and uniform condition. (p. 65)

The role of the entrepreneur is one of Cantillon's great contributions to economic understanding. He speaks of the entrepreneur in the classic sense of the undertaker of great business adventures, but Cantillon also has a theoretical distinction between those who work for a fixed return or wages and those who face uncertain returns, including farmers,[22] independent craftsmen, merchants, and manufacturers. These entrepreneurs purchase inputs at a given price to produce and sell later at an uncertain price.[23] In the pursuit of profit, the entrepreneur must bear risks as he faces the pervasive uncertainty of the market.[24] For example, the farmer has fixed expenses but:

> The price of these products will depend partly on the weather, partly on demand; if corn is abundant relative to consumption it will be dirt cheap, if there is scarcity it will be dear. Who can foresee the number of births and deaths of the people in a State in the course of the year? Who can foresee the increase or reduction of expense that may come about in the families? And yet the price of the Farmer's produce depends naturally upon these unforeseen circumstances, and consequently he conducts the enterprise of his farm at an uncertainty.[25]

The unsuccessful entrepreneur will live poorly or go bankrupt, while the successful entrepreneur will obtain a profit or advantage and cause entry into the market, "and so it is that the Undertakers of all kinds adjust themselves to risks in a State."[26] The entrepreneur brings prices and production into line with demand; in well organized societies, government officials can even fix prices of basic items without too much complaint.[27]

Cantillon has a sophisticated understanding of the price system containing most of the elements of modern Austrian analysis. Price is determined by demand and relative scarcity. Demand is a subjective concept based on the "humors" and "fancies" of the people. It is the "consent of the people" along with the relative scarcity of a product that determines

---

[22]See ibid., pp. 48–49.

[23]Ibid., p. 51.

[24]Cantillon laid the groundwork for Turgot and the theory of profit. See Renee Prendergast, "Cantillon and the Emergence of the Theory of Profit," *History of Political Economy* 23 (Fall 1991): 429.

[25]Cantillon, *Essai*, p. 49. His use of the word "naturally" shows that the changes he refers to cause a predictable change in price.

[26]Ibid., p. 53.

[27]Ibid., p. 31. When he refers to well-organized societies, Cantillon seems to be referring to an advanced market economy in which monetary exchange and banking services have been long and thoroughly established.

the market price, where market price is understood to be the price paid to the seller. Likewise, the market value of metals "varies with their plenty or scarcity, according to the demand."[28]

Cantillon makes an important distinction between price and market price, and between value and market value, that has served as a source of confusion concerning the meaning of his economics. Market price and market value are the real prices that occur in the market based on forces of supply and demand. Price and value are separate and distinct concepts from market prices. They are related to Cantillon's term "intrinsic value," and are used to describe the opportunity cost of resources used to produce the particular good in question, the specific land and labor that were sacrificed to produce the good.[29]

The term intrinsic value has been a source of confusion. Commentators have often been led to deride his value theory, consider him an objective value theorist, and to misplace him in the history of economic thought. Cantillon recognized the potential for this confusion:

> in this *Essai* I have always used the term Intrinsic Value to signify the amount of Land and Labor which enter into Production, not having found any term more suitable to express my meaning. I mention this only to avoid misunderstanding.[30]

What is very clear from a close reading of the *Essai* is that intrinsic value does not refer to the objective properties of the good (such as the purity of a gold bar), or to some long-run equilibrium value, but rather to the resources sacrificed to produce a particular good. As Hayek observed:

> What is most significant about Cantillon's achievement in the field of value and price theory is his down-playing the quest for rules and formulae that might account for the "normal" relationship between the value or price of various goods, and concentrating instead on the forces and mechanisms that are consistently at work in restoring these normal relationships.[31]

---

[28]Ibid., p. 97.

[29]Hülsmann, "Cantillon as a Proto-Austrian," p. 3, defends Cantillon by noting he clearly did not think that market prices were determined by cost, in terms of land and labor, and that intrinsic value is merely being used as a measure of the quantity of land and labor. Cantillon thus avoided the errors of later economists who claimed that land and labor were measures of value. His views are similar to Austrian economists who hold that only exchange ratios and market prices permit economic calculation.

[30]Cantillon, *Essai*, p. 107.

[31]Hayek, "Richard Cantillon," p. 263.

Most importantly, Cantillon was naming and describing a concept for which a term did not already exist in the Western world, for Cantillon knew many different languages.

Cantillon's conception of cost as the sacrifice of land and labor foregone is far more advanced than the land theory of cost and value advanced by the Physiocrats, or the labor theory of cost and value advanced by the classical economists. But Cantillon had a far richer understanding of cost than a simple measure of the quantity of land and labor that went into production. Cantillon stressed two important concepts throughout the *Essai* that provide greater depth to his conception of cost. First, Cantillon viewed all resources as heterogeneous. Each piece of land was of a different quality, and each laborer was also of a different quality. Therefore, while intrinsic value was a measure of cost, it was not possible in fact to simply count the number of hours and acres except in an abstract way or in simple illustrations. In fact, after establishing a preliminary land-and-labor theory of value in part one, he notes at the very beginning of part two that for specific goods in the real economy, it is "impossible to fix their respective intrinsic values."[32]

The other concept that he stressed was the alternative use of resources. Land could be used to grow corn or to provide hay for horses. Labor could toil on the farm or be trained in a craft. Cantillon clearly saw that when a landlord chose to own more horses, what he was giving up was the production (and sale) of grain, and that if France wished to import fine lace, then she would have to forego a large amount of wine produced from her vineyards. Cantillon understood the concept of opportunity cost, and his *Essai* was an attempt to construct the concept to explain economic choice.[33] The discovery of opportunity cost by this important precursor of the Austrian School truly marks the origin of economic theory.

Cantillon made pathbreaking contributions to the subjective theory of population. As part of his overall model of the economy, population density and distribution are determined by the tastes of the owners of productive resources. The prince and the landowners can greatly affect population by their consumption choices, thus helping to determine

---

[32]Cantillon, *Essai*, p. 115. He does note, however, that a specific intrinsic value is one that does not change.

[33]This point was first suggested to me by Professor Hébert; see Hébert, "Was Richard Cantillon an Austrian Economist?" p. 272. Spengler also hints at this in Joseph J. Spengler, "Richard Cantillon: First of the Moderns II," *Journal of Political Economy* 62, no. 5 (October 1954): 407; also see Michael D. Bordo, "Some Aspects of the Monetary Economics of Richard Cantillon," *Journal of Monetary Economics* 12, no. 2 (August 1983): 235–58.

how labor-intensive the land will be used. Culture and religion also play a role in population determination, while technology and resource endowments are important determinants of population density.

Cantillon took a scientific approach to population. He recognized that humans might multiply like "mice in a barn if they have unlimited means of subsistence," or that population might fall substantially over time.[34] Cantillon even recognized that international trade would affect the level and distribution of population, as land-poor countries could export manufactured goods to land-rich countries in return for food, fiber, and raw materials, and thus support a larger population than otherwise. Here, Cantillon is often mistakenly labeled a mercantilist, but Cantillon remains a value-free economist on the subject of population size.[35] However, he does offer the prince technical advice of a nationalist nature on how to achieve a greater population, which supposedly is good for national defense. For example, he bemoans the export of large amounts of French wine in order to pay the very high market price of a small amount of lace imported from Brussels.[36]

Despite this, Cantillon's analysis is far superior to those he influenced, like Malthus and Smith. They were concerned about population because, in their thinking, economic growth would result in a larger population of miserable people living at the subsistence level. According to Professor Tarascio, "Smith and Malthus do not reflect the spirit of Cantillon's *Essai*. Hence the message has been lost to subsequent readers of the later authors."[37] Smith and Malthus extended the idea of the subsistence wage to industrial workers, while Cantillon recognized that

---

[34]Cantillon, *Essai*, p. 83.

[35]Brewer, "Cantillon and the Land Theory of Value," p. 452; and Cantillon, *Essai*, p. 85.

[36]What Frenchman wouldn't be concerned with this issue? Cantillon is clearly not against luxury per se, as he defines wealth as consumption on the first page of the *Essai*, including the conveniences and superfluities of life. What he is concerned with is production. It is not possible to continue to consume, or to consume greater amounts, without production. According to Cantillon, the comparative greatness of States is their reserve stock, which is savings measured in both money and materials in order to improve the State and to offset bad harvests and wars. For the State, gold is the true reserve stock, because with gold you can even buy the implements of war from your enemy. See Cantillon, *Essai*, pp. 89, 91.

[37]Vincent J. Tarascio, "Cantillon's Theory of Population Size and Distribution," *Atlantic Economic Journal* 9, no. 2 (July 1981): 12–18, is perceptive in noticing that Cantillon's contribution was lost, and that neoclassical economics did not adopt the classical-population theory because real wages were clearly rising for a long time before the origins of neoclassical economics.

there would be a tendency towards higher wages for trained workers or for those in risky occupations.[38] In fact, Cantillon generally wrote of a maintenance wage that was not a subsistence wage at all, but rather a wage sufficient to maintain the worker in his current job.[39] In his model, economic growth led to higher wages and a better standard of living.

Another area in which Cantillon made an important contribution was spatial economics, a subject that permeated much of the *Essai*. Cantillon explained the economic geography of a state, the center of which was the capital city where the prince and government resided. Cities are regional centers with large markets and population, surrounded by market towns where the produce of the villages and farms are brought for sale. Cantillon explained that villagers bring their output to market in order to get the best price and to reduce transaction costs. He was masterful in using the role of transportation costs to explain why raw materials were more expensive near the cities, why heavy manufacturing was located near the source of raw materials, and why perishables should be produced near population centers. The role of transportation costs is a central issue in his writing on money and banking because the banker (like Cantillon himself) served as an intermediary to reduce the risk and transportation costs of shipping large amounts of money over great distances. Cantillon was the first economist to apply the principles of spatial economics in a general economic treatise. He "made original and lasting contributions to spatial economics . . . in the nature of first principles readily applicable to the fields of location theory and spatial pricing."[40]

Cantillon's successful career in banking played a major role in his monetary economics, which Hayek considered his greatest achievement.[41] Cantillon was a hard-money man who understood that the nature of money as a medium of exchange drove the evolution of money to precious metals, and that princes cannot introduce imaginary money or successfully debase money.[42] Central to his Austrian-style analysis was his rejection of the aggregate approach of the naive quantity theory of money in favor of a microeconomic-process approach to the study of the money. He showed that the type of change in the money supply and where it entered the economy were crucial to determining what the effects would

---

[38]See Cantillon, *Essai*, pt. 1, chaps. 7 and 8.

[39]See ibid., pt. 1, chap. 9; esp. Higgs, p. 25.

[40]Robert F. Hébert, "Richard Cantillon's Early Contributions to Spatial Economics," *Economica* 48, no. 189 (February 1981): 71–77.

[41]Hayek, *Economic History*, p. 264.

[42]See Bordo, "Some Aspects," p. 236; and Cantillon, *Essai*, pp. 111, 113.

be. A big gold discovery would raise the prices of goods demanded by gold mine owners and miners. Any large increase in money will give a new turn to consumption, thus changing relative prices, velocity, and the distribution of income.

New money can also affect the interest rate if the money comes into the hands of lenders. Cantillon rejected the Lockean–mercantilist view that the rate of interest was a purely monetary phenomenon. Like Mises, he found that the interest rate was based on the forces of supply and demand in the market for loanable funds, and that if the new money increased supply it would lower the interest rate.[43]

Cantillon thoroughly describes the forces that cause changes in interest rates, and shows the interest rate to be a normal and important aspect of the economy. He defends the earning of high rates of interest via comparison to earning profits and rents of even higher rates.[44] On the basis of his description of interest rates and what causes rates to be high, Cantillon ridicules the notion that government should regulate interest rates with usury laws.[45]

Cantillon presented a theory of the business cycle very similar to the Austrian theory when he analyzed changes in the money supply. Increased money supply is the boom phase that kicks off the business cycle. His descriptions of this phase of the cycle are what many commentators have used to label Cantillon a mercantilist, because more money is seen as leading to a higher level of economic activity.[46] However, problems sooner or later arise. The basic problem revolves around price inflation and the collapse of domestic industry. Cantillon's Austrian lesson is that mercantilist policy is a shortrun expediency that fails in the long run.

Cantillon was the first to describe the workings of the famous specie-flow price mechanism, a crucial component of the Austrian theory of the business cycle, normally attributed to Hume.[47] Here he analyzes

---

[43]Likewise, if the money comes into the hands of spenders first, the increased consumption will stimulate investment demand and raise interest rates (as prices rise, the nominal rate will increase as well).

[44]Remember Cantillon was a banker. When he was charged with usury in the wake of the South Sea Bubble, part of his defense was to defend high interest rates.

[45]"Nothing is more amusing than the multitude of Laws and Canons made in every age on the subject of the Interest of Money, always by Wiseacres who were hardly acquainted with trade and always without effect." Cantillon, *Essai*, p. 211.

[46]Anthony Brewer, "Cantillon and Mercantilism," *History of Political Economy* 20, no. 3 (Fall 1988): 447–60.

[47]Hume was published before Cantillon, but we now know that Cantillon wrote before Hume, and that Hume had probably read Cantillon.

changes in the domestic money supply brought about by changes in the balance of payments in a similar fashion to changes in the domestic gold supply described above. He suggests ways in which the prince might try to offset the negative effects of monetary inflation or to forestall them, but theoretically the reversal is inevitable, and Cantillon is not confident in the government's ability to micromanage the adjustment process.[48]

In discussing the topics of foreign trade, the balance of payments, and banking, Cantillon clearly shows how countries that develop a skilled workforce in manufacturing, participate in foreign trade, and avoid national banks will prosper. However, his commentary also seems mercantilist when he laments the buying of fancy lace from Brussels as "burdensome and unprofitable to France," and uses this as an example of how foreign trade can be usefully regulated.[49]

Although he comes across as supporting mercantilism, it is plausible that the basis for the support of such policy lies in theoretical analysis and his empirical observations of the world economy, not in mercantilism. He showed that manufactured goods are produced by skilled workers who earn higher real wages than unskilled farm workers. By exporting high-valued manufactured goods, average wage rates would be higher, the burden of transportation costs would be lower, and the economy could import either money or a much larger volume of food and raw materials. Cantillon shows that if the money is quickly spent, prices will rise and the positive impact of the money will quickly turn negative. Here he suggests that the foreign money be saved by the prince for purposes of national defense and to account for years of bad harvests. Presumably, the additional cash could be invested in the domestic economy.

Finally, Cantillon showed that monetizing the economy was good, but that you could get too much of a good thing, thus exposing the greatest error of mercantilism. Like modern Austrian economists, Cantillon rejected the mercantilist–monetarist policy goal of forever increasing the money supply. He thought that a set amount of money was sufficient, and that amount need only change as an economy switched from barter to monetary exchange, although there were several factors that would naturally reduce the need for money, such as banking services and an increased velocity of money.

Cantillon showed why bimetallism would create shortages of money, and warned against the use of paper money and national banks.[50] He also

---

[48]Cantillon, *Essai*, pp. 185, 323.

[49]Ibid., pp. 231, 233.

[50]Ibid., p. 319.

saw the problems of general banks of a public and private nature such as the South Sea Company, the Bank of England, and the yet-to-exist Federal Reserve System. He closed his *Essai* with an indictment of John Law and his system, which serves as a warning that continues to be important (and unheeded) to this day:

> It is then undoubted that a Bank with the complicity of a Minister is able to raise and support the price of public stock and to lower the rate of interest in the State at the pleasure of this Minister when the steps are taken discreetly, and thus pay off the State debt. But these refinements which open the door to making large fortunes are rarely carried out for the sole advantage of the State, and those who take part in them are generally corrupted. The excess banknotes, made and issued on these occasions, do not upset the circulation, because being used for the buying and selling of stock they do not serve for household expenses and are not changed into silver. But if some panic or unforeseen crisis drove the holders to demand silver from the Bank the bomb would burst and it would be seen that these are dangerous operations.[51]

No short essay can provide a complete picture of Richard Cantillon and his contributions to economics. For example, he presented a very good theory of prohibition; he had an excellent analysis of government debt; and he provided an interesting and useful perspective on the economics of slavery. Cantillon has been misunderstood as a mercantilist and objective (i.e., intrinsic) value theorist, but in fact he exposed the errors of mercantilism, and clearly understood the concept of opportunity cost, the fundamental principle in economic theory. Cantillon and his *Essai* are the origins of economic theory and that theory is clearly that of the latter-day Austrian School.[52]

## SELECTED READINGS

Bordo, Michael D. 1983. "Some Aspects of the Monetary Economics of Richard Cantillon." *Journal of Monetary Economics* 12, no. 2 (August ): 235–58.

Brewer, Anthony. 1992. *Richard Cantillon: Pioneer of Economic Theory.* London: Routledge.

---

[51]Ibid., p. 323.

[52]See Hébert, "Was Richard Cantillon an Austrian Economist?" It is worth noting that the historians of economic thought who have hailed Cantillon's accomplishments have been Austrian economists, such as Hayek and Rothbard, or have been fellow travelers and sympathizers, such as Schumpeter. An interesting fact is that a copy of the *Essai* can be found in Carl Menger's library, and also a German language edition (1931) is in Ludwig von Mises's library. It seems clear that the Austrian School drew much of its inspiration from Cantillon.

——. 1988. "Cantillon and the Land Theory of Value." *History of Political Economy* 20, no. 1 (Spring): 1–14.

——. 1988. "Cantillon and Mercantilism." *History of Political Economy* 20, no. 3 (Fall): 447–60.

Cantillon, Richard. [1755] 1959. *Essai sur la Nature du Commerce en Général* [and other essays]. Henry Higgs, ed. and trans. London: Frank Cass.

Hayek, F.A. [1931] 1991. "Richard Cantillon (c.1680–1734)." Introduction to Richard Cantillon, *Essai sur la Nature du Commerce en Général*, Grete Heinz, trans. Reprinted in Hayek, *Economic History*. Vol. 3. *The Collected Works of F.A. Hayek*. W.W. Bartley, III, and Stephen Kresge, eds. Chicago: University of Chicago Press.

——. [1931] 1985. "Richard Cantillon," Micheál Ó. Súilleabháin, trans. *Journal of Libertarian Studies* 7, no. 2 (Fall): 217–48.

Hébert, Robert F. 1985. "Was Richard Cantillon an Austrian Economist?" *Journal of Libertarian Studies* 7, no. 2 (Fall): 269–80.

——. 1981. "Richard Cantillon's Early Contributions to Spatial Economics." *Economica* 48, no. 189 (February): 71–77.

Higgs, Henry. 1892. "Cantillon's Place in Economics." *Quarterly Journal of Economics* 6:436–56.

——. 1891. "Richard Cantillon." *Economic Journal* 1:262–91.

Hone, Joseph. 1944. "Richard Cantillon, Economist-Biographical Note." *Economic Journal* 54:96–100.

Hülsmann, Jörg Guido. 1997. "Cantillon As A Proto-Austrian: Further Evidence." Working Paper.

Liggio, Leonard P. 1985. "Richard Cantillon and the French Economists: Distinctive French Contributions to J.B. Say." *Journal of Libertarian Studies* 7, no. 2 (Fall): 295–304.

Murphy, Antoin E. 1986. *Richard Cantillon: Entrepreneur and Economist*. New York: Oxford University Press.

——. 1985. "Richard Cantillon: Banker and Economist." *Journal of Libertarian Studies* 7, no. 2 (Fall): 185–216.

——. 1984. "Richard Cantillon: An Irish Banker in Paris." *Hermathena* 135: 45–74.

O'Mahony, David. 1985. "Richard Cantillon—A Man of His Time: A Comment on Tarascio." *Journal of Libertarian Studies* 7, no. 2 (Fall): 259–68.

Prendergast, Renee. 1991. "Cantillon and the Emergence of the Theory of Profit."*History of Political Economy* 23 (Fall): 419–29.

Rothbard, Murray N. 1995. *Economic Thought Before Adam Smith*. Vol. 1. *An Austrian Perspective on the History of Economic Thought*. Cheltenham, U.K.: Edward Elgar.

Salerno, Joseph T. 1985. "The Influence of Cantillon's *Essai* on the Methodology of J.B. Say." *Journal of Libertarian Studies* 7, no. 2 (Fall): 305–16.

——. 1978. "Comment on the French Liberal School." *Journal of Libertarian Studies* 2, no. 3 (Winter): 65–68

Schumpeter, Joseph. [1914] 1991. *Epochen der Dogmen-und Methodengeschichte, Grundriz der Sozialökonomik.* 1st ed. Tübingen: J.C.B. Mohr. Vol. 1, Pt. 1, P. 143, as quoted in F.A. Hayek (1991). Pp. 258–59.

Spengler, Joseph J. 1954. "Richard Cantillon: First of the Moderns I." *Journal of Political Economy* 62, no. 4 (August): 281–95.

——. 1954. "Richard Cantillon: First of the Moderns II." *Journal of Political Economy* 62, no. 5 (October): 406–24.

Tarascio, Vincent J. 1985. "Cantillon's *Essai*: A Current Perspective." *Journal of Libertarian Studies* 7, no. 2 (Fall): 249–58.

——. 1981. "Cantillon's Theory of Population Size and Distribution." *Atlantic Economic Journal* 9, no. 2 (July): 12–18.

Waddell, D.A.G. 1958. "Charles Davenant (1656–1714): A Biographical Sketch." *Economic History Review* 2nd Series, 11, no. 1: 279–88.

# 3
# A.R.J. TURGOT: BRIEF, LUCID, AND BRILLIANT[1]

MURRAY N. ROTHBARD

ANNE ROBERT JACQUES TURGOT'S career in economics was an all too brief but brilliant one, and in every way remarkable. In the first place, he died a rather young man, and second, the time and energy he devoted to economics was comparatively little. He was a busy man of affairs, born in Paris to a distinguished Norman family which had long served as important royal officials. Turgot's father, Michel-Etienne, was a Councillor of the Parliament of Paris, a master of requests, and top administrator of the city of Paris. His mother was the famous intellectual and aristocratic Dame Magdelaine-Françoise Martineau.

*A.R.J. Turgot*
*1727–1781*

Turgot had a sparkling career as a student, earning honors at the Seminary of Saint-Sulpice, and then at the great theological faculty of the University of Paris, the Sorbonne. As a younger son of a distinguished but not wealthy family, Turgot was expected to enter the Church, the preferred path of advancement for someone in that position in eighteenth-century France. But although he became an Abbé, Turgot decided instead to become magistrate, master of requests, *intendant*, and, finally, a short-lived and controversial minister of finance (or "controller-general") in a heroic but ill-fated attempt to sweep away statist restrictions on the market economy in a virtual revolution from above.

---

[1]This article is an edited version of a 1986 booklet by Murray N. Rothbard entitled *The Brilliance of Turgot* (Auburn, Ala.: Ludwig von Mises Institute).

Not only was Turgot a busy administrator, but his intellectual interests were wide-ranging, and most of his spare time was spent in reading and writing, not in economics, but in history, literature, philology, and the natural sciences. His contributions to economics were brief, scattered, and hasty. His most famous work, "Reflections on the Formation and Distribution of Wealth" (1766), comprised only fifty-three pages. This brevity only highlights the great contributions to economics made by this remarkable man.

In the history of thought, the style is often the man, and Turgot's clarity and lucidity of style mirrors the virtues of his thought, and contrasts refreshingly to the prolix and turgid prose of the Physiocrat School.

### LAISSEZ-FAIRE AND FREE TRADE

Turgot's mentor in economics and in administration was his great friend Jacques Claude Marie Vincent, Marquis de Gournay (1712–1759). It is fitting, then, that Turgot developed his laissez-faire views most fully in one of this early works, the "Elegy to Gournay" (1759), a tribute offered when the Marquis died young after a long illness.[2] Turgot made it clear that the network of detailed mercantilist regulation of industry was not simply intellectual error, but a veritable system of coerced cartelization and special privilege conferred by the State. For Turgot, freedom of domestic and foreign trade followed equally from the enormous mutual benefits of free exchange. All the restrictions "forget that no commercial transactions can be anything other than reciprocal," and that it is absurd to try to sell everything to foreigners while buying nothing from them in return.

Turgot then goes on, in his "Elegy," to make a vital pre-Hayekian point about the uses of indispensable particular knowledge by individual actors and entrepreneurs in the free market. These committed, on-the-spot participants in the market process know far more about their situations than do intellectuals aloof from the fray.

In proceeding to a more detailed analysis of the market process, Turgot points out that self-interest is the prime mover of the process, and that individual interest in the free market must *always* coincide with the general interest. The buyer will select the seller who will give him the lowest price for the most suitable product, and the seller will sell his best merchandise at the highest competitive price. Governmental restrictions

---

[2]Turgot wrote the "Elegy" in a few days, as material for Gournay's official eulogist, writer Jean François Marmontel. Marmontel simply took extracts from Turgot's essay, and published them as the official eulogy.

and special privileges, on the other hand, compel consumers to buy poorer products at higher prices. Turgot concludes that "the general freedom of buying and selling is therefore . . . the only means of assuring, on the one hand, the seller of a price sufficient to encourage production, and, on the other hand, the consumer of the best merchandise at the lowest price." Turgot concluded that government should be strictly limited to protecting individuals against "great injustice" and the nation against invasion. "The government should always protect the natural liberty of the buyer to buy, and the seller to sell."

It is possible, Turgot conceded, that, on the free market, there will sometimes be "a cheating merchant and a duped consumer." But then, the market will supply its own remedies: "the cheated consumer will learn by experience and will cease to frequent the cheating merchant, who will fall into discredit and thus will be punished for his fraudulence." Turgot, in fact, ridiculed attempts by government to insure against fraud or harm to consumers.

To expect the government to prevent such fraud from ever occurring would be like wanting it to provide cushions for all the children who might fall. To assume it to be possible to prevent successfully, by regulation, all possible malpractices of this kind is to sacrifice to a chimerical perfection the whole progress of industry.

Turgot added that all such regulations and inspections "always involve expenses, and that these expenses are always a tax on the merchandise, and as a result overcharge the domestic consumer and discourage the foreign buyer." Turgot concludes with a splendid flourish: "To suppose all consumers to be dupes, and all merchants and manufacturers to be cheats, has the effect of authorizing them to be so, and of degrading all the working members of the community."

Turgot goes on once more in the Hayekian theme of greater knowledge by the particular actors in the market. Gournay's entire laissez-faire doctrine, he points out, "is grounded on the continuous inspection of a multitude of transactions which by their immensity alone could not be fully known, and which, moreover, are continually dependent on a multitude of ever changing circumstances which cannot be managed or even foreseen." Turgot concludes his elegy to his friend and teacher by noting Gournay's belief that most people were "well disposed toward the sweet principles of commercial freedom," but prejudice and a search for special privilege often bar the way. Every person, Turgot pointed out, wants to make an exception to the general principle of freedom, and "this exception is generally based on their personal interest."

Turgot's final writings on economics were written while he was *intendant* at Limoges, in the years just before becoming Controller-General in 1774. They reflect his embroilment in a struggle for free trade within the royal bureaucracy. In his last work, the "Letter to the Abbé Terray [the Controller-General] on the Duty of Iron" (1773), Turgot trenchantly lashes out at the system of protective tariffs as a war of all-against-all using State monopoly privilege as a weapon, at the expense of the consumers.

Turgot indeed, in anticipation of Bastiat seventy-five years later, calls this system a "war of reciprocal oppression, in which the government lends its authority to all-against-all." He concludes that "Whatever sophisms are collected by the self-interest of a few merchants, the truth is that all branches of commerce ought to be free, equally free, and entirely free."[3]

Turgot was close to the physiocrats, not only in advocating freedom of trade, but also in calling for a single tax on the "net product" of land. Even more than in the case of the physiocrats, one gets the impression with Turgot that his real passion was in getting rid of the stifling taxes on all other walks of life, rather than in imposing them on agricultural land. Turgot's views on taxes were most fully, if still briefly, worked out in his "Plan for a Paper on Taxation in General" (1763), an outline of an unfinished essay he had begun to write as *intendant* at Limoges for the benefit of the Controller-General. Turgot claimed that taxes on towns were shifted backward to agriculture, and showed how taxation crippled commerce, distorted the location of towns, and led to the illegal evasion of duties. Privileged monopolies, furthermore, raised prices severely and encouraged smuggling. Taxes on capital destroyed accumulated thrift and hobbled industry. Turgot's eloquence was confined to pillorying bad taxes rather than elaborating on the alleged virtues of the land tax. Turgot's summation of the tax system was trenchant and hard-hitting: "It seems that Public Finance, like a greedy monster, has been lying in wait for the entire wealth of the people."

## VALUE, EXCHANGE AND PRICE

One of the most remarkable contributions by Turgot was an unpublished and unfinished paper, "Value and Money," written around 1769.

[3]In the course of arguing in this letter for free trade in iron, Turgot anticipated the great Ricardian doctrine of comparative advantage, in which each region concentrates on producing that commodity which it can make efficiently relative to other regions.

Turgot developed an Austrian-type theory first of Crusoe economics, then of an isolated two-person exchange, which he later expanded to four persons, and then to a complete market. By concentrating first on the economics of an isolated Crusoe figure, Turgot was able to work out economic laws that transcend exchange and apply to all individual actions.

First, Turgot examines an isolated man, and works out a sophisticated analysis of his value or utility scale. By valuing and forming preference scales of different objects, Crusoe confers value upon various economic goods, and compares and chooses between them on the basis of their relative worth to him, not only between various present uses of goods but also between consuming them now and accumulating them for "future needs." Like his French precursors, Turgot sees that the subjective utility of a good diminishes as its supply to a person increases; and like them, he lacks only the concept of the marginal unit to complete the theory. But he went far beyond his predecessors in the precision and clarity of his analysis. He also sees that the subjective values of goods will change rapidly on the market, and there is at least a hint in his discussion that he realized that this subjective value is strictly ordinal and not subject to measure.

Turgot saw that a "comparison of *value*, this evaluation of different objects, changes continually with the need of the person." Turgot proceeds not only to diminishing utility, but to a strong anticipation of diminishing *marginal* utility, since he concentrates on the *unit* of the particular goods: "When the savage is hungry, he values a piece of game more than the best bearskin; but let his appetite be satisfied and let him be cold, and it will be the bearskin that becomes valuable to him."

After bringing the anticipation of future needs into his discussion, Turgot deals with diminishing utility as a function of abundance. Armed with this tool of analysis, he helps solve the value paradox:

> Water, in spite of its necessity and the multitude of pleasures which it provides for man, is not regarded as a precious thing in a well-watered country; man does not seek to gain its possession since the abundance of this element allows him to find it all around him.

Turgot then proceeds to a truly noteworthy discussion, anticipating the modern concentration on economics as the allocation of scarce resources to a large and far-less-limited number of alternative ends:

> To obtain the satisfaction of these wants, man has only an even more limited quantity of strength and resources. Even a particular object of enjoyment costs him trouble, hardship, labor, and, at the very least,

> time. It is this use of his resources applied to the quest for each object which provides the offset to his enjoyment, and forms as it were the cost of the thing.

Although Turgot called the cost of a product its "fundamental value," he comes down generally to a rudimentary version of the later Austrian view that all costs are really "opportunity costs," sacrifices foregoing a certain amount of resources that would have been produced elsewhere. Thus, Turgot's actor (in this case an isolated one) appraises and evaluates objects on the basis of their significance to himself. First, Turgot says that this significance, or utility, is the importance of his "time and toil" expended, but then he treats this concept as equivalent to productive opportunity foregone: as "the portion of his resources which he can use to acquire an evaluated object without thereby sacrificing the quest for other objects of equal or greater importance."

Having analyzed the actions of an isolated Crusoe, Turgot brings in Friday; that is, he now assumes two men and sees how an exchange will develop. Here, in a perceptive analysis, he works out the Austrian theory of isolated two-person exchange, virtually as it would be arrived at by Carl Menger a century later. First, he has two savages on a desert island, each with valuable goods in his possession, but the goods being suited to different wants. One man has a surplus of fish, the other of hides, and the result will be that each will exchange part of his surplus for the other's, so that both parties to the exchange will benefit. Commerce, or exchange, has developed.

Turgot then changes the conditions of his example, and supposes that the two goods are corn and wood, and that each commodity could therefore be stored for future needs, so that each would not be automatically eager to dispose of his surplus. Each man will then weigh the relative "esteem" to him of the two products until the two parties agree on a price at which each man will value what he obtains in exchange more highly than what he gives up. Both sides will then benefit from the exchange.

Turgot then unfortunately goes off the subjective-value track by adding, unnecessarily, that the terms of exchange arrived at through this bargaining process will have "equal exchange value," since otherwise the person cooler to the exchange "would force the other to come closer to his price by a better offer." It is unclear here what Turgot means by saying that "each gives equal value to receive equal value"; there is perhaps an inchoate notion here that the price arrived at through bargaining will be halfway between the value-scales of each. He is, however, perfectly correct in pointing out that the exchange increases the wealth of both parties. He then brings in the competition of two sellers for each of the products and shows how the competition affects the value-scales of the participants.

A few years earlier in his most important work, "The Reflections of the Formation and Distribution of Wealth,"[4] Turgot had pointed out the bargaining process, where each party wants to get as much as he can and give up as little as possible in exchange. The price of any good will vary in accordance with the urgency of need among the participants; there is no "true price" toward which the market tends.

Finally, in his repeated analysis of human action as the result of expectations, rather than in equilibrium or as possessing perfect knowledge, Turgot anticipates the Austrian emphasis on expectations as the key to actions on the market. Turgot's very emphasis on expectations, of course, implies that they can be and often are disappointed in the market.

## THE THEORY OF PRODUCTION AND DISTRIBUTION

In one sense, Turgot's theory of production followed the physiocrats—only agriculture is productive, so there should be a single tax on land. But the major thrust of his theory of production was quite different from that of physiocracy. Even though only land was supposed to be productive, Turgot readily conceded that natural resources must be transformed by human labor, and that labor must enter into each stage of the production process. Here Turgot had worked out the rudiments of the crucial Austrian theory that production takes *time* and that it passes through various *stages*, each of which takes time, and that therefore the basic classes of factors of production are land, labor, and time.

One of Turgot's most remarkable contributions to economics, the significance of which was lost until the twentieth century, was his brilliant and almost offhand development of the laws of diminishing returns. This gem arose out of a contest which he had inspired to be held by the Royal Agricultural Society of Limoges, for essays on indirect taxation. Unhappiness with the winning physiocratic essay by Guerineau de Saint-Peravy led him to develop his own views in "Observations on a Paper by Saint-Peravy" (1767). Here, Turgot went to the heart of the physiocratic error of assuming a fixed proportion of the various expenditures of different classes of people. But, Turgot pointed out, not only are the proportions of factors to product variable, but also after a point,

[4]The "Reflections" (1766), remarkably, were scribbled hastily in order to explain to two Chinese students in Paris questions that Turgot was preparing to ask them about the Chinese economy. Rarely has a work so important arisen from so trivial a cause.

"all further expenditures would be useless, and that such increases could even become detrimental. In this case, the advances would be increased without increasing the product. There is therefore a *maximum* point of production which it is impossible to pass." Furthermore, it is "more than likely that as the advances are increased gradually past this point up to the point where they return nothing, each increase would be less and less productive." On the other hand, if the farmer reduces the factors from the point of maximum production, the same changes in proportion would be found.

In short, Turgot had worked out, in fully developed form, an analysis of the law of diminishing returns which would not be surpassed, or possibly equaled, until the twentieth century.[5] Increasing the quantity of factors raises the marginal productivity (the quantity produced by each increase of factors) until a maximum point is reached, after which the marginal productivity falls, eventually to zero, and then becomes negative.

## THE THEORY OF CAPITAL, ENTREPRENEURSHIP, SAVINGS, AND INTEREST

In the roster of Turgot's outstanding contributions to economic theory, the most remarkable was his theory of capital and interest, which, in contrast to such fields as utility, sprang up virtually fullblown unrelated to preceding contributions. Not only that, but Turgot worked out almost completely the Austrian theory of capital and interest a century before it was set forth in definitive form by Eugen von Böhm-Bawerk.

Turgot's theory of capital proper was echoed in the British classical economists as well as the Austrians. In his great "Reflections," Turgot pointed out that wealth is accumulated by means of consumed and saved annual produce. Savings are accumulated in the form of money, and then invested in various kinds of capital goods. Furthermore, as Turgot pointed out, the "capitalist–entrepreneur" must first accumulate saved capital in order to "advance" his payment to laborers while the product is being worked on. In agriculture, the capitalist–entrepreneur must save funds to pay workers, buy cattle, pay for buildings and equipment, etc., until the harvest is reaped and sold and here can recoup his advances. And so it is in every field of production.

Some of this was picked up by Adam Smith and the later British classicists, but they failed to absorb two vital points. One was that Turgot's capitalist was a capitalist–*entrepreneur*. He not only advanced savings to workers and other factors of production, he also, as Cantillon had

[5] According to Schumpeter, not until a journal article by Edgeworth in 1911.

first pointed out, bore the risks of uncertainty of the market. Cantillon's theory of the entrepreneur as a pervasive risk-bearer facing uncertainty, thereby equilibrating market conditions, had lacked one key element: an analysis of capital and the realization that the major driving force of the market economy is not just any entrepreneur but the *capitalist*–entrepreneur, the man who combines both functions. Yet Turgot's memorable achievement in developing the theory of the capitalist–entrepreneur, has, as Professor Hoselitz pointed out, "been completely ignored" until the twentieth century.

If the British classicists totally neglected the entrepreneur, they also failed to absorb Turgot's proto-Austrian emphasis on the crucial role of *time* in production, and the fact that industries may require many stages of production and sale. Turgot anticipated the Austrian concept of opportunity cost, and pointed out that the capitalist will tend to earn his imputed wages and the opportunity that the capitalist sacrificed by not investing his money elsewhere. In short, the capitalist's accounting profits will tend to a long-run equilibrium plus the imputed wages of his own labor and skill. In agriculture, manufacturing, or any other field of production, there are two basic classes of producers in society: (a) the entrepreneurs / owners of capital, and (b) the workers.

At this point, Turgot incorporated a germ of valuable insight from the physiocrats—invested capital must continue to return a steady profit through continued circulation of expenditures, or dislocations in production and payments will occur. Integrating his analyses of money and capital, Turgot then pointed out that before the development of gold or silver as money, the scope for entrepreneurship had been very limited. For, to develop the division of labor and stages of production, it is necessary to accumulate large sums of capital, and to undertake extensive exchanges, none of which is possible without money.

Seeing that advances of savings to factors of production are a key to investment, and that this process is only developed in a money economy, Turgot then proceeded to a crucial Austrian point: since money and capital advances are indispensable to all enterprises, laborers are therefore willing to *pay* capitalists a discount out of production for the service of having money paid them in advance of future revenue. In short, the interest return on investment is the payment by laborers to the capitalists for advancing them present money so they do not have to wait for years for income.

The following year, in his scintillating comments on the paper by Saint-Peravy, Turgot expanded his analysis of savings and capital to set forth an excellent anticipation of Say's Law. Turgot rebutted pre-Keynesian fears of the physiocrats that money not spent on consumption would "leak" out of the circular flow and thereby wreck the economy. As a result, the physiocrats tended to oppose savings per se. Turgot, however, pointed out that advances of capital are vital in all enterprises, and where might the advances come from, if not out of savings? He also noted that it made no difference if such savings were supplied by landed proprietors or by entrepreneurs. For entrepreneurial savings to be large enough to accumulate capital and expand production, profits have to be higher than the amount required to merely maintain the current capital stock.

Turgot goes on to point out that the physiocrats assume without proof that savings simply leak out of circulation. Instead, he says, money will return to circulation immediately; savings will be used either (a) to buy land, (b) to be invested as advances to workers and other factors, or (c) to be loaned out at interest. All of these uses of savings return money to the circular flow. Advances of capital, for example, return to circulation in paying for equipment, buildings, raw materials, or wages. The purchase of land transfers money to the seller of land, who in turn will either buy something with the money, pay his debts, or relend the amount. In any case, the money returns promptly to circulation.

Turgot then engaged in a similar analysis of spending flows if savings are loaned at interest. If consumers borrow the money, they borrow in order to spend, and so the money expended returns to circulation. If they borrow to pay debts or buy land, the same thing occurs. And if entrepreneurs borrow the money, it will be poured into advances and investments, and the money will once again return to circulation. Money saved, therefore, is not lost; it returns to circulation. Furthermore, the value of savings invested in capital is far greater than that piled up in hoards, so that money will tend to return to circulation quickly. Turgot pointed out, even if increased savings actually withdrew a small amount of money from circulation for a considerable time, the lower price of the produce will be more than offset for the entrepreneur by the increased advances and the consequent greater output and lowering of the cost of production. Here, Turgot had the germ of the much later Mises–Hayek analysis of how savings narrows but lengthens the structure of production.

The acme of Turgot's contribution to economic theory was his sophisticated analysis of interest. We have already seen Turgot's remarkable insight in seeing interest return on investment as a price paid by laborers to capitalist–entrepreneurs for advances of savings in the form of present money. Turgot also demonstrated—far ahead of his time—the relationship between this natural rate of interest and the interest on money loans. He showed, for example, that the two must tend to be equal on the market, since the owners of capital will continually balance their expected returns in different channels of use, whether they be money loans or direct investment in production. The lender sells the use of his money now, and the borrower buys the use, and the "price" of those loans, i.e., the loan rate of interest, will be determined, as in the case of any commodity, by the higgling and haggling of supply and demand on the market. Increased demand for loans will raise interest rates; increased supply of loans will lower them. People borrow for many reasons—to try to make an entrepreneurial profit, to purchase land, pay debts, or consume—while lenders are concerned with just two matters—interest return and the safety of their capital.

While there will be a market tendency to equate loan rates of interest and interest returns on investment, loans tend to be a less risky form of channeling savings. So that investment in risky enterprises will only be made if entrepreneurs expect that their profit will be greater than the loan rate of interest. He also pointed out that government bonds will tend to be the least risky investment, so that they will earn the lowest interest return. Turgot went on to declare that the "true evil" of government debt is that it presents advantages to the public creditors but channels their savings into "sterile" and unproductive uses, and maintains a high interest rate in competition with productive uses.

Pressing on to an analysis of the nature and use of lending at interest, Turgot engaged in an incisive and hardhitting critique of usury laws, which the physiocrats were still trying to defend. A loan, Turgot pointed out, "is a reciprocal contract, free between the two parties, which they make only because it is advantageous to them." Turgot moved in for the clincher: "Now on what principle can a crime be discovered in a contract advantageous to two parties, with which both parties are satisfied, and which certainly does no injury to anyone else?" There is no exploitation in charging interest just as there is none in the sale of any commodity. To attack a lender for "taking advantage" of the borrower's need for money by demanding interest "is as absurd an argument as saying that a baker who demands money for bread he sells, takes advantage of the buyer's need for bread."

It is true, Turgot says to the anti-usury wing of the Scholastics, that money employed successfully in enterprises yields a profit, or invested in land yields revenue. The lender gives up, during the term of the loan, not only possession of the metal but also the profit he could have obtained by investment. The "profit or revenue he would have been able to procure by it, and the interest which indemnified him for this loss cannot be looked on as unjust." Thus, Turgot integrates his analysis and justification for interest with a generalized view of opportunity cost, that is, of income foregone from lending money. And then, above all, Turgot declares, there is the property right of the lender, a crucial point that must not be overlooked.

Turgot, in the highly influential "Paper on Lending at Interest" (1770), focused on the crucial problem of interest: *why* are borrowers willing to pay the interest premium for the use of money? The opponents of usury, he noted, hold that the lender, in requiring more than the principal to be returned, is receiving a value in excess of the value of the loan, and that this excess is somehow deeply immoral. But then Turgot came to the critical point: "It is true that in repaying the principal, the borrower returns exactly the same weight of the metal which the lender had given him." But why, he adds, should the weight of the money metal be the crucial consideration, and not the "value and usefulness it has for the lender and the borrower?" Specifically, arriving at the vital Böhm-Bawerkian—Austrian concept of time preference, Turgot urges us to compare "the difference in usefulness which exists at the date of borrowing between a sum currently owned and an unequal sum which is to be received at a distant date." The key is time preference—the discounting of the future and the concomitant placing of a premium upon the present. Turgot points to the well-known motto, "a bird in the hand is better than two in the bush." Since a sum of money actually owned now "is preferable to the assurance of receiving a similar sum in one or several years' time," the same sum of money paid and returned is scarcely an equivalent value, for the lender "gives the money and receives only an assurance." But cannot this loss in value "be compensated by the assurance of an increase in the sum proportioned to the delay?" Turgot concluded that "this compensation is precisely the rate of interest." He added that what has to be compared in a loan transaction is *not* the value of the money loaned with the sum of money repaid, but the "value of the *promise* of a sum of money compared to the value of money available now." For a loan is precisely the transfer of a sum of money in the future. Hence, a maximum rate of interest imposed by law would deprive virtually all risky enterprises of credit.

In addition to developing the Austrian theory of time preference, Turgot was the first person, in his "Reflections," to point to the corollary concept of *capitalization*; that is, the present capital value of land or other capital good on the market tends to equal the sum of its expected annual future rents, or returns, discounted by the market rate of time preference, or rate of interest.

As if this were not enough to contribute to economics, Turgot also pioneered a sophisticated analysis of the relation between the interest rate and the quantity of money. There is little connection he pointed out, between the value of currency in terms of prices and the interest rate. The supply of money may be plentiful, and hence the value of money low in terms of commodities, but interest may at the same time be very high. Perhaps following David Hume's similar model, Turgot asks what would happen if the quantity of silver money in a country suddenly doubled, *and* that increase were magically distributed in equal proportions to every person. Turgot then points out that prices will rise, perhaps doubling, and that therefore the value of silver in terms of commodities will fall. But, he adds, it by no means follows that the interest rate will fall if people's expenditure proportions remain the same.

Indeed, Turgot points out that, depending on how the spending–saving proportions are affected, a rise in the quantity of money could *raise* interest rates. Suppose, he says, that all wealthy people decide to spend their incomes and annual profits on consumption and spend their capital on foolish expenditures. The increased consumption spending will raise the prices of consumer goods, and there being far less money to lend or to spend on investments, interest rates will rise along with prices. In short, spending will accelerate and prices rise, while, at the same time, time-preference rates rise, people spend more and save less, and interest rates will increase. Thus, Turgot is over a century ahead of his time in working out the complex Austrian relationship between what Mises would call the "money-relation"—the relation between the supply and demand for money, which determines prices or the price level—and the rates of time preference, which determine the spending–saving proportion and the rate of interest. Here, too, was the beginning of the rudiments of the Austrian theory of the business cycle, of the relationship between expansion of the money supply and the rate of interest.

As for the movements in the rate of time preference or interest, an increase in the spirit of thrift will lower interest rates and increase the amount of savings and the accumulation of capital; a rise in the spirit of luxury will do the opposite. The spirit of thrift, Turgot notes, has been steadily rising in Europe over several centuries, and hence interest rates have tended to fall. The various interest rates and rates of return on loans, investments, and land will tend to equilibrate throughout the market and tend toward a single rate of return. Capital, Turgot notes, will move out of lower-profit industries and regions and into higher-profit industries and regions.

## THEORY OF MONEY

While Turgot did not devote a great deal of attention to the theory of money, he had some important contributions to make. In addition to continuing the Hume model and integrating it with his analysis of interest, Turgot was emphatic in his opposition to the now dominant idea that money is purely a conventional token. In contrast, Turgot declared, "it is not at all by virtue of a convention that money is exchanged for all the other values: it is itself an object of commerce, a form of wealth, because it has value, and because of value exchanges in trade for an equal value."

In his unfinished dictionary article on "Value and Money," Turgot developed his monetary theory further. Drawing on his knowledge of linguistics, he declared that money is a kind of language, bringing forms of various conventional things into a "common term or standard." The common term of all currencies is the actual value, or prices, or the objects they try to measure. These "measures," however, are hardly perfect, Turgot acknowledged, since the values of gold and silver always vary in relation to commodities as well as each other. All moneys are made of the same materials, largely gold and silver, and differ only on the units of currency. And all these units are reducible to each other, as are other measures of length or volume, by expressions of weight in each standard currency. There are two kinds of money, Turgot noted, *real* money —coins, pieces of metal marked by inscriptions—and *fictitious* money, serving as units of account or *numeraires*. When real money units are defined in terms of the units of account, the various units are then linked to each other and to specific weights of gold or silver.

Problems arise, Turgot showed, because the real moneys in the world are not just one metal but two—gold and silver. The relative values of gold and silver on the market will then vary in accordance with the relative scarcity of gold and silver in the various nations.

## INFLUENCE

One of the striking examples of injustice in the historiography of economic thought is the treatment accorded to Turgot's brilliant analysis of capital and interest by the great founder of Austrian capital-and-interest theory, Eugen von Böhm-Bawerk. In the 1880s, Böhm-Bawerk set out, in the first volume of his *Capital and Interest*, to clear the path for his own theory of interest by studying and demolishing previous, competing theories.

Unfortunately, instead of acknowledging Turgot as his forerunner in the pioneering Austrian theory, Böhm-Bawerk brusquely dismissed the Frenchman as a mere physiocratic land-productivity theorist. This unfairness to Turgot is all the more heightened by recent information that Böhm-Bawerk, in his first evaluation of Turgot's theory of interest in a still-unpublished seminar paper in 1876, reveals the enormous influence of Turgot's views on his later developed thought. Perhaps we must conclude that, in this case as in others, Böhm-Bawerk's need to claim originality and to demolish all of his predecessors took precedence over the requirements of truth and justice.

In the light of Böhm-Bawerk's mistreatment, it is heartwarming to see Schumpeter's appreciative summation of Turgot's great contributions to economics. Concentrating almost exclusively on Turgot's "Reflections," Schumpeter declares that his theory of price formation is "almost faultless, and, barring explicit formulation of the marginal principle, within measurable distance of that of Böhm-Bawerk." The theory of saving, investment, and capital is "the first serious analysis of these matters" and "proved almost unbelievably hardy. It is doubtful whether Alfred Marshall had advanced beyond it, certain that John Stuart Mill had not. Böhm-Bawerk no doubt added a new branch to it, but substantially he subscribed to Turgot's proposition." Turgot's interest theory is "not only by far the greatest performance . . . the eighteenth century produced but it clearly foreshadowed much of the best thought of the last decades of the nineteenth."

## SELECTED READINGS

Böhm-Bawerk, Eugen von. 1959. *Capital and Interest*. Vol. 1. South Holland, Ill.: Libertarian Press. Pp. 39–45.

Fetter, Frank A. 1977. *Capital, Interest, and Rent: Essays in the Theory of Distribution*. Murray N. Rothbard, ed. Kansas City: Sheed Andrews and McMeel. Pp. 39–45.

Groenewegen, Peter D. 1983. "Turgot's Place in the History of Economic Thought: A Bicentenary Estimate." *History of Political Economy* 115 (Winter): 611–15.

——. 1977. *The Economics of A.R.J. Turgot*. The Hague, Holland: Martinus Nijhoff. Pp. xxix–xxx.

——. 1971. "A Reinterpretation of Turgot's Theory of Capital and Interest." *Economic Journal* 81: 327–28, 333, 339–40.

Rothbard, Murray N. 1995. *Economic Thought Before Adam Smith*. Vol. 1. *An Austrian Perspective on the History of Economic Thought*. Cheltenham, U.K.: Edward Elgar. Pp. 383–463.

Schumpeter, Joseph. 1954. *History of Economic Analysis*. New York: Oxford University Press.

Turgot, A.R.J. 1921. *Reflections on the Formation and Distribution of Riches*. New York: Augustus M. Kelley.

# 4
# JEAN-BAPTISTE SAY: NEGLECTED CHAMPION OF LAISSEZ-FAIRE

LARRY J. SECHREST

*Jean-Baptiste Say*
*1767–1832*

BEYOND SOME RUDIMENTARY facts, very little is available in English about the life of J.B. Say.[1] He was born in Lyons, France, to middle-class Huguenot parents, and spent most of his early years in Geneva and London. As a young man, he returned to France in the employ of a life insurance company, and soon became an influential member of a group of strongly pro-free-market intellectuals.[2] Indeed, Say was the first editor of *La Décade Philosophique*, a journal published by the group. After the Napoleonic Wars, he held a Chair of Political Economy at the *Conservatoire des Arts et Métiers*, and again, later, at the *Collège de France*. In addition to his famous *Treatise*, his works included *Cours Complet d'Économie Politique Pratique* and *Letters to Mr. Malthus*. By means of his writing, his influence spread to Italy, Spain, Germany, Russia, Latin America, Great Britain, and the United States, in which latter country his admirers included Thomas Jefferson and James Madison. His devotion to laissez-faire principles appears to have been maintained throughout his life. Say died in Paris.

J.B. Say deserves to be remembered, especially by Austrian economists, as a pivotal figure in the history of economic thought. Yet, one

[1]One recent book may rectify that deficiency. See R.R. Palmer, *J.B. Say: An Economist in Troubled Times* (Princeton, N.J.: Princeton University Press, 1997).

[2]This group was inspired by the work of Abbé Etienne Bonnot de Condillac, and it included such men as Destutt de Tracy and Pierre Jean Georges Cabanis as well as Say.

finds him discussed very briefly, if at all. In fact, even Austrians have devoted little attention to Say's contributions.[3]

Mainstream history-of-thought texts usually mention Say only briefly, and then only in connection with his law of markets, thereby implicitly trivializing much of his work. One of the exceptions is *A History of Economic Thought* by Eric Roll.[4] Roll treats Say with notable respect, but, unfortunately, partly because he misinterprets Say as an ancestor of modern general-equilibrium, positivistic, neoclassical economists.

In all fairness, one could argue that this lack of both attention and appreciation might be traced, at least in part, to Say himself. After all, Say did explicitly represent his work as being mainly an elaboration and popularization of Adam Smith's *Wealth of Nations* for the benefit of continental European readers. Taking Say at his word, many economists seem never to have bothered to investigate more closely. Upon close reading of Say's principal work, *A Treatise on Political Economy*,[5] one will find that, although Say frequently praises Smith, he also departs from Smithian doctrine on a number of important points. In fact, Say even sharply criticizes Adam Smith on more than one occasion. Rather than thinking of Say as a slight variation on Smith, it is much more accurate to recognize that these two men represent two meandering, but generally divergent, paths embedded within classical economics.

Smith leads one to David Ricardo, John Stuart Mill, Alfred Marshall, Irving Fisher, John Maynard Keynes, and Milton Friedman. Say leads from A.R.J. Turgot and Richard Cantillon to Nassau Senior, Frank A. Fetter, Carl Menger, Ludwig von Mises, and Murray Rothbard. The reader should keep in mind, however, that these two paths, or progressions, have often been circuitous and nonlinear. That is to say, J.B. Say was in a number of ways truly a *precursor* of the Austrian School, but one must not leap to the conclusion that he was a fullfledged Austrian who

---

[3]Of course, Murray N. Rothbard does discuss Say in detail and with great respect in *Classical Economics*, vol. 2, *An Austrian Perspective on the History of Economic Thought* (Cheltenham, U.K.: Edward Elgar, 1995), pp. 3–45.

[4]Eric Roll, *A History of Economic Thought* (Englewood Cliffs, N.J.: Prentice-Hall, [1956] 1961).

[5]This was first published in French in 1803 as *Traité d Économie Politique*. There were five editions of this enormously popular book published during Say's life, the last being in 1826. See Jean-Baptiste Say, *A Treatise on Political Economy: or the Production, Distribution, and Consumption of Wealth*, C.R. Prinsep and Clement C. Biddle, trans. (New York: Augustus M. Kelley, [1880] 1971), p. 111. It has been translated into a number of other languages.

was simply ahead of his time. One should not read Say and expect, at all points, to find Mises.

## METHODOLOGY

Say's approach to economics is, in philosophical terms, that of a realist and an essentialist.[6] He combines a healthy skepticism regarding the usefulness of statistical investigations with an emphasis on observing the facts of reality. A statistical description "does not indicate the origin and consequences of the facts it has collected."[7] For Say, only a causal analysis based on the essential natures of the entities involved can achieve that end, and such an analysis is the core task of political economy. He sees economics as a genuine science capable of establishing "absolute truths,"[8] but insists that it "has only become a science since it has been confined to the results *of inductive* investigation."[9] In fact, Say declares that political economy "forms a part of experimental science" and is, thus, rather similar to chemistry and natural philosophy.[10]

Taxonomically, he divides all facts into (a) those that refer to objects and (b) those that refer to events or interactions. The former is the domain of descriptive science (e.g., botany); while the latter is the domain of experimental science (e.g., chemistry or physics).

Above all, Say seeks to be practical; for "[n]othing can be more idle than the opposition of theory to practice!"[11] To that end, he attempts always to employ language that is precise and yet as simple as possible, so that any literate, reasonably intelligent person can comprehend his meaning.[12] For Say, as for most modern Austrians, economics is not a shadowy realm to be penetrated only by the expert, but a subject of enormous practical importance accessible to all. It is thus no surprise to find that Say, in keeping with such a goal of lucidity and intelligibility, criticizes Adam Smith's *Wealth of Nations* for being "destitute of method,"

---

[6]It is not clear, however, whether Say adopts the Aristotelian position that "essences" are metaphysically real, that is, that particular objects "partake of" the essence of the class of objects, or the position of contextual realism that "essence" is a necessary epistemological device, but possesses no metaphysical reality. See David Kelley, *The Evidence of the Senses: A Realist Theory of Perception* (Baton Rouge: Louisiana State University Press, 1986).

[7]Say, *Treatise*, p. xix.

[8]Ibid., p. xlix.

[9]Ibid., p. xxxvi, emphasis added.

[10]Ibid., p. xviii.

[11]Ibid., p. xxi.

[12]Ibid., p. xlvi.

obscure, vague, and disjointed as well as for containing too many long and distracting digressions on topics such as war, education, history, and politics.[13]

## MONEY AND BANKING

Say's discussion of money opens with what is now a standard argument about the "double coincidence of wants" problem and how a medium of exchange solves it. His explanation of how one highly demanded commodity spontaneously evolves into an accepted exchange medium is reminiscent of Carl Menger's more famous treatment of the same issue,[14] although it predates Menger by almost seventy years. Historically, money appears due to self-interest, not government decree, and its form should be left to the interaction of consumers' preferences. "[C]ustom, therefore, and not the mandate of authority, designates the specific product that shall pass exclusively as money."[15]

He then reviews the list of properties a medium of exchange should (ideally) possess: durability, portability, divisibility, high purchasing power per unit, and uniformity. From this presentation, Say draws the familiar conclusion that the precious metals (gold and silver) are excellent choices as monetary substances. In other words, if individuals are left free to choose, it is highly likely that they will choose a commodity money (specie). While it is true that Say is a strong proponent of gold and silver as money, it is provocative to notice that he does allow for the possibility that they could be replaced by something else if "new and rich veins of ore should be discovered."[16] In short, Say is not unalterably wedded to the proposition that "money" means gold or silver. However, if money consists of precious metal coinage, then he does agree that monetary units, such as the dollar, should be renamed in terms of the mass of gold or silver contained in the coin. For example, if a coin denominated as one French franc is supposed to contain 5 grams of silver, then it should be named "5 grams of silver," not "one franc."[17]

According to Say, the only justifiable intervention by the State into monetary matters is the minting of coins. In fact, Say thought this should be monopolized by the State "because there would probably be more

[13]Ibid., p. xliv.

[14]Carl Menger, *Principles of Economics,* James Dingwall and Bert F. Hoselitz, trans. (New York: New York University Press, [1871] 1976), pp. 257–62.

[15]Say, *Treatise,* p. 220.

[16]Ibid., p. 222.

[17]Ibid., p. 256.

difficulty in detecting the frauds of private issuers."[18] In particular, in any system in which gold and silver coexisted as monetary metals, governments should studiously avoid setting an official exchange rate between the two, contrary to what was done in historical episodes of bimetallism.[19] Say clearly understood why the practice under bimetallism always led to disaster. That is, the officially *over*priced money drove the officially *under*priced money out of circulation, a principle known as Gresham's Law.[20] Say emphatically states that money is ruled by supply and demand, just like all commodities. Money's purchasing power "rises and falls in proportion to the relative demand and supply."[21] Therefore, exchange rates between gold coinage and silver coinage should be allowed to change with market conditions. Say seems to favor a "parallel" metallic system, much like that suggested by Murray Rothbard.[22]

With regard to banking, Say distinguishes between "banks of deposit" and "banks of circulation," but treats them both as legitimate institutions.[23] The former function as warehouses for money. They hold one-hundred-percent reserves at all times, and provide convenience as well as security in that they effect transactions on behalf of their depositors by transferring funds from one customer's account to another's, for which services they charge a fee.[24] The latter function as true financial intermediaries. They hold fractional reserves, issue banknotes, and generate an interest income by discounting promissory notes and bills of exchange. The banknotes issued by such institutions must be backed by specie or short-term securities, but if so, then "[t]he holders of the notes of a bank issuing convertible money

---

[18]Ibid., p. 229.

[19]Ibid., p. 254.

[20]This is an application of the textbook treatment of price controls, but to money. Simultaneously, a price ceiling is imposed on one form of money and a price floor on the other. This, of course, creates a shortage of the former (that is, it disappears into savings) and a surplus of the latter (it is used for daily transactions).

[21]Say, *Treatise*, p. 226.

[22]Murray N. Rothbard, *The Case for a 100 Percent Gold Dollar* (Auburn, Ala.: Ludwig von Mises Institute, [1962] 1991), p. 28.

[23]This is certainly not the case with all Austrians. Murray Rothbard was especially hostile to fractional-reserve banking, and frequently condemned it as "inherently fraudulent." See ibid., pp. 42–51; also Murray N. Rothbard, *The Mystery of Banking* (New York: Richardson and Snyder, 1983), pp. 97–98; and idem, *Man, Economy, and State* (Los Angeles: Nash Publishing, [1962] 1970), p. 700.

[24]Say, *Treatise*, pp. 268–69.

run little or no risk, so long as the bank is well administered, and independent of the government."[25] In fact, Say even argues that these fractional-reserve-holding banks of circulation bestow a benefit upon society because they provide "the advantage of economizing capital, by reducing the amount of the sum kept in reserve."[26] And if it happens that such fractional-reserve banknotes also supplant part of the specie that had been in circulation, then "the functions of the specie, that has been withdrawn, are just as well performed by the paper substituted in its stead."[27]

There are two additional insights on monetary topics that one must not overlook. First, Say emphasizes that as the division of labor extends ever farther, horizontally and vertically, through the society, that is, as individuals specialize ever more, the number and the importance of exchanges will increase. And this requires an identifiable medium of exchange. Briefly put, money is an integral part of the rise of modern civilization.[28] Second, Say agrees with Mises and Rothbard, who insist that *any* nominal supply of money is "optimal," as long as prices are free to adjust, because any increase or decrease in nominal terms will simply change the purchasing power per unit in inverse proportion. Thus the real money supply will remain the same.[29]

## SAY'S LAW OF MARKETS

Without question, the one thing for which Say is best known is "Say's Law," also referred to as his theory of markets (*la théorie des débouchés*) or law of markets (*loi des débouchés*). This principle was, and still is, one of the key building blocks of the classical school of economics.[30] It remains, in some guise or other, essential to any defense of free markets. Moreover, all collectivists attempt to refute it in the course of their assault on liberty and the free society. And yet, some writers have questioned the profundity of Say's Law. Alexander Gray refers to "this theory, which

---

[25]Ibid., p. 278.

[26]Ibid., p. 272.

[27]Ibid., p. 274.

[28]This poses a problem for Karl Marx and those other socialists who have wished to abolish money but somehow retain the productive benefits of a division of labor.

[29]Say, *Treatise*, p. 151.

[30]See Thomas Sowell, *Say's Law: An Historical Analysis* (Princeton, N.J.: Princeton University Press, 1972); idem, *Classical Economics Reconsidered* (Princeton, N.J.: Princeton University Press, 1974); also, George Reisman, *Capitalism: A Treatise on Economics* (Ottawa, Ill.: Jameson Books, 1996).

perhaps does not come to much."[31] Even Murray Rothbard calls it a "relatively minor facet of his [Say's] thought."[32]

Most textbooks truncate Say's Law into the transparently false proposition "supply creates its own demand." At minimum, this should be given as "*aggregate* supply creates its own *aggregate* demand," because the claim is not that the production of commodity X necessarily results in an equivalent demand for X, but that the production of X leads to demand for commodities A, B, C, and so forth. The production, or supply, of commodities (and complementary services) *in general* leads to the consumption of, or demand for, commodities (and complementary services) *in general*.[33] It is certainly possible for there to exist either a shortage or a surplus of any particular commodity, but general overproduction or general underproduction can be no more than momentary phenomena. "It is because the production of some commodities has declined, that all other commodities are superabundant," and such maladjusted production results from "some violent means . . . a political or natural convulsion."[34] Left to its own devices, the market will correct such imbalances.

Say identifies two means by which the corrective process operates. Principally, he argues that, though individuals do save part of the income derived from production, as long as those savings are reinvested in "productive employment," in the aggregate there need be no decreases in production, income, or consumption.[35] This process of reinvestment is fueled by differences in the profits earned by entrepreneurs. Those goods that are relatively more scarce, and thus rising in price, attract additional investment, while those that are relatively less scarce, and thus falling in price, discourage investment. And even if one hoards money or buries it, "the ultimate object is always to employ it in a purchase of some kind,"[36] so there still cannot be deficient demand as long as real economic values are being produced. In order for consumers to exist, there must first be producers.

Throughout his discussion of production and consumption, Say consistently maintains that money is merely a neutral conduit through which aggregate supply is translated into aggregate demand, or

---

[31]Alexander Gray, *The Development of Economic Doctrine: An Introductory Survey* (London: Longmans, Green, [1931] 1961), p. 268.

[32]Rothbard, *Classical Economics*, p. 27.

[33]Say, *Treatise*, pp. 132–40.

[34]Ibid., p. 135.

[35]Ibid., p. 110.

[36]Ibid., p. 133.

"money is but the agent of the transfer of values."[37] There seems to be no recognition of the transmission mechanism by which changes in the supply of money alter the relative prices of goods and, thereby, redirect the entire interrelated structure of production. From a modern Austrian perspective, Say's failure to grasp the non-neutrality of money must be deemed a deficiency of some note.

On the other hand, Say eloquently expresses a clear understanding that it is wholly beneficial for a society to experience generally *falling* prices whenever such declining prices are the result of productivity gains. Not only does this circumstance indicate, contrary to popular belief, "that a country is rich and plentiful,"[38] but also that "products formerly within reach of the rich alone have been made accessible to almost every class of society."[39] Moreover, Say correctly perceives that (a) the prices of goods reflect their *utility* to the buyer, (b) the prices of the factors of production are derived or "imputed" from the prices of the goods produced, and therefore (c) costs of production represent an interface between the utility of the good and the productivity of the factors of production.[40]

## ENTREPRENEURS, CAPITAL, AND INTEREST

Rothbard has suggested that the world of economics should bestow blessings upon Say for reintroducing the entrepreneur into economic thought,[41] and so it should. With pen and ink, Adam Smith made the entrepreneur invisible. J.B. Say brings him back to life and to the center of the stage.[42] What do these entrepreneurs do? They use their "industry" (a term Say prefers to "labor") to organize and direct the factors of production so as to achieve the "satisfaction of human wants."[43]

But they are not merely managers. They are forecasters, project appraisers, and risk-takers as well.[44] Out of their own financial capital, or that borrowed from someone else, they advance funds to the owners of labor, natural resources ("land"), and machinery ("tools"). These payments,

[37]Ibid.

[38]Ibid., p. 303.

[39]Ibid., p. 288.

[40]Ibid., p. 287–88.

[41]Rothbard, *Classical Economics*, p. 25.

[42]For the benefit of those who might be reading Say's *Treatise* for the first time, it should be pointed out that the commonly found text is a reprint of the American edition of 1880, and in that edition the French word "entrepreneur" is translated as "adventurer." See Say, *Treatise*, p. 78n.

[43]Ibid., p. 83.

[44]Ibid., p. 82–85.

or "rents," are recouped only if the entrepreneurs succeed in selling the product to consumers. Entrepreneurial success is not only sought after by the individual, but also essential to the society as a whole. "[A] country well stocked with intelligent merchants, manufacturers, and agriculturists has more powerful means of attaining prosperity, than one devoted chiefly to the pursuit of the arts and sciences."[45]

Say's use of the word "capital" can be confusing, because it is used to mean, as the context requires, either (a) capital goods that are integral to the production of further, final goods, or (b) the financial capital that constitutes the enterprise's funding.[46] The former are the result of some earlier production process and, when combined with the industry of the entrepreneur, generate *profit* (or loss). The latter is the result of saving some portion of the income from past productive activity and generates *interest*.

The analysis of interest rates is very perceptive and, in most respects, remarkably Austrian. First, Say realizes that the interest rate is not the price of money, but the price of credit, or "capital lent."[47] Therefore, it is false that "the abundance or scarcity of money regulates the rate of interest."[48] Of course, Say is thinking of the real rate of interest, not the nominal, or market, rate. He also clearly sees that interest rates will include some risk premium as a sort of insurance to protect against loss due to default.[49] Such a risk premium will become very large when, for example, laws are imposed so that creditors have no legal recourse against a debtor who defaults.[50] Furthermore, Say identifies the fact that there are "political risk" differentials between nations that lead to an international array of nominal interest rates.[51] Overall, in terms of public policy, Say adopts the same stance with regard to credit markets that he exhibits elsewhere: namely, the state should not meddle. The "rate of interest ought no more to be restricted, or determined by law, than . . . the price of wine, linen, or any other commodity."[52]

It has been argued that the one glaring flaw in Say's understanding of interest rates is his failure to anchor them on the bedrock of "time

---

[45]Ibid., p. 82.

[46]Ibid., p. 343.

[47]Ibid.

[48]Ibid., p. 353.

[49]Ibid., p. 344.

[50]Ibid., p. 345–46.

[51]Ibid., p. 347.

[52]Ibid., p. 352.

preferences,"[53] that is, to explain interest rates as founded on the rate at which individuals prefer to trade present goods for future goods.[54] While Say does indeed fail explicitly to connect interest rates with time preferences, he seems to possess at least an embryonic notion of time preference itself. He observes, for instance, that there often exists an "inducement to every one to consume the whole of his income . . . [during] times of political turbulence and confusion."[55] And when discussing the impact of increased frugality (a falling rate of time preference?) on the accumulation of capital, he even concludes that "the low rate of interest proves the existence of more abundant capital."[56]

### VALUE AND UTILITY

For Say, the foundation of value is utility or the capacity of a good or service to satisfy some human desire. Those desires—and the preferences, expectations, and customs that lie behind them—must be taken as givens, as data, by the analyst. The task is to reason from those data. Say is most emphatic in denying the claims of Adam Smith, David Ricardo, and others that the basis for value is labor, or "productive agency."[57] Economists who subscribe to a labor theory of value have the matter precisely backwards. "[I]t is the ability to create the utility . . . that gives value to productive agency."[58]

The two categories of value are "exchange-value" and "use-value."[59] Exchange-value lies within the domain of economics, because it is a measure of what one must give up in order to acquire a good in the market. In economic terms, "[t]he only fair criterion of the value of an object is, the quantity of other commodities at large, that can be readily obtained for it in exchange."[60] Those things which possess exchange-value would today be called "economic goods," but Say calls them "social wealth." In contrast, some things, such as air, water, and sunlight, possess only use-value, because they are present in such abundance that

---

[53]Rothbard, *Classical Economics*, p. 23.

[54]One might also think of this as the rate at which an individual prefers to consume now as opposed to saving for the future.

[55]Say, *Treatise*, p. 348.

[56]Ibid., p. 116.

[57]Ibid., pp. xxxi, xl, 287.

[58]Ibid., p. 287.

[59]For a discussion of value that bears some strong similarities to Say's, see Menger, *Principles*, pp. 114–21, 295–302.

[60]Say, *Treatise*, p. 285.

they cannot command a price. These are now known as "free goods," but Say labels them "natural wealth."[61]

Unfortunately, by adhering to the above taxonomy of values, Say plunges into a most regrettable error. He concludes that since the measure of a good's economic value is literally and precisely its market price,[62] then all market transactions must involve the exchange of equal values. This, of course, must imply that neither buyer nor seller gains. Or, in other words, all market transactions are a "zero-sum game." "When Spanish wine is bought at Paris, equal value is really given for equal value: the silver paid, and the wine received, are worth one the other."[63] Austrians are adamant in maintaining that exchanges, as long as they are voluntary, must be *mutually beneficial* in terms of the expected utilities of each the buyer and the seller. If that is not the case, then why would buyer and seller agree to trade?

### TAXES AND THE STATE

Nowhere is Say's radicalism more evident than in his critique of government intervention into the economy.[64] Most succinctly stated, he declares that self-interest and the search for profits will push entrepreneurs toward satisfying consumer demand. "[T]he nature of the products is always regulated by the wants of society," therefore "legislative interference is superfluous altogether."[65]

Say's comments on one particular series of legislative acts is very instructive. The first of the British Navigation Acts was passed in 1581; these Acts were strengthened in 1651 and 1660; and the last was not repealed until 1849. Their purpose was to reserve Britain's international trade exclusively for the shipowners of the British merchant marine. Say argues that such monopolization of the "carrying trade" diminishes national wealth because it often reduces the profits of those merchants shipping their goods to market.

He recognizes that defenders of such statutes may grant this, but still insist that the restrictions are justified on the grounds of national security. Say retorts that this is so only if

---

[61]Ibid., p. 286.

[62]Ibid., p. 285.

[63]Ibid., p. 67.

[64]Murray N. Rothbard, in his *Power and Market: Government and the Economy* (Kansas City: Sheed Andrews and McMeel, [1970] 1977), provides a superb analysis of this issue from a modern Austrian perspective. One cannot but believe that Say would have applauded this work quite heartily.

[65]Say, *Treatise*, p. 144.

> it is an advantage to one nation to domineer over others.... The love of domination never attains more than a factitious elevation, that is sure to make enemies of all its neighbors. It is this that engenders national debt, internal abuse, tyranny and revolution; while the sense of mutual interest begets international kindness, extends the sphere of useful intercourse, and leads to a prosperity, permanent, because it is natural.[66]

The foregoing reveals how well Say comprehends the proposition that free trade and peace go hand in hand.

As for taxation, Say divides it into two types. Direct taxes are those levied on income or wealth. Indirect taxes are those such as sales taxes, excise taxes, and tariffs. Regardless of its specific form or method of collection, "all taxation may be said to injure reproduction, inasmuch as it prevents the accumulation of productive capital."[67] Therefore, contrary to what some economists have claimed, "[i]t is a glaring absurdity to pretend, that taxation... enriches the nation by consuming part of its wealth."[68]

Today, one will find many writers who insist that high rates of taxation, and the concomitant high levels of government spending, somehow cause a society to be more prosperous. Naturally, Say knows this to be false, despite the fact that, from a statistical standpoint, prosperity and taxation may be positively correlated. He explains that such assertions commit the error of reversing cause and effect. That is, "[a] man is not rich, because he pays largely; but he is able to pay largely, because he is rich."[69] Prosperous nations, if they remain prosperous, do so despite heavy tax burdens, not because of them. Anyone who reads Say's *Treatise* should not overlook the fact that the discussion of taxes and government appears in the section headed "consumption." That is no accident, for Say does not hesitate to identify government spending as "unproductive consumption." And "[e]xcessive taxation is a kind of suicide."[70]

It is true that Say either overlooked or misunderstood certain points of theory dear to the hearts of Austrian economists. He does not believe that market exchanges represent utility gains for both buyer and seller; he does not see the relationship between interest rates and time preference; he offers no theory of business cycles. On the other hand, he is cognizant of the limitations of statistical investigations; he is very much

---

[66]Ibid., p. 104.

[67]Ibid., p. 455.

[68]Ibid., p. 447.

[69]Ibid., p. 448.

[70]Ibid., p. 450.

in favor of commodity money and free banking; he knows that entrepreneurs and the accumulation of capital are essential to economic advancement; he correctly identifies both government regulation and taxation as threats to prosperity, indeed, even as threats to civil society itself.

Jean-Baptiste Say has much to offer any reader, whether Austrian or not, whether an economist or not. He saw many important truths with clarity, and wrote of them with passion and lucidity. Say once called economics "this beautiful, and above all, useful science."[71] He left economics both more beautiful and more useful than he had found it.

### SELECTED READINGS

Gray, Alexander. [1931] 1961. *The Development of Economic Doctrine: An Introductory Survey*. London: Longmans, Green.

Kelley, David. 1986. *The Evidence of the Senses: A Realist Theory of Perception*. Baton Rouge: Louisiana State University Press.

Menger, Carl. [1871] 1976. *Principles of Economics*. Translated by James Dingwall and Bert F. Hoselitz. New York: New York University Press.

Mises, Ludwig von. [1957] 1969. *Theory and History: An Interpretation of Social and Economic Evolution*. New Rochelle, N.Y.: Arlington House.

——. [1960] 1976. *Epistemological Problems of Economics*. Translated by George Reisman. New York: New York University Press.

——. [1949] 1966. *Human Action: A Treatise on Economics*. Chicago: Henry Regnery.

Palmer, R.R. 1997. *J.B. Say: An Economist in Troubled Times*. Princeton, N.J.: Princeton University Press.

Reisman, George. 1996. *Capitalism: A Treatise on Economics*. Ottawa, Ill.: Jameson Books.

Roll, Eric. [1956] 1961. *A History of Economic Thought*. Englewood Cliffs, N.J.: Prentice-Hall.

Rothbard, Murray N. [1962] 1993. *Man, Economy, and State*. Auburn, Ala.: Ludwig von Mises Institute.

——. [1962] 1991. *The Case for a 100 Percent Gold Dollar*. Auburn, Ala.: Ludwig von Mises Institute.

——. 1983. *The Mystery of Banking*. New York: Richardson and Snyder.

——. [1970] 1977. *Power and Market: Government and the Economy*. Kansas City: Sheed Andrews and McMeel.

——. 1995. *Classical Economics*. Vol. 2. *An Austrian Perspective on the History of Economic Thought*. Cheltenham, U.K.: Edward Elgar.

---

[71]Ibid., p. lii.

Say, Jean-Baptiste. [1880] 1971. *A Treatise on Political Economy: or the Production, Distribution and Consumption of Wealth.* Translated by C.R. Prinsep and Clement C. Biddle. New York: Augustus M. Kelley.

Sowell, Thomas. 1972. *Say's Law: An Historical Analysis.* Princeton, N.J.: Princeton University Press.

——. 1974. *Classical Economics Reconsidered.* Princeton, N.J.: Princeton University Press.

# 5

# FRÉDÉRIC BASTIAT: BETWEEN THE FRENCH AND MARGINALIST REVOLUTIONS

THOMAS J. DILORENZO

*Claude Frédéric Bastiat*
*1801–1850*

CLAUDE FRÉDÉRIC BASTIAT was a French economist, legislator, and writer who championed private property, free markets, and limited government. Perhaps the main underlying theme of Bastiat's writings was that the free market was inherently a source of "economic harmony" among individuals, as long as government was restricted to the function of protecting the lives, liberties, and property of citizens from theft or aggression. To Bastiat, governmental coercion was only legitimate if it served "to guarantee security of person, liberty, and property rights, to cause justice to reign over all."[1]

Bastiat emphasized the plan-coordination function of the free market—a major theme of the Austrian School—because his thinking was influenced by some of Adam Smith's writings and by the great French free-market economists Jean-Baptiste Say, Françiois Quesnay, Destutt de Tracy, Charles Comte, Richard Cantillon (who was born in Ireland and emigrated to France), and Anne Robert Jacques Turgot. These French economists were among the precursors to the modern Austrian School, having first developed such concepts as the market as a dynamic, rivalrous

[1]Frédéric Bastiat, "The Law," in *Selected Essays on Political Economy*, George B. de Huszar, ed. (Irvington-on-Hudson, N.Y.: Foundation for Economic Education, 1995), p. 52.

process, the free-market evolution of money, subjective value theory, the laws of diminishing marginal utility and marginal returns, the marginal productivity theory of resource pricing, and the futility of price controls in particular and of the government's economic interventionism in general.

## BASTIAT'S INTELLECTUAL BACKGROUND

Bastiat was orphaned at age ten, and was raised and educated by his paternal grandparents. He left school at age seventeen to work in the family exporting business in the town of Bayonne, where he learned firsthand the evils of protectionism by observing all the closed-down warehouses, the declining population, and the increased poverty and unemployment caused by trade restrictions.

When his grandfather died, Bastiat, at age twenty-five, inherited the family estate in Mugron, which enabled him to live the life of a gentleman farmer and scholar for the next twenty years. Bastiat hired people to operate the family farm so he could concentrate on his intellectual pursuits. He was a voracious reader, and he discussed and debated with friends virtually all forms of literature. His closest friend was his neighbor, Felix Coudroy.

> Coudroy and Bastiat, worked their way through a tremendous number of books on philosophy, history, politics, religion, travel, poetry, political economy, biography, and so on. . . . It was in these conversations that the ideas of Bastiat developed and his thoughts matured.[2]

Coudroy was initially a follower of Rousseau and, like most of Rousseau's admirers, then as now, was a socialist. But Bastiat, who always said he preferred a one-on-one conversation to giving a speech to thousands of people, converted Coudroy to classical liberalism.

Bastiat's first published article appeared in April of 1834. It was a response to a petition by the merchants of Bordeaux, Le Havre, and Lyons to eliminate tariffs on agricultural products but to maintain them on manufacturing goods. Bastiat praised the merchants for their position on agricultural products, but excoriated them for their hypocrisy in wanting protectionism for themselves. "You demand privilege for a few," he wrote, whereas "I demand liberty for all."[3] He then explained why all tariffs should be abolished completely.

---

[2]Dean Russell, *Frédéric Bastiat: Ideas and Influence* (Irvington-on-Hudson, N.Y.: Foundation for Economic Education, 1969), pp. 22–23.

[3]Ibid., p. 24.

Bastiat continued to hone his arguments in favor of economic freedom by writing a second essay in opposition to all domestic taxes on wine, entitled "The Tax and the Vine," and a third essay opposing all taxes on land and all forms of trade restrictions. Then, in the summer of 1844, Bastiat sent an unsolicited manuscript on the effects of French and English tariffs to the most prestigious economics journal in France, the *Journal des Economistes*. The editors published the article, "The Influence of English and French Tariffs," in the October 1844 issue, and it unquestionably became the most persuasive argument for free trade in particular, and for economic freedom in general, that had ever appeared in France, if not all of Europe.

In this article, Bastiat first displayed his mastery of the accumulated wisdom of the economists of the pre-Austrian tradition, and established himself as a brilliant synthesizer and organizer of economic ideas. He immediately gained national and international fame and, as a fellow advocate of free trade, began a friendship with Richard Cobden, the leader of the British Anti-Corn Law League, which succeeded in abolishing all trade restrictions in England by 1850. Bastiat organized a similar organization in France—the French Free-Trade Association—which was instrumental in France's elimination of most of its trade barriers in 1860, ten years after Bastiat's death. Bastiat was especially effective in spreading his influence as editor of the Free Trade Association's newspaper, *Le Libre-Exchange*.

After twenty years of intense intellectual preparation, articles began to pour out of Bastiat, and soon took the form of his first book, *Economic Sophisms*, which to this day is still arguably the best literary defense of free trade available.[4] He quickly followed with his second book, *Economic Harmonies*,[5] and his articles were reprinted in newspapers and magazines all over France. In 1846, he was elected a corresponding member of the French Academy of Science, and his work was immediately translated into English, Spanish, Italian, and German. Free-trade associations soon began to sprout up in Belgium, Italy, Sweden, Prussia, and Germany, and were all based on Bastiat's French Free Trade Association.

---

[4]Frédéric Bastiat, *Economic Sophisms* (Irvington-on-Hudson, N.Y.: Foundation for Economic Education, 1966).

[5]Frédéric Bastiat, *Economic Harmonies* (Irvington-on-Hudson, N.Y.: Foundation for Economic Education, 1966).

## BASTIAT'S AUSTRIAN SCHOOL IDEAS

While Bastiat was shaping economic opinion in France, Karl Marx was writing *Das Kapital,* and the socialist notion of "class conflict"—that the economic gains of capitalists necessarily came at the expense of workers—was gaining in popularity. Bastiat's *Economic Harmonies* explained why the opposite is true—that the interests of mankind are essentially harmonious if they can be cultivated in a free society where government confines its responsibilities to suppressing thieves, murderers, and special-interest groups who seek to use the state as a means of plundering their fellow citizens.

### *Capital Theory*

Bastiat contributed to Austrian capital theory by masterfully explaining how the accumulation of capital results in the enrichment *of the workers* by raising labor's marginal productivity and, consequently, its remuneration. Capital accumulation, wrote Bastiat, would also result in cheaper and better quality consumer goods, which would also raise real wages. He also explained how the interest on capital declines as it becomes more plentiful.

Thus, the interests of capitalists and labor are indeed harmonious, and government interventions into capital markets will impoverish the workers as well as the owners of capital. Bastiat also explained why in a free market no one can accumulate capital unless he uses it in a way that benefits others, i.e., consumers. In reality, wrote Bastiat, capital is always used to satisfy the desires of people who do not own it. In sharp contrast to most of his predecessors, Bastiat believed that "it is necessary to view economics from the viewpoint of the consumer. . . . All economic phenomena . . . must be judged by the advantages and disadvantages they bring to the consumer."[6] Mises repeated this point in *Human Action* when he noted that although bankers may seem to "control" the allocation of capital by their day-by-day decisions, it is the consumers who are the "captains" of the economic ship, because it is their preferences to which successful businesses cater.

### *Subjective Cost*

Bastiat's greatest contribution to subjective value theory was how he rigorously applied the theory in his essay, "What is Seen and What is Not Seen."[7] In that essay, Bastiat, by relentlessly focusing on the hidden

---

[6]Russell, *Ideas and Influence,* p. 32.

[7]Bastiat, "What is Seen and What is Not Seen," in *Selected Essays,* pp. 1–50.

opportunity costs of governmental resource allocation, destroyed the proto-Keynesian notion that government spending can create jobs and wealth. In the first edition of *Economics in One Lesson*, Henry Hazlitt wrote that

> My greatest debt, with respect to the kind of expository framework on which the present argument is hung, is Frédéric Bastiat's essay, "What is Seen and What is Not Seen." The present work may, in fact, be regarded as a modernization, extension and generalization of the approach found in Bastiat's pamphlet.[8]

*The Science of Human Action*

The way in which Bastiat described economics as an intellectual endeavor is virtually identical to what modern Austrians label the science of human action, or praxaeology. Bastiat wrote in his *Harmonies* of how

> The subject of political economy is MAN . . . [who is] endowed with the ability to compare, judge, choose, and act. . . . This faculty . . . to work for each other, to transmit their efforts and to exchange their services through time and space . . . is precisely what constitutes Economic Science.[9]

As with contemporary Austrians, Bastiat viewed economics as "the Theory of Exchange" where the desires of market participants "cannot be weighed or measured. . . . Exchange is necessary in order to determine value."[10] Thus, to Bastiat, as with contemporary Austrians, value is subjective, and the only way of knowing how people value things is through their demonstrated preferences as revealed in market exchanges. Voluntary exchange, therefore, is necessarily mutually advantageous. This was an important theoretical innovation in the history of economic theory, for many of the British economists had succumbed to the "physical fallacy"—the misguided notion that value is determined by the production of physical objects alone.

The understanding that value is created by voluntary exchange, Murray Rothbard pointed out, "led Bastiat and the French school to stress the ways in which the free market leads to a smooth and harmonious organization of the economy."[11] Rothbard himself developed

---

[8]Henry Hazlitt, *Economics in One Lesson* (New York: Harper and Brothers, 1946), p. 1.

[9]Bastiat, *Economic Harmonies*, p. 35.

[10]Ibid., p. 36.

[11]Murray N. Rothbard, *Classical Economics*, vol. 2, *An Austrian Perspective on the History of Economic Thought* (Cheltenham, U.K.: Edward Elgar, 1995), p. 446.

Bastiat's subjectivist theory of exchange much more fully a century later in his devastating critique of modern welfare economics.

Another Rothbardian theme in Bastiat's work (or a Bastiat theme in Rothbard's work) has to do with land rent. In Bastiat's time, socialists made the argument that no one was entitled to land rent because it was God, after all, who created the land, not the current landowners. Bastiat's response was that land rent was indeed legitimate because landowners have rendered a valuable service by clearing the land, draining it, and making it suitable for agriculture. If all these investment costs are capitalized, explained Bastiat, then it is clear that landowners were not earning an exceptional income through land rent after all, but were providing a valuable public service. Murray Rothbard would later develop this idea more fully in his defense of "homesteading" as an appropriate means of establishing property rights.

*Governmental Plunder*

While establishing the inherent harmony of voluntary trade, Bastiat also explained how governmental resource allocation is necessarily antagonistic and destructive of the free market's natural harmony. Since government produces no wealth of its own, it must necessarily take from some to give to others—robbing Peter to pay Paul is the essence of government, as Bastiat described it. Moreover, as special-interest groups seek more and more of other peoples' money through the aegis of the state, they undermine the productive capacities of the free market by engaging in politics rather than in productive behavior. "The state," wrote Bastiat, "is the great fictitious entity by which everyone seeks to live at the expense of everyone else."[12]

Bastiat is perhaps best known for his work in the field of political economy—the study of the interaction between the economy and the state—as opposed to pure economic theory. He sought to understand how the state operated—what incentives drive it—and he did so as well as anyone ever has. There is no space here for a in-depth discussion of Bastiat's ideas on political economy, but a few examples will suffice. Government was necessary, according to Bastiat, but only if restricted to its "essential" functions. He believed that "no society can exist unless the laws are respected to a certain degree," but at the same time that could only occur if the laws themselves were respectable.[13]

---

[12]Bastiat, *Selected Essays*, p. 144.

[13]Russell, *Ideas and Influence*, p. 5.

The moral justification for a law, moreover, can never be based on a majority vote, because "since no individual has the right to enslave another individual, then no group of individuals can possibly have such a right."[14] All income redistribution through majoritarian democracy is therefore "legal plunder" and is, by definition, immoral.

The slogan, "if goods don't cross borders, armies will," is often attributed to Bastiat because he so forcefully made the case that free trade was perhaps the surest route to peace as well as prosperity. He understood that throughout history, tariffs had been a major cause of war. Protectionism, after all, is an attempt by governments to inflict on their own citizens in peacetime the same kinds of harm their enemies attempt (with naval blockades) during wars.

*Competitive Discovery*

Bastiat understood that free-market competition was a "dynamic discovery procedure," to use a Hayekian phrase, in which individuals strove to coordinate their plans to achieve their economic goals. All forms of government intervention interrupt and distort that process because once a law or regulation is issued,

> the people no longer need to discuss, to compare, to plan ahead; the law does all this for them. Intelligence becomes a useless prop for the people; they cease to be men; they lose their personality, their liberty, their property.[15]

*Phony Altruism*

Bastiat also saw through the phony "philanthropy" of the socialists who constantly proposed helping this or that person or group by plundering the wealth of other innocent members of society through the aegis of the state. All such schemes are based on "legal plunder, organized injustice."[16]

Like today's neo-conservatives, nineteenth-century socialists branded classical liberals with the name "individualist," implying that classical liberals are opposed to fraternity, community, and association. But, as Bastiat astutely pointed out, he (like other classical liberals) was only opposed to forced associations, and was an advocate of genuine, voluntary communities and associations. "[E]very time we object to a

[14]Ibid.

[15]Ibid., p. 11.

[16]Ibid.

thing being done by government, the socialists [mistakenly] conclude that we object to its being done at all."[17]

*Natural Rights and Freedom of Exchange*

Bastiat can also be seen as a link between the seventeenth- and eighteenth-century natural-rights theorists and some members of the modern Austrian School, most notably Murray Rothbard, who based their defense of free markets on natural rights, rather than merely on utilitarian arguments.[18] To Bastiat, collectivism in all its forms was both morally reprehensible (being based on legalized theft) and an impediment to the natural harmonization of human interests that is facilitated by free markets and private property.

Bastiat not only believed that collectivism constituted legal plunder; he also believed that private property was essential to fulfill man's nature as a free being who, by nature, acts in his own self-interest to satisfy his (subjective) wants. To argue against the right to private property would be to argue that theft and slavery were morally "correct." Thus, the protection of private property is the primary (if not the only legitimate) function of government. The politician has "no authority over our persons and our property, since they pre-exist him, and his task is to surround them with guarantees."[19]

Bastiat authored what is to this day the strongest defense of free trade ever produced. His case was built on myriad economic concepts, but what the case for free trade really comes down to,

> has never been a question of customs duties, but a question of right, of justice, of public order, of property. Because [government-created] privilege, under whatever form it is manifested, implies the denial or the scorn of property rights.

And "the right to property, once weakened in one form, would soon be attacked in a thousand different forms."[20]

---

[17]Ibid., p. 12. Also, see Bastiat's essay, "Justice and Fraternity," in *Selected Essays*, pp. 116–39.

[18]Because Hayek's defense of liberty was based largely on expediency (does it promote the efficient use of knowledge in society?) and utilitarianism (do "social" benefits outweigh "social" costs, as determined by an "impartial judge"?), he came to endorse virtually all of the government interventions that define the American (or Swedish) welfare state. This is something natural-rights-based theorists, such as Rothbard and Bastiat, would never have done.

[19]Bastiat, "Property and Law," in *Selected Essays*, pp. 97–115.

[20]Ibid., p. 111.

In *Economic Sophisms*, Bastiat masterfully created the most complete case for free trade ever constructed up to that time, which applied such economic concepts as the mutual advantage of voluntary trade, the law of comparative advantage, the benefits of competition to the producer as well as the consumer, and the historical link between trade barriers and war. Free trade, Bastiat explained, would mean

> an abundance of goods and services at lower prices; more jobs for more people at higher real wages; more profits for manufacturers; a higher level of living for farmers; more income to the state in the form of taxes at the customary or lower levels; the most productive use of capital, labor, and natural resources; the end of the "class struggle" that . . . was based primarily on such economic injustices as tariffs, monopolies, and other legal distortions of the market; the end of the "suicidal policy" of colonialism; the abolition of war as a national policy; and the best possible education, housing, and medical care for all the people.[21]

Bastiat was a genius at explaining all these economic principles and outcomes by the use of satire and parables, the most famous of which is "The Candlemaker's Petition," which "requested" a law to mandate

> the covering of all windows and skylights and other openings, holes, and cracks through which the light of the sun is able to enter houses. This free sunlight is hurting the business of us deserving manufacturers of candles.

Another of Bastiat's most memorable satires is his destruction of the protectionist argument that a "balance of trade" is necessarily desirable. A French merchant is said to have shipped $50,000 worth of goods to the U.S., sold them for a $17,000 profit, and purchased $67,000 worth of U.S. cotton, which he then imported into France. Since France had therefore imported more than it exported, it "suffered" an "unfavorable" balance of trade. A more "favorable" situation, Bastiat sarcastically wrote, would have been one where the merchant attempted a second transaction in the U.S., but had his ship sunk by a storm as it left the harbor. The customs house at the harbor would therefore have recorded more exports than imports, creating a very "favorable" balance of trade. But since storms are undependable, Bastiat reasoned, the "best" policy would be to have the government throw all the merchants' goods into the sea as they left French harbors, thereby guaranteeing a "favorable balance of trade"! It is this kind of display of literary genius that must have motivated Henry Hazlitt to take up Bastiat's fallen mantle a century after his death.

---

[21]Russell, *Ideas and Influence*, p. 42.

## BASTIAT'S INTELLECTUAL LEGACY TO THE AUSTRIAN SCHOOL

Bastiat's writing constitutes an intellectual bridge between the ideas of the pre-Austrian economists, such as Say, Cantillon, de Tracy, Comte, Turgot, and Quesnay, and the Austrian tradition of Carl Menger and his students. He was also a model of scholarship for those Austrians who believed that general economic education—especially the kind of economic education that shatters the myriad myths and superstitions created by the state and its intellectual apologists—is an essential function (if not duty) of the economist. Mises was a superb role model in this regard, as were Henry Hazlitt and Murray Rothbard, among other Austrian economists. As Mises said, the early economists "devoted themselves to the study of the problems of economics," and in "lecturing and writing books they were eager to communicate to their fellow citizens the results of their thinking. They tried to influence public opinion in order to make sound policies prevail."[22]

To this day, Bastiat's work is not appreciated as much as it should be because, as Murray Rothbard explained, today's intemperate critics of economic freedom "find it difficult to believe that anyone who is ardently and consistently in favor of laissez-faire could possibly be an important scholar and economic theorist."[23] It is bizarre that even some contemporary Austrian economists seem to believe that the act of communicating economic ideas—especially economic policy ideas—to the general public is somehow unworthy of a practitioner of "economic science." For that is exactly the model of scholarship that Mises himself adopted, which was carried forward most aggressively and brilliantly by Murray Rothbard, all in the tradition of the great French Austrian economist, Frédéric Bastiat.

## SELECTED READINGS

Bastiat, Frédéric. 1995. *Selected Essays on Political Economy*. George B. de Huszar, ed. Irvington-on-Hudson, N.Y.: Foundation for Economic Education.

——. 1966. *Economic Sophisms*. Irvington-on-Hudson, N.Y.: Foundation for Economic Education.

——. 1966. *Economic Harmonies*. Irvington-on-Hudson, N.Y.: Foundation for Economic Education.

---

[22]Ludwig von Mises, *Human Action: A Treatise on Economics*, 3rd rev. ed (Chicago: Henry Regnery, 1963), p. 869.

[23]Rothbard, *Classical Economics*, p. 449.

Hazlitt, Henry. 1946. *Economics in One Lesson*. New York: Harper and Brothers.

Mises, Ludwig von. 1963. *Human Action: A Treatise on Economics*. 3rd rev. ed. Chicago: Henry Regnery.

Rothbard, Murray. 1995. *Classical Economics*. Vol. 2. *An Austrian Perspective on the History of Economic Thought*. Cheltenham, U.K.: Edward Elgar.

Russell, Dean. 1969. *Frédéric Bastiat: Ideas and Influence*. Irvington-on-Hudson, N.Y.: Foundation for Economic Education.

# 6
# CARL MENGER: THE FOUNDING OF THE AUSTRIAN SCHOOL

JOSEPH T. SALERNO

*Carl Menger*
*1840–1921*

DESPITE THE MANY illustrious forerunners in its six-hundred-year prehistory, Carl Menger was the true and sole founder of the Austrian School of economics *proper*. He merits this title if for no other reason than that he created, out of whole cloth, the system of value and price theory that constitutes the core of Austrian economic theory. But Menger did more than this: he also originated and consistently applied the correct, praxeological method for pursuing theoretical research in economics. Thus, in its method and core theory, Austrian economics always was and will forever remain *Mengerian* economics.

Menger's position as the originator of the fundamental doctrines of Austrian economics has been recognized and hailed by all eminent authorities on the history of Austrian economics. In his eulogy of Menger written upon the latter's death in 1921, Joseph Schumpeter averred that "Menger is nobody's pupil and what he created stands. . . . Menger's theory of value, price, and distribution is the best we have up to now."[1] Ludwig von Mises wrote that

> What is known as the Austrian School of Economics started in 1871 when Carl Menger published a slender volume under the title *Grundsätze der*

[1]Joseph A. Schumpeter, "Carl Menger," *Ten Great Economists: From Marx to Keynes* (New York: Oxford University Press, 1969), p. 86.

> *Volkswirtschaftslehre* [Principles of economics]. . . . Until the end of the [1870s] there was no "Austrian School." There was only Carl Menger.[2]

For F. A. Hayek, the Austrian School's

> fundamental ideas belong fully and wholly to Carl Menger. . . . [W]hat is common to the members of the Austrian School, what constitutes their peculiarity and provided the foundations for their later contributions, is their acceptance of the teaching of Carl Menger.[3]

While there is no dispute regarding Menger's role as creator of the defining principles of Austrian economics, there does exist some confusion regarding the precise nature of his contribution. It is not always fully recognized that Menger's endeavor to radically reconstruct the theory of price on the basis of the law of marginal utility was not inspired by a vague subjectivism in outlook. Rather, Menger was motivated by the specific and overarching aim of establishing a causal link between the subjective values underlying the choices of consumers and the objective market prices used in the economic calculations of businessmen. The classical economists had formulated a theory attempting to explain market prices as the outcome of the operation of the laws of supply and demand, but they were compelled to restrict their analysis to the monetary calculations and choices of businessmen while neglecting consumer choice for the lack of a satisfactory theory of value. Their theory of "calculated action" was correct as far as it went, and was used to telling effect in demolishing the protectionist and interventionist schemes of sixteenth- and seventeenth-century mercantilists and the statist fantasies of nineteenth-century Utopian socialists.[4] Thus, Menger's ultimate

---

[2]Ludwig von Mises, *The Historical Setting of the Austrian School of Economics* (New Rochelle, N.Y.: Arlington House, 1969), pp. 9–10. Mises also wrote that "in 1871 the writings of Carl Menger and William Stanley Jevons inaugurated a new epoch of economic studies" (Ludwig von Mises, *Theory and History: An Interpretation of Social and Economic Evolution* [Auburn, Ala.: Ludwig von Mises Institute, 1985], p. 124).

[3]F.A. Hayek, "Carl Menger (1840–1921)," in *The Fortunes of Liberalism: Essays on Austrian Economics and the Ideal of Freedom*, vol. 4, *The Collected Works of F.A. Hayek*, Peter G. Klein, ed. (Chicago: University of Chicago Press, 1992), p. 62.

[4]This weakness of classical economics was noted by Mises:

> Because the classical economists were able to explain only the action of businessmen and were helpless in the face of everything that went beyond it, their thinking was oriented toward bookkeeping, the supreme expression of the rationality of the businessman (but not that of the consumer). (Ludwig von Mises, *Epistemological Problems of Economics*, George Reisman, trans. [New York: New York University Press, 1981], p. 175)

But, as Mises also recognized, this theory, though incomplete, was an essential step forward in the construction of the comprehensive system of praxeological economics:

goal was not to destroy classical economics, as has sometimes been suggested, but to complete and firm up the classical project by grounding the theory of price determination and monetary calculation in a general theory of human action.

## LIFE AND WORK[5]

Carl Menger was born on February 28, 1840, in Galicia, which is today a part of Poland. He was the scion of an old Austrian family which included craftsmen, musicians, civil servants, and army officers, and which had emigrated from Bohemia a generation before his birth. His father, Anton, was a lawyer, and his mother, Caroline (née Gerzabek), was the daughter of a wealthy Bohemian merchant. He had two brothers, Anton and Max: the former, an eminent socialist author and fellow professor in the Law Faculty of the University of Vienna; and the latter, a lawyer and a Liberal deputy in the Austrian Parliament. The Menger family had been ennobled, but Carl himself dropped the title "von" in early adulthood.

After studying economics at the Universities of Prague and Vienna from 1859 to 1863, Menger went to work as a journalist in the summer of 1863. The young Menger quickly attained prominence in the journalistic profession, writing a number of novels and comedies (which were apparently serialized for newspapers) and, in 1865, meeting and sharing confidences with the Liberal Austrian prime minister R. Belcredi. In the Fall of 1866, he left the *Wiener Zeitung*, an official newspaper for which he

---

> [M]ercantilists had placed goods in the center of economics, which in their eyes was a theory of objective wealth. It was the great achievement of the Classics in this respect that beside the goods they set up economic man [i.e., the calculating businessman]. They thus prepared the way for modern Economics which puts man and his subjective valuations into the center of its system. (Ludwig von Mises, *Socialism: An Economic and Sociological Analysis*, J. Kahane, trans. [Indianapolis, Ind.: LibertyClassics, 1981], p. 293)

Indeed, the classical economic theory was effectively a praxeological theory that dealt narrowly with actions whose means and ends were calculable in monetary terms: "The first comprehensive system of economic theory, that brilliant achievement of the classical economists, was essentially a theory of calculated action" (Ludwig von Mises, *Human Action: A Treatise on Economics* [Chicago: Henry Regnery, 1966], p. 231).

[5]Details of Menger's life can be found in Hayek, "Carl Menger"; Erich W. Streissler, "The Influence of German Economics on Menger and Marshall," in *Carl Menger and His Legacy in Economics*, Bruce J. Caldwell, ed. (Durham, N.C.: Duke University Press, 1990); Streissler, "Menger's Treatment of Economics in the Rudolph Lectures," in *Carl Menger's Lectures to Crown Prince Rudolf Erich*, W. Streissler and Monika Streissler, eds. (Cheltenham, U.K.: Edward Elgar, 1994), pp. 3–25; and Kiichiro Yagi, "Menger's *Grundsätze* in the Making," *History of Political Economy* 25 (Winter 1993): 697–724.

was then working as a market analyst, in order to prepare for his oral examination for a doctorate in law. After passing this examination, Menger went to work as an apprentice lawyer in May 1867, receiving his law degree from the University of Krakow in August 1867. However, he soon returned to work as an economic journalist and helped to found a daily newspaper.[6]

It was in September 1867, immediately after receiving his law degree, that, reported Menger, he "threw [himself] into political economy."[7] Over the next four years, he painstakingly worked out the system of thought that would so profoundly reshape economic theory when it came to fruition in 1871 with the publication of the *Principles*. As an economic journalist, Menger had observed a sharp contrast between the factors that classical economics had identified as most important in explaining price determination and the factors that experienced market participants believed exerted the greatest influence in shaping the pricing process. Whether or not this observation was the original inspiration for Menger's sudden and deep absorption in economic questions after 1867, it surely is consistent with his ultimate goal of reconstructing price theory.[8]

In 1870, Menger obtained a civil service appointment in the press department of the Austrian cabinet (the *Ministerratspraesidium*), which was then composed of members of the Liberal Party. With a published work in hand and the successful completion of his *Habilitation* examination in 1872, Menger fulfilled the requirements for an appointment as a *Privatdozent*—basically an unpaid lecturer with complete professorial privileges—in the Faculty of Law and Political Science at the University of Vienna.[9] Upon his promotion to the position of a paid, full-time associate

---

[6]This was the *Wiener Tagblatt*. Its successor, the *Neue Wiener Tagblatt*, established itself as one of Vienna's most influential newspapers for many years to come.

[7]Quoted in Yagi, "Menger's *Grundsätze*," p. 700.

[8]See Hayek, "Carl Menger," p. 69.

[9]Mises describes the institution of the *Privatdozent* in the following terms:

> A doctor who had published a scholarly book could ask the faculty to admit him as a free and private teacher of his discipline; if the faculty decided in favor of the petitioner, the consent of the Minister [of Worship and Instruction] was still required; in practice this consent was [before the early 1880s] always given. The duly admitted *Privatdozent* was not, in this capacity, a civil servant. Even if the title of professor was accorded to him, he did not receive any compensation from the government. A few *Privatdozents* could live from their own funds. Most of them worked for their living. (Mises, *Historical Setting of the Austrian School*, p. 13)

professor (*Professor Extraordinarius*)[10] in Autumn 1873, Menger resigned from the ministerial press department, but continued his private-sector journalistic activities until 1875.

In 1876, Menger won an appointment as one of the tutors of the eighteen-year-old Crown Prince, Rudolf von Habsburg. Over the course of the next two years, Menger tutored Rudolf while traveling with him throughout Europe.[11] Upon his return to Vienna, Menger was appointed by the Emperor Franz Joseph, Rudolf's father, to the Chair of Political Economy in Vienna's Law Faculty, where he took up his duties in 1879 as a *Professor Ordinarius* or Full Professor.

Secure in a prominent academic position, Menger was now able to concern himself with formulating a clarification and defense of the theoretical method he had adopted in his *Principles.* The latter book had been ignored in Germany because, by the 1870s, German economics had come almost completely under the sway of the younger Historical School, which was led by Gustav Schmoller and was bitterly hostile to Menger's (and the Classical School's) "abstract" style of economic theorizing. The fruits of Menger's methodological research were published in 1883 in a book entitled *Untersuchungen uber die Methode der Sozialwissenschaften und der politischen Ökonomie insbesondere* (Investigations into the method of the social sciences with special reference to economics).[12] Where the earlier book had been coldly ignored, the *Investigations* precipitated a furor among German economists, who heatedly responded with derisive attacks on Menger and the "Austrian School." In fact, this latter term was originated and applied by the German Historicists in order to emphasize the isolation of Menger and his followers from the mainstream of German economics. Menger responded in 1884 with a scathing pamphlet, *Irrthumer des Historismus in der deutschen Nationalökonomie* (The errors of historicism in German economics), and the famous *Methodenstreit*, or methodological debate, between the Austrian School and the German Historical School was on.[13]

---

[10]It is Streissler, in his "Influence of German Economics," p. 4, who renders this academic rank as "associate professor" in English; Mises, in *Historical Setting of the Austrian School*, p. 11, translates it as "assistant professor."

[11]Menger's lectures to the Crown Prince, as recorded in the latter's notebooks, can be found in Streissler and Streissler, eds., *Carl Menger's Lectures to Crown Prince Rudolf.*

[12]Carl Menger, *Investigations into the Method of the Social Sciences with Special Reference to Economics*, Louis Schneider, ed., Francis J. Nock, trans. (New York: New York University Press, 1985).

[13]On the conflict between the Austrian and German Historical Schools, see Mises, *Historical Setting of the Austrian School*, pp. 20–39. For a critique of historicism in all its forms, see Mises, *Theory and History*, pp. 198–239.

In the meantime, Menger's writing and teaching had begun by the mid-1870s to attract a number of brilliant followers, most notably Eugen von Böhm-Bawerk and Friedrich von Wieser. Between 1884 and 1889, the works of these men and of numerous others also influenced by Menger began to pour forth in great abundance, leading to a coalescence of an identifiable Austrian School. By the late 1880s, Mengerian doctrines were also being introduced to non-German speaking economists in France, the Netherlands, the United States, and Great Britain.

After he retired from active participation in the *Methodenstreit* in the late 1880s, Menger's interests shifted back from methodological concerns to questions of pure economic theory and applied economics. In 1888, he published a notable article on capital theory, *Zur Theorie des Kapitals*. Also during this period, Menger served as the leading member of a commission charged with reforming the Austrian monetary system, a role which stimulated him to ponder deeply problems of monetary theory and policy. The result was a spate of articles on monetary economics published in 1892, including *Geld* (Money), a pathbreaking contribution to monetary theory.[14] Menger continued in academic life until he resigned his professorship in 1903, but, unfortunately, despite the fact that he lived until 1921, there were no more major works to come from his pen.

## THE CLASSICAL SCHOOL AND THE STATE OF ECONOMIC THEORY ON THE EVE OF THE PUBLICATION OF MENGER'S *PRINCIPLES*

When Menger seriously turned his attention to economic theory in 1867, there existed a mighty though deeply flawed system of economic theory that had been constructed mainly by the British Classical School, namely David Hume, Adam Smith, and David Ricardo. To their undying credit, the classical economists were successful in demonstrating that price phenomena—product prices, wages, and interest rates—were not the product of historical accident or the arbitrary whim of sellers, but were determined by universal and immutable economic law, viz., the law of supply and demand. They also showed how prices, through the calculations and actions of profit-seeking businessmen, effectively regulated the production process. In those industries where the selling price exceeded the average cost of the product by a greater than normal margin, business owners were motivated by prospective profits to expand their

[14]For a survey of these and other writings of Menger on money, see Hans F. Sennholz, "The Monetary Writings of Carl Menger," in *The Gold Standard: Perspectives in the Austrian School*, Llewellyn H. Rockwell, Jr., ed. (Auburn, Ala.: Ludwig von Mises Institute, 1992), pp. 19–34.

output from existing enterprises, while additional output was forthcoming from new enterprises initiated by capitalist-investors eager to share in the supranormal profits. Conversely, in those industries where product prices failed to cover per unit costs, the universal quest for profit and aversion to loss among businessmen led existing firms to contract their output or discontinue production altogether, while discouraging entry by new competitors into the industry. Moreover, as the production of goods expanded in those industries where higher-than-normal profits were being reaped, supply increased relative to demand and the profit rate tended to diminish back to a normal level as prices declined toward their "natural" level in relation to production costs. In the case of industries where production was shrinking due to losses, the decrease in supply relative to demand drove prices up toward (and beyond) average costs to their natural level, causing losses to disappear and a normal level of profit to emerge in the process.

In the classical view, then, both prices and production behaved according to definite laws of cause and effect. Prices were determined by the interaction of all market participants, so that the actual price of any good reflected the momentary equilibrium of supply and demand; the allocation of resources to the various processes of production was governed by the calculations and choices of profit-seeking (and loss-avoiding) businessmen, which meant that, in the long run, resources were allocated among the various branches of production so as to ensure a tendency to equalize at some normal or natural level the "rate of profit" or rate of return on all capital investment. Classical economics, therefore, did indeed contain an embryonic theory of human action, which was incomplete because it focused narrowly on the calculating businessman, the proverbial "economic man" who "bought in the cheapest and sold in the dearest markets." In other words, the classical theory of prices and production was a theory of calculable action only, i.e., of action in the marketplace, a realm where all means and ends, costs and benefits, and profits and losses could be calculated in terms of money. While this was a great achievement and a bold step forward in economic science, it left out of account the subjective and nonquantifiable valuations and preferences of the consumer, the *raison d'être* of all economic activity.

To explain this neglect, we turn to the aforementioned great flaw in classical economics: its value theory. In attempting to analyze the value of goods as a foundation for its theory of price, the classical economists commenced by focusing on abstract categories or classes of goods, e.g., bread, iron, diamonds, water, etc., and their general usefulness to humankind instead of focusing on a specific quantity of a concrete good and its perceived importance to a choosing individual. They were thus at a loss to resolve the famous "paradox of value": or why the market price of one pound of bread is almost negligible compared to the price of an equal weight of gem-quality diamonds, despite the fact that bread is indispensable in sustaining human life while diamonds are useful only for aesthetic enjoyment or ostentatious display. To proceed any further in their analysis, the classical economists were thus forced to sever value into two categories, "use value" and "exchange value." The former referred to the importance of a good in serving human wants, while the latter indicated simply the market price of the good. Dismissing use value as a given and unexplained precondition of exchange value, they went on to concentrate their analysis exclusively on exchange value. This approach to value theory naturally prevented the classical economists from developing a complete theory of human action that integrated valuations and choices of consumers with the calculations and choices of businessmen.

Unable to ground their price theory in the subjective values of consumers, the classical economists turned to objective costs of production to close their theoretical system and, in so doing, accorded the technical conditions under which goods are produced equal status with human choices as the *active* determinants of economic activity. This resulted in a bifurcated and contradictory price theory. According to this theory, as we noted above, market prices—prices that were actually paid in everyday transactions—are determined by supply and demand. However, only supply was actually explained, as the result of the monetary calculations of profit-maximizing businessmen, while the demands for the various consumer goods were taken as given. While human choices determined day-to-day market prices for all goods, in the long run the exchange value of "reproducible" goods was driven inexorably toward the "natural" price established by their costs of production, which themselves remained unexplained. "Scarcity" goods, those whose supplies could not be augmented by the production process, such as antiques, rare coins, paintings of the Old Masters, and so on, were treated as a separate and relatively unimportant category of goods whose exchange values were governed entirely by supply and demand. Thus, the split in classical value and price theory. But there also existed an unresolved contradiction, at least in the case of reproducible goods: although the emergence of actual prices at every moment are completely accounted for by human calculation and action, they also harbor a mysterious tendency to gravitate toward a level determined by factors wholly unrelated to human volition.

Regarding the question of the determination of the incomes of the factors of production, the classical analysis was almost completely worthless because, once again, it was conducted in terms of broad and homogeneous classes, such as "labor," "land," and "capital." This diverted the classical theorists from the important task of explaining the market value or actual prices of specific kinds of resources in favor of a chimerical search for the principles by which the aggregate income shares of the three classes of factor owners—laborers, landlords, and capitalists—are governed. The Classical School's theory of distribution was thus totally disconnected from its quasi-praxeological theory of price, and focused almost exclusively on the differing objective qualities of land, labor, and capital as the explanation for the division of aggregate income among them. Whereas the core of classical price and production theory included a sophisticated theory of calculable action, classical distribution theory crudely focused on the technical qualities of goods alone.

This was the unsatisfactory state in which Menger found economic theory in the late 1860s. It is true that a subjective-value school, which traced its roots back through J.B. Say, A.R.J. Turgot, and Richard Cantillon to the Scholastic writers of the Middle Ages, flourished on the Continent during the whole period of the Classical School's ascendancy in Great Britain. And Menger himself, a renowned bibliophile, was nurtured and steeped in the writings of the German-language branch of this subjective-value tradition. However, while writers associated with this tradition repeatedly emphasized that "utility" and "scarcity" are the sole determinants of market prices and, in some cases, even formulated the concept of marginal utility, none before Menger was able to systematically elaborate these insights into a comprehensive theory of the pricing process and of the economy in general.[15]

---

[15]For a sweeping and erudite treatment of the entire pre-Mengerian subjective-value tradition see Murray N. Rothbard, *Economic Thought Before Adam Smith*, vol. 1, *An Austrian Perspective on the History of Economic Thought* (Cheltenham, U.K.: Edward Elgar, 1995), pp. 65–133. Alejandro A. Chafuen, *Christians for Freedom: Late Scholastic Economics* (San Francisco: Ignatius Press, 1986), provides the definitive account of the Scholastic pioneers in this tradition. Murray N. Rothbard, "New Light on the Prehistory of the Austrian School," in *The Foundations of Modern Economics*, Edwin G. Dolan, ed. (Kansas City: Sheed and Ward, 1976), pp. 52–74, is also a noteworthy source on the Scholastic contributions. Joseph T. Salerno, "The Neglect of the French Liberal School in Anglo-American Economics: A Critique of Received Explanations," *Review of Austrian Economics* 2 (1987): 113–56, deals with Say's successors in the French Liberal School, while Streissler, "Influence of German Economics," details the German subjectivist influences on Menger.

## MENGER'S RECONSTRUCTION OF ECONOMIC THEORY[16]

### *The Nature and Scope of Economic Theory*

As noted above, Menger emphatically did not intend to overthrow classical economics. He was quite comfortable with its emphasis on the universality and immutability of economic law, its theory of short-run price determination, and the laissez-faire policy conclusions it derived therefrom.[17] Rather, Menger's intentions were to reconstruct classical economics on firmer foundations by grounding the supply-and-demand theory of price and the theory of monetary calculation in the choices and actions of consumers and to repair its superstructure by healing the rift between the theory of price and the theory of distribution. Menger boldly proclaimed his intention of subsuming all the branches of economics under a reconstructed price theory in his Preface to *Principles*, writing

> I have devoted special attention to the investigation of the causal connections between economic phenomena involving products and the corresponding agents of production, not only for the purpose of establishing a price theory based upon reality and placing all price phenomena (including interest, wages, ground rent, etc.) together under one unified point of view, but also because of the important insights we thereby gain into many other economic processes heretofore completely misunderstood.[18]

---

[16]The nearly simultaneous and completely independent co-discovery of the principle of marginal utility in the early 1870s by Menger, the Briton William Stanley Jevons, and the Frenchman Léon Walras is generally referred to as the "marginalist revolution." However, although this principle played an essential role in Menger's reconstruction of economic theory, as we shall see, the method by which he arrived at the principle and the use he made of it mark Mengerian economics as paradigmatically distinct from the theoretical systems that developed out of Jevons's and Walras's writings. On this point, see especially Emil Kauder, *A History of Marginal Utility Theory* (Princeton, N.J.: Princeton University Press, 1965); and William Jaffé, "Menger, Jevons, and Walras De-Homogenized," *Economic Inquiry* 14 (December 1976): 511–24. On the marginalist revolution in general, see Richard S. Howey, *The Rise of the Marginal Utility School: 1870–1889* (New York: Columbia University Press, 1989); and *The Marginal Revolution in Economics: Interpretation and Evaluation*, R.D. Collison Black, A.W. Coats, and Craufurd D.W. Goodwin, eds. (Durham, N.C.: Duke University Press, 1973).

[17]Menger's attitude toward the Classical School is reflected in the fact that "The whole framework of the lectures [to Crown Prince Rudolf] and most of the arguments are taken from Adam Smith's . . . *Wealth of Nations*." See Streissler, "Menger's Treatment of Economics in the Rudolf Lectures," p. 6.

[18]Menger, *Principles*, p. 49.

Menger recognized that at the center of "a price theory based upon reality" and of economic theory in general is human action—and human action alone. As Menger epigrammatically put it in preliminary notes written while *Principles* was in preparation: "Man himself is the beginning and the end of every economy" and "Our science is the theory of a human being's ability to deal with his wants."[19] While the centrality of human want satisfaction had been affirmed by earlier writers in the subjective-value tradition,[20] Menger alone was successful in forging a method of economic theorizing—it was later to be dubbed "praxeology" by Ludwig von Mises—that was consistent with this insight. Thus, he began his scientific inquiry by meditating upon the nature of human striving to satisfy wants, and then deducing its immediate implications. By proceeding in this way, Menger was able to perceive immediately that the process of want satisfaction is not purely cognitive and internal to the human mind, but depends crucially upon the external world and, therefore, upon the law of cause and effect. This explains why Menger began his economic treatise with the statement that "All things are subject to the law of cause and effect."[21] Without reference to this great law of objective reality, the human striving to attain goals is logically inconceivable, because, as Menger argued, subjective states of satisfaction are links in the same causal chain that includes objective states of the world:

> One's own person, moreover, and any of its states are links in this great universal structure of relationships. It is impossible to conceive of a change of one's person from one state to another in any way other than one subject to the law of causality. If, therefore, one passes from a state of need to a state in which the need is satisfied, sufficient causes for this change must exist. There must be forces in operation within one's organism that remedy the disturbed state, or there must be external things acting upon it that by their nature are capable of producing the state we call satisfaction of our needs.[22]

---

[19]Menger, quoted in Yagi, "Menger's *Grundsätze*," pp. 720–21.

[20]Especially Frédéric Bastiat, William E. Hearn, Amasa Walker, and Arthur Latham Perry. See Salerno, "Neglect of the French Liberal School" for a discussion of these economists.

[21]Menger, *Principles*, p. 51.

[22]Ibid., pp. 51–52. As Mises points out in *Human Action*, pp. 22–23,

> Man is in a position to act because he has the ability to discover causal relations which determine change and becoming in the universe. Acting requires and presupposes the category of causality. . . . [I]n order to act, man must know the causal relationship between events, processes, or states of affairs. And only as far as he knows this relationship, can his action attain the ends sought.

But the direction of causation is not one-way, from objective states of the world to subjective states of satisfaction. For Menger, it is two-way, because, by conceiving the law of cause and effect, man is able to recognize his total dependence on the external world, and transform the latter into means to attain his ends. Man, himself, thus becomes the ultimate cause—as well as the ultimate end—in the process of want satisfaction. In his notes, Menger expressed and emphasized the causal interrelationships between the subjective and the objective aspects of action by means of parallel trinities of linked concepts: "ends–means–realization/man–external world–subsistence/wants–goods–satisfaction."[23]

*The Theory of Goods*

Menger's emphasis on the law of causality led him to devote the first twenty-five pages of the *Principles* to explicating "the general theory of the good," in the course of which he radically reformulated the concept of a good in praxeological terms.[24] For Menger, goods are those elements of the external world that are integral to the causal process of want satisfaction and upon which action operates.[25] Once again, passages in Menger's pre-*Principles* notebooks are illuminating:

> Our general dependence on the external world: in its entirety the external world is presented to us as a whole in which we live. Dependence

[23]Menger, quoted in Yagi, "Menger's *Grundsätze*," p. 704. These conceptual trinities, especially the last, reflect the influence of the French Liberal economist Frédéric Bastiat on Menger, who cited Bastiat twice in his *Principles*. "Wants, Efforts, Satisfaction" was the title of the second chapter of Bastiat's unfinished treatise on political economy. See Frédéric Bastiat, *Economic Harmonies*, George B. de Huszar, ed., W. Hayden Boyers, trans. (Irvington-on-Hudson, N.Y.: Foundation for Economic Education, 1964), pp. 20–33. Bastiat also used these three terms in his definition of the science of political economy (p. 31). Elsewhere in the chapter, Bastiat stated that "The subject of political economy is man" (p. 25), words that resound in Menger's statement, quoted above in the text, that "Man himself is the beginning and the end of every economy." For Bastiat and the Liberal School's profound influence on Continental economics in the nineteenth century, see Salerno, "Neglect of the French Liberal School," pp. 119–24.

[24]It was standard practice for German textbook writers before Menger to begin by discussing "the theory of goods." See Yagi, "Menger's *Grundsätze*," p. 703; and Streissler, "Influence of German Economics," p. 49.

[25]Mises, in *Human Action*, p. 93, referred to goods as "the substratum of action." From a doctrinal point of view, Hayek, in "Carl Menger," p. 70, noted that

> [Menger's] careful initial investigation of the causal relationship between human needs and the means for their satisfaction . . . is typical of the particular attention which, the widespread impression to the contrary notwithstanding, the Austrian School has always given to the technical structure of production.

> on *certain portions* of this external world, or on some relationships in it, which must be brought into *certain relations* to us. To this end, these portions must be particularly *suited*. Such *things* are called goods, insofar as they have the capacity to satisfy human wants (serving ends amounts to the same thing).[26]

Having identified the nature of a good, Menger proceeds to elucidate what he calls "the causal connections between goods," with the goal of identifying "the place that each good occupies in the causal nexus of goods."[27] "Goods of the lowest order" are consumer goods, like bread for instance, which are used to directly satisfy human wants. In Menger's words, "the causal connection between bread and the satisfaction of one of our needs is . . . a direct one." Factors of production, on the other hand, are "goods of higher order," having only "an indirect causal connection with human needs." For example, flour and the services of ovens and bakers' labor are second-order goods whose goods-character stems from the fact that, when they are combined in the process of production to yield a quantity of bread, they operate as an indirect cause of the satisfaction of the human want for bread. Likewise, wheat, grain mills, and millers' labor constitute third-order goods which attain their goods-character from their usefulness in the production of second-order goods. The same applies to fourth- and fifth-order goods in the production of bread. In short, according to Menger,

> The process by which goods of higher order are progressively transformed into goods of lower order and by which these are directed finally to the satisfaction of human needs is . . . not irregular but subject, like all other processes of change, to the law of causality.[28]

Thus, it is their position in this causal order of want satisfaction that endows elements of the external world with their goods-character.

Menger draws a further distinction: between those goods whose available quantity exceeds the amount necessary to satisfy all human wants for them, and those available in a quantity that is insufficient to fully satisfy human wants for them. The former Menger designates "non-economic goods," and the latter, "economic goods." In the case of non-economic goods, because of their superabundance relative to wants, people need take no definite action with regard to them. With regard to economic goods, however, an individual must undertake to *economize* them in order to satisfy his wants for them as fully as possible.

---

[26]Menger, quoted in Yagi, "Menger's *Grundsätze*," p. 705. [Emphasis is Menger's.]

[27]Menger, *Principles*, p. 56.

[28]Ibid., p. 67.

Economizing involves, among other things, ranking the wants for a particular good according to their greatest urgency or importance and then choosing to allocate units of the good only to those uses that serve the most important wants, while leaving unsatisfied the less important wants. Also, just as in the case of their goods-character, the economic character of higher-order goods also derives from the economic character of the lower-order good which they cooperate in producing. Thus, for example, in a region where pure water is naturally superabundant for all human purposes, neither water nor man-made reservoirs and water pumps, pipes, and filters need be economized. For Menger, then, the operation of economizing is nothing more or less than purposive behavior or *action*, as this latter term is understood by Mises and the proponents of the modern praxeological paradigm. Both Menger's "economizing man" and Mises's "acting man" apply scarce means so as to attain their most highly valued ends.

Inherent in the idea of economizing is the notion of *property*. For Menger, "human economy and property have a joint economic origin," which is rooted in the condition of scarcity.[29] Thus, property is neither "an arbitrary invention" nor merely an aggregation of heterogeneous objects. It is a praxeological category that refers to a purposively created structure of goods that is adjusted through the operations of economizing to serve the structure of ends aimed at by an individual actor. According to Menger,

> [A person's] property is not . . . an arbitrarily combined quantity of goods, but a direct reflection of his needs, an integrated whole, no essential part of which can be diminished or increased without affecting realization of the end it serves.[30]

It is no exaggeration to say that Mengerian economics is as much about goods and property as it is about knowledge and expectations.[31]

Menger's analyses of the order and of the economic character of goods taken together demolish the foundations of the classical cost-of-production theory. First, the proposition that the economic character of lower-order goods is derived from the fact that the goods of a higher order employed in producing them possess an economic character established prior to the causal production process, according to Menger,

[29]Ibid., p. 97.

[30]Ibid., p. 76.

[31]I am indebted to Hans-Hermann Hoppe for first suggesting to me that goods and property play a central, though egregiously underappreciated, role in Mengerian economics.

> contradict[s] . . . all experience, which teaches us that, from goods of higher order whose economic character is beyond all doubt, completely useless things may be produced, and in consequence of economic ignorance actually are produced.[32]

In other words, the cost-of-production theory is at a loss in explaining how scarce and valuable resources can be and are used to produce products whose market value is zero because they are not useful, directly or indirectly, in serving human wants. This problem aside, the fatal flaw in a theory which seeks to explain the economic character of lower-order goods in terms of the economic character of goods of a higher order is that it is merely a "pseudo-explanation." As Menger argued,

> If we explain the economic character of goods of first order by that of goods of second order, the latter by the economic character of goods of third order, this again by the economic character of goods of fourth order, and so on, the solution of the problem is not advanced fundamentally by a single step, since the question as to the last and true cause of the economic character of goods always still remains unanswered.[33]

## THE THEORY OF VALUE

This brings us to the question of value which so vexed, and ultimately defeated, the classical economists. Because they were tragically unable to grasp that specific quantities and not entire classes of goods were the object of human action, the classical economists dropped use value from their analysis. But Menger, with his unblinking focus on individual action, easily recognized the profound significance of the concept of the *marginal unit*—the quantity of a good relevant to choice—for the whole of economic theory.

In his notes, Menger compared "species value," the value of an abstract class of goods, to the "individual value" or "concrete value" attaching to specific units of a good. Dismissing the former as completely irrelevant to action in the real world, Menger argued that,

> In the case of species value, we compare, on the one hand, the properties of a good without considering its quantity, and on the other, human wants without taking into account individuality. . . . In real life there are only concrete goods and concrete wants.[34]

---

[32]Menger, *Principles*, p. 108.

[33]Ibid.

[34]Menger, quoted in Yagi, "Menger's *Grundsätze*," p. 709.

In fact, the subjective ranking of the different satisfactions yielded by a definite quantity of a good is implied by the very notion of action. As Menger explained:

> The varying importance that satisfaction of separate concrete needs has for men is not foreign to the consciousness of any economizing man. . . . Wherever men live, and whatever level of civilization they occupy, we can observe how economizing individuals weigh the relative importance of satisfaction of their various needs in general, how they weigh especially the relative importance of the separate acts leading to the more or less complete satisfaction of each need, and how they are finally guided by the results of this comparison into activities directed to the fullest possible satisfaction of their needs (economizing).[35]

By cogitating on the essence of economizing or action, Menger was thus able to conclusively demonstrate that the want for any good is actually a series of wants for a definite unit of the good to the satisfaction of which the individual is constrained by scarcity to attach differing degrees of importance. And, by implication, only actual units of a good are relevant to human choice: "Not species as such, but only concrete things are *available* to economizing individuals. Only the latter, therefore, are *goods*, and only goods are the *objects of our economizing* and of our *valuation*."[36]

Having established that only specific wants and specific units of goods pertain to the valuational process, Menger proceeded to define value as "the importance that individual goods or quantities of goods attain for us because we are conscious of being dependent on command of them for the satisfaction of our needs."[37] In other words, "the value of all goods is merely an imputation of this importance [of satisfying our needs] to economic goods."[38] It follows, then, for Menger, that "value does not exist outside the consciousness of men. . . . [T]he value of goods . . . is entirely subjective in nature."[39] One would be wrong to interpret this last statement as a radical subjectivist dismissal of the realm of external reality. For Menger's emphatic distinction between the value of a thing and the thing itself is actually intended as a means of elucidating the indissoluble ontological link between the realm of cognition and the realm of objective causal processes that comes into being by virtue of valuation and economizing. The value of goods is therefore nothing

---

[35]Menger, *Principles*, p. 128.

[36]Ibid., p. 116, n. 3

[37]Ibid., p. 115.

[38]Ibid., p. 122.

[39]Ibid., p. 121.

arbitrary, but always the necessary consequence of human knowledge that the maintenance of life, of well-being, or of some ever so insignificant part of them, depends upon control of a good or a quantity of goods.[40]

If value consists in a judgment about the significance of "concrete" things in producing satisfaction of "concrete" wants, how are such judgments arrived at? That is, what is the value of a specific thing to a person who seeks to employ it to satisfy his wants? It was in his answer to this question that Menger not only solved the paradox of value, but laid the foundations for the reconstruction of price theory, and, hence, of all of economic science.

Menger brilliantly answered the question by restating it: "[W]hich satisfaction would not be attained if the economizing individual did not have the given unit at his disposal—that is, if he were to have command of a total amount smaller by that one unit?"[41] In light of Menger's discussion of economizing, the obviously correct answer to this question is "only the least of all the satisfactions assured by the whole available quantity." In other words, regardless of which particular physical unit of his supply was subtracted, the actor would economize by choosing to reallocate the remaining units so as to continue to satisfy his most important wants and to forego the satisfaction of only the least important want of those previously satisfied by the larger supply. It is, thus, always the least important satisfaction that is dependent on a unit of the actor's supply of a good and, that, therefore, determines the value of each and every unit of the supply. This value-determining satisfaction soon came to be known as the "marginal utility."[42] As Menger formulated the law of marginal utility:

> Accordingly, in every concrete case, of all the satisfactions secured by means of the whole quantity of a good at the disposal of an economizing individual, only those that have the least importance to him are dependent on the availability of a given portion of the whole quantity. Hence the value to this person of any portion of the whole available quantity of the good is equal to the importance to him of the satisfactions of least importance among those assured by the whole quantity and achieved with an equal portion.[43]

---

[40]Ibid., pp. 120–21.

[41]Ibid., p. 131.

[42]The term was coined by Menger's follower and fellow Austrian economist, Friedrich von Wieser, and Menger himself appears never to have used it in his published work.

[43]Menger, *Principles*, p. 132.

Thus, by applying the law of marginal utility, Menger was able to provide a straightforward and incontrovertible resolution to the paradox of value that had so bedeviled classical economics and prevented its development into a full-blown theory of human action. According to Menger, it is because diamonds and gold are extremely rare while water tends to be abundantly available that:

> Under ordinary circumstances, therefore, no human need would have to remain unsatisfied if men were unable to command some particular quantity of drinking water. With gold and diamonds, on the other hand, even the least significant satisfactions assured by the total quantity available still have a relatively high importance to economizing men. Thus concrete quantities of drinking water usually have *no* value to economizing men but concrete quantities of gold and diamonds a *high* value.[44]

Having thus repaired the classical split between use value and exchange value and firmly rooted price theory in consumer valuations and choices, Menger turned his attention to the bifurcation perpetrated by the classical economists between price theory and distribution theory, or between the pricing of consumer goods and the pricing of the factors of production. Once again, Menger used the law of marginal utility to provide a solution of absolute and universal validity. He also refuted, once and for all, the classical contention that, in the long run at least, price is determined by costs of production.

Menger began by pointing out that only satisfaction of wants is directly significant to human beings.[45] Consumer goods, or goods of the first order, attain value, therefore, only because people are cognizant of their dependence on specific quantities of these goods for the satisfaction of specific wants, and, hence, "impute" to these goods the importance of the satisfactions that depend upon them. Goods of higher orders, the factors of production that cooperate in the production of consumer goods, have no immediate connection with the satisfaction of human wants, but through the causal production process they do indirectly bear on the process of want satisfaction. Thus, the value of a certain quantity of consumer goods is imputed to the goods of the second order employed in its production, because the latter are a necessary, if indirect, cause of the satisfaction which is directly attributable to the stock of consumer goods. The same value-imputation analysis applies to the value of goods of the third, fourth, and higher orders. Concluded Menger:

---

[44]Ibid., p. 140.

[45]Ibid., pp. 151–52.

> Thus, as with goods of first order, the factor that is ultimately responsible for the value of goods of higher order is merely the importance we attribute to those satisfactions with respect to which we are aware of being dependent on the availability of the goods of higher order whose value is under consideration. But due to the causal connections between goods, the value of goods of higher order is not measured directly by the expected importance of the final satisfaction, but rather by the expected value of the corresponding goods of lower order.[46]

If "the value of goods of higher order is dependent upon the expected value of goods of lower order they serve to produce," then, as Menger argued, costs of production, which are nothing but the sums of the prices paid for various kinds of higher-order goods, cannot possibly determine the prices of consumer goods, because the costs themselves are ultimately determined by these prices.[47] Furthermore, as Menger pointed out, the cost-of-production theory of price determination cannot account for the prices of the services of land and of labor, which are nature given and, hence, have no costs of production themselves.[48] In contrast, the Mengerian theory of value imputation easily explains these prices in the same manner as the prices of any other species of concrete goods: as proximately derived from the value of the lower-order goods or—if they themselves are goods of the first-order—of the satisfactions that are directly dependent upon them.

While up to this point Menger's analysis succeeds in identifying consumer valuations as the general cause of the values and prices of both consumer goods and productive factors, it still leaves unexplained the prices of individual factors. The reason is that a good of a lower order can only be produced by "complementary" quantities of higher-order goods. As Menger realized, by its very nature, production must involve more than one kind of factor of production.[49] Now it would appear, therefore, that it is impossible to impute partial quotas of the value of the lower-order good to each of the various higher-order goods that cooperate in its production. However, once again, with dazzling analytical acumen, Menger wielded the law of marginal utility to hit upon the correct solution.

Menger pointed out that, in most production processes, higher-order goods need not be combined in the rigidly fixed proportions that

---

[46]Ibid., p. 152.

[47]Ibid., p. 151.

[48]Ibid., p. 149.

[49]For a praxelogical proof of Menger's insight, see Murray N. Rothbard, *Man, Economy, and State: A Treatise on Economic Principles*, 2nd ed. (Auburn, Ala.: Ludwig von Mises Institute, 1993), pp. 10–11, 28–29.

characterizes chemical reactions. In other words, if one of the complementary factors that cooperates in the production of grain, let us say, fertilizer, is partially or completely withdrawn, then there will result a reduction of the output of grain rather than a nullification of the entire production process. This implies, Menger argued, that the share of the value of a particular quantity of a higher-order good can be isolated from the aggregate value of the complementary goods combined in the given production process. Thus, if a diminution of a hundredweight of fertilizer, all other things equal, causes a drop in a grain harvest of ten sacks, then the value of this unit of fertilizer to the farmer is precisely equal to the marginal utility of ten sacks of grain, comprising the satisfactions he chooses to forego as a result of the loss of the ten sacks.

Menger summarized the "general law of the determination of the value of a concrete quantity of a good of higher order" as follows:

> Assuming . . . that all available goods of higher order are employed in the most economic fashion, the value of a concrete quantity of a good of higher order is equal to the difference in importance between the satisfactions that can be attained when we have command of the given quantity of the good of higher order whose value we wish to determine and the satisfactions that would be attained if we did not have this quantity at our command.[50]

## TIME, PROPERTY, AND ENTREPRENEURSHIP

Because Menger conceived the processes of transforming higher-order into lower-order goods (production) and of imputing value from lower-order to higher-order goods (imputation) as conjoint causal processes, he accorded time an integral role in both. According to Menger, "The idea of causality . . . is inseparable from the idea of time."[51]

If, indeed, "the time period lying between command of goods of a higher order and possession of the corresponding goods of lower order can never be eliminated," then the production process is inherently uncertain. For factors beyond the actor's technical knowledge or control, such as changes in soil properties or in weather, may affect the quality or quantity of the first-order goods that are yielded by the production process. This technical uncertainty associated with production can be greatly mitigated but never completely extinguished by the improvement of technological knowledge, which, in effect, provides the actor with better *foresight* of the outcome of a time-consuming causal process.

---

[50]Menger, *Principles*, pp. 164–65.

[51]Ibid., p. 67.

But technological knowledge cannot ameliorate other kinds of uncertainty that are inextricably bound up with production. Since any production process is undertaken to satisfy future wants, the actor must be able to foresee these wants. Indeed, as Menger pointed out, "its success will be dependent principally upon correct foresight of the quantities of goods they [actors] will find necessary in future time periods," while "a complete lack of foresight would make any planning of activity directed to the satisfaction of human needs completely impossible."[52] Nonetheless, despite the fact that people are unable to foresee their future circumstances with perfect certainty, Menger did not believe that they are utterly ignorant of their future wants.[53] Recourse to previous experience permits them to foresee with approximate certainty many wants that they will experience during their planning period. About other wants, e.g., for medicines and fire extinguishers, they remain "more or less in doubt." But despite their "deficient foresight," people do act successfully to satisfy even these wants. Menger concluded that

> The circumstance that it is uncertain whether a need for a good will be felt during the period of our plans does not, therefore, exclude the possibility that we will provide for its eventual satisfaction, and hence does not cause the reality of our requirements for goods necessary to satisfy such needs to be in question.[54]

Thus uncertainty for Menger is not an obstacle to but a condition of action.[55]

For Menger, "The second factor that determines the success of human activity is the knowledge gained by men of the means available to them for the attainment of the desired ends."[56] As a prerequisite of want-satisfaction, actors are concerned "to measure and take inventory of the goods at their disposal."[57] The more exact is the knowledge regarding the kinds and quantities of existing higher-order goods provided by these operations, the more accurate will be the forecasts of consumer goods forthcoming to satisfy future wants during the planning period.

---

[52]Ibid., p. 89.

[53]Ibid., pp. 81–82.

[54]Ibid., p. 82.

[55]This is implied in Hayek, "Carl Menger," p. 71, where Hayek characterizes Menger's view of economic activity: "To him economic activity is essentially planning for the future, and his discussion of the period, or rather different periods, to which human forethought extends as regards different wants has a definitely modern ring."

[56]Menger, *Principles*, p. 89.

[57]Ibid., p. 90.

The acquisition of such data is especially important for production planning in a developed market economy where the ownership and location of the supplies of various higher-order goods tend to be dispersed. But even if we consider "the lowest levels of civilization . . . a complete lack of this knowledge would make impossible any provident activity of men directed to the satisfaction of their needs."[58]

Now, a causal production process must be "planned and conducted . . . by an economizing individual." The set of functions necessary for actuating such a process Menger designates as "entrepreneurial activity."[59] As we have just seen, for Menger, the entrepreneur's most important function is anticipating future wants, estimating their relative importance, and acquiring the technological knowledge and knowledge of currently available means. In the absence of such entrepreneurial foresight and knowledge, there could be no imputing of value from satisfactions to higher-order goods, and rational resource allocation would be impossible.[60]

Entrepreneurial activity comprises a number of additional functions bound up with the praxeological category of property.[61] These include "economic *calculation*," involving the various computations needed to ensure the technical efficiency of the production process, i.e., the most valuable use of property. A third entrepreneurial function is "the *act of will*" by which higher-order goods are purposively allocated to the chosen production process. Finally, there is "*supervision* of the execution of the production plan so that it may be carried through as economically as possible." Clearly, the last two functions entail property-ownership and, therefore, mark the Mengerian entrepreneur as a capitalist–entrepreneur. Menger states explicitly that "command of the services of capital" is a "necessary prerequisite" for performing economic activity.[62] Moreover, in large firms, although he may employ "several helpers" whose activities are quite extensive, the entrepreneur himself will continue to perform all four characteristic functions enumerated above, "even if they are ultimately confined . . . to determining the allocation of portions of wealth to particular productive purposes only by general categories, and to the selection and control of persons."[63]

---

[58]Ibid.

[59]Ibid., p. 160.

[60]Ibid., p. 151.

[61]Ibid., pp. 159–61.

[62]Ibid., p. 172.

[63]Ibid., pp. 160–61.

The four functions Menger describes as the core of entrepreneurship are simply the praxeological implications of property in higher-order goods. This explains why, in Menger's view, the knowledge an actor acquires and the expectations he forms are not autonomous but are strictly governed by the structure of goods constituting his property and his chosen ends.[64] Moreover, as an "economizing man" who actuates and guides an uncertain causal process, Menger's entrepreneur is a dynamic actor who profits by actively seeking out the most valuable uses for his property, and is not merely a passive "risk-bearer" whose profits represent a reward for investing in risky ventures.[65]

---

[64]Guido Hülsmann, in his pathbreaking article "Knowledge, Judgment, and the Use of Property," *Review of Austrian Economics* 10, no. 1 (1997): 23–48, elaborates a thoroughly Mengerian perspective on knowledge. On pp. 43–44, Hülsmann says,

> knowledge as such is never scarce. Knowledge problems thus do have a place in economics only insofar as knowledge has to be selected for application. Yet the selection of knowledge depends entirely on the property of the acting person. . . . [O]ur choices imply a judgment upon the *importance* of our technological knowledge under the expected conditions of our action. . . . Yet, without reference to our property we could not possibly select knowledge in terms of importance. Moreover once we own property we then know which kind of knowledge could be useful. It is this property that directs our learning toward useful channels.

[65]Thus Menger criticizes his eminent predecessor in the German subjective-value tradition, Hans von Mangoldt, for characterizing "'risk-bearing' as the essential function of entrepreneurship." For Menger, risk is "only incidental" to the planning and operation of the causal production process, whose goal and driving force is the satisfaction of the actor's most important wants. See Menger, *Principles*, p. 161.

Mises offered an analogous critique of the "popular fallacy" that entrepreneurial profit represents "a reward for risk-taking." In *Human Action*, pp. 809–10, Mises writes,

> Every word in this reasoning is false. The owner of capital does not choose between more risky, less risky, and safe investments. He is forced, by the very operation of the market economy, to invest his funds in such a way as to supply the most urgent needs of the consumers to the best possible extent. . . . The fact that a capitalist as a rule . . . prefers to spread out his funds among various classes of investment, does not suggest that he wants to reduce his "gambling risk." He wants to improve his chances of earning profits.

Indeed the four functions that Menger associated with entrepreneurial activity are all embodied in Mises's concept of the "promoter–entrepreneur" (ibid., pp. 289–315). The only error Menger made in his discussion of entrepreneurship was to incorrectly categorize entrepreneurial activity as (nonexchangeable) labor services. See Menger, *Principles*, p. 172.

## THE THEORY OF PRICE

We now turn to price theory, the capstone of Mengerian economics. Menger viewed the explanation of prices on the basis of the law of marginal utility as the final step in linking the classical theory of monetary calculation to the general process of human want satisfaction. For if the active element in determining the prices of goods of all orders is marginal utility, and if entrepreneurs base their economic calculations on these prices, it can then be demonstrated that purposeful actions undertaken to satisfy human wants are the ultimate determinant of resource allocation and income distribution in the market economy.

As a prelude to elaborating his theory of price, Menger was forced to clarify the cause and essence of exchange. Unfortunately, because of their tendency to conceive the human want for a good abstractly and generically rather than concretely and individually, Adam Smith and the classical economists had no alternative but to identify the motive to exchange with an alleged innate proclivity of human beings to "truck and barter." It was thus left to Menger to elaborate a theory of exchange in terms of human wants.

Once again resorting to the law of marginal utility, Menger was able to provide a simple and definitive solution to the problem. Menger illustrated this solution with an example along roughly the following lines[66]: Suppose that there exist two farmers, A and B, each of whom owns a supply of a different good, horses and cows. Assuming that A possesses six horses and B, six cows, Menger posed the question: "How many horses and cows would A and B agree to exchange?" In answer, Menger argued that the two parties would continue to exchange one horse for one cow as long as the value of the good each received exceeded the value of the good he gave up, that is, as long as the two parties valued the goods they exchanged in inverse order. As Menger summed up his analysis,

> This limit [to exchange] is reached when one of the two bargainers has no further quantity of goods which is of less value to him than a quantity of another good at the disposal of the second bargainer who, at the same time, evaluates the two quantities of goods inversely.[67]

The cessation of exchange also implies that the two parties have exhausted the mutual benefits from trade. These benefits consist in the opportunity of each trader to satisfy more important wants with his restructured property than he was able to satisfy with his initial, pre-exchange supplies of goods. Exchange, for Menger, is therefore as much a

---

[66]Ibid., pp. 183–87.

[67]Ibid., p. 187.

part of the causal process of want satisfaction as production is. Menger used this insight to demonstrate the fallacy of the classical position that exchange and the activities of middlemen are unproductive, arguing that

> The effect of an economic exchange of goods upon the economic position of each of the two traders is always the same as if a new object of wealth had entered his possession. . . . For the end of the economy is not the physical augmentation of goods but always the fullest possible satisfaction of human needs.[68]

In the course of demonstrating the limits to exchange, Menger originated the praxeological method of analyzing the real-world pricing process. Since every causal process has a beginning and an end, a complete explanation of the process involves a description of the factors that precipitate it and maintain it in motion and the factors that cause its cessation. Central to this analytical method is the concept of what Böhm-Bawerk called "momentary equilibrium" and Mises called "the state of rest."[69] In the example above, the exchange process continues as along as A and B rank the values of the two goods in inverse order; the process is suspended and the state of rest emerges when the inverse valuations no longer hold. In the real world, it is true, individual valuations of goods are in constant flux due to changes in consumer wants and the technical conditions of production, thus continually recreating the conditions of further exchange. However, this does not nullify Menger's analysis. In fact, it is precisely the notion of the state of rest that is necessary to delimit a particular act of exchange. As Menger explained:

> the foundations of economic exchanges are constantly changing, and we therefore observe the phenomenon of a perpetual succession. . . . But even in this chain of transactions we can, by observing closely, find *points of rest* at particular times, for particular persons, and with particular kinds of goods. At these *points of rest*, no exchange of goods takes place because an economic limit to exchange has already been reached.[70]

Menger's explanation of how prices are determined follows naturally from his analysis of exchange. Menger defined prices as "the quantities of goods actually exchanged." As part of the overall want satisfaction

---

[68]Ibid., pp. 184, n. 4, and 190.

[69]See Mises, *Human Action*, pp. 334–35, for a description of this method, which, Mises stated, "we owe to Gossen, Carl Menger, and Böhm-Bawerk." While Böhm-Bawerk was Menger's student, the German writer Heinrich Hermann Gossen's classic work appeared in 1854, well before Menger published his *Principles*, although it does not appear that Menger had ever read this work.

[70]Menger, *Principles*, p. 188, emphasis added.

process, however, "Prices are only incidental manifestations of [economic] activities, symptoms of an economic equilibrium between the economies of individuals."[71] This means that the emergence of a realized price—i.e., an actual exchange of definite quantities of two goods—coincides not only with the consummation of the exchange process but also with the attainment of a momentary state of rest by the parties involved in the exchange. In the example above, if A pays the sum of four horses for four of B's cows, this constitutes both the realized price of the transaction and the exchange of the specific quantities of goods necessary to establish a temporary exchange equilibrium between A and B with respect to horses and cows. Similarly, in a modern monetary economy, at any moment in time, every money price actually observed indicates the exchange of the quantities of goods necessary to facilitate the achievement of catallactic states of rest by each pair of transactors. For each individual, this state takes the form of a temporary lull, of longer or shorter duration, before the market is reentered and another exchange is initiated. It is during this interlude that the mutual advantages of exchange are perceived to be exhausted. For example, a consumer exiting a supermarket is, at least momentarily, in a state of rest with respect not only to the various items of food she has purchased, but with respect to her money assets and all other species of exchangeable goods that compose her property. This state of catallactic quiescence will be disturbed, sooner or later, when she again finds herself confronting a prospective seller whose valuations of a good and its purchase price are the inverse of her own.

Menger used this method of analysis to demonstrate that prices are determined exclusively by the subjective valuations of market participants. He began with a simple analysis of exchange between two isolated individuals. Person A1 owns a horse while Person B1 owns a supply of wheat. If, based on his estimations of the relative marginal utilities of the two goods to him, B1 will pay up to a maximum of eighty bushels of wheat to obtain the horse and A1 will part with the horse for no less than ten bushels of wheat—again, based on considerations of marginal utility —then the basis for exchange exists, because, for prices between ten and eighty bushels of wheat per horse, A1 and B1 value the horse and the wheat inversely. This being the case, and assuming A1 and B1 are known to each other, the price paid under these conditions will settle somewhere in the range of ten to eighty bushels per horse. The exact price will be the subject of higgling between the two and will depend upon their relative

---

[71]Ibid., pp. 191–92.

bargaining skills. At the instant the exchange takes place, the price is realized and vanishes, and a state of rest immediately ensues for the two parties that is characterized by an improvement in the want satisfaction of each and a temporary pause in their catallactic activities.

Let us now introduce two more prospective horse buyers into this market, B2 and B3, whose maximum purchase prices for a horse are sixty and fifty bushels of wheat, respectively. Assuming B1's maximum buying price remains constant at eighty, the equilibrium price range must contract to sixty-one to eighty bushels, as competition on the buyer's side drives the price up to a level sufficiently high to exclude all but the single most capable buyer. Only a price of sixty-one bushels on above will cause a distribution of goods that is consistent with a state of rest for all participants in the market. For example, at a price of seventy bushels, only B1, the buyer, ranks the horse above the purchase price, while A1, the seller, and B2 and B3, the excluded buyers, all rank the purchase price above the horse and are content to depart the market without it. If the example is altered so that A1 now brings two horses to market, with minimum selling prices of thirty and ten bushels, respectively, then the equilibrium price range will fall and shrink further to fifty-one to sixty bushels of wheat, with B1 and B2 each buying a horse at this price. For it is only a realized price in this range that is capable of producing the lull in the catallactic process that follows from a redistribution of goods in accordance with the complete exploitation of the mutual benefits from exchange.

Menger summed up the general principle of price formation under "monopoly trade," i.e., a market in which, as above, one side of the market consists of a single seller, as follows:

> Price formation takes place between limits that are set by the equivalent of one unit of the monopolized good to the individual least eager and least able to compete who still participates in the exchange [B2, in the above example] and the equivalent of one unit of the monopolized good to the individual most eager and best able to compete of the competitors who are economically excluded from the exchange [B3, in the example].[72]

Menger recognized, moreover, that the same principle that underlies price formation in the case of monopoly does not only apply to "monopoly," but is an absolutely true and exact law of economics that applies universally to the formation of price in all markets. According to this law, dubbed the law of "marginal pairs" by Böhm-Bawerk, in every

---

[72]Ibid., p. 207.

market the actual price will always settle at a level that completely dissipates the mutual gains from additional exchange and culminates in a state of rest.[73] Wrote Menger:

> Each given economic situation sets definite limits within which price formation and the distribution of goods must take place, and any price and distribution of goods that is outside these limits is economically impossible. . . . Whether a given quantity of a commodity is sold by a monopolist or by several competitors in supply, and independently of the way in which the commodity was originally distributed among the competing sellers, the effect on price formation and on the resultant distribution of the commodity among the competing buyers is exactly the same.[74]

It is his overarching concern with the causal process of want satisfaction that explains why Menger gives equal emphasis in this passage to "price formation" and "the distribution of goods." Goods are the proximate cause of want satisfaction and, therefore, the immediate motive for engaging in exchange. This also explains Menger's focus on historically realized prices, because these prices are, in Menger's words, simply "quantities of goods actually exchanged"; hence, it is their payment that generates the mutual improvement of satisfaction among market participants. The momentary "points of rest" that loom so large in Menger's price theory are the states that prevail immediately after these prices have been paid, when there exist no further opportunities for the mutual enhancement of satisfaction among market participants.

Since the *Principles* was intended as the first general part of a multivolume treatise that Menger never completed, it does lack an explicit and detailed discussion of the pricing of the factors of production and, thus, of the money costs of production that are used in the economic calculations of entrepreneurs.[75] This gap in Mengerian price theory was ably filled by Böhm-Bawerk who, in 1886, elaborated the "law of costs" —today we call it the law of marginal productivity—which explained

---

[73]Eugen von Böhm-Bawerk, *Capital and Interest*, vol. 2, *The Positive Theory of Capital*, trans. George D. Huncke (South Holland, Ill.: Libertarian Press, 1960), p. 225. According to Mises:

> The notion of the plain state of rest as developed by the elementary [i.e., Mengerian] theory of prices is a faithful description of what comes to pass in the market at every instant. Any deviation of a market price from the height at which supply and demand are equal is—in the unhampered market—self-liquidating. (*Human Action*, p. 762)

[74]Menger, *Principles*, pp. 216, 219.

[75]Hayek, "Carl Menger," p. 69. As Hayek points out, this is "really [the] only one major point at which Menger's exposition leaves a serious gap" (p. 73).

pricing in factor markets in a manner fully consistent with Menger's explanation of the pricing of consumer goods by the law of marginal utility.[76] With the completion of the Mengerian theory of the pricing process, business entrepreneurship and monetary calculation are finally integrated with consumer choice into a general theory of human action.

This then is Menger's greatest achievement and the essence of his "revolution" in economics: the demonstration that prices are no more and no less than the objective manifestation of causal processes purposefully initiated and directed to satisfying human wants. It is, thus, price theory that is the heart of Mengerian and, therefore, of Austrian economics. In a profoundly insightful passage in his eulogy, Schumpeter emphasized this aspect of Menger's contribution:

> What matters, therefore, is not the discovery that people buy, sell, or produce goods because and insofar as they value them from the point of view of satisfaction of needs, but a discovery of quite a different kind: the discovery that this simple fact and its sources in the laws of human needs are wholly sufficient to explain the basic facts about all complex phenomena of the modern exchange economy, and that in spite of striking appearances to the contrary, human needs are the driving force of the economic mechanism beyond the Robinson Crusoe economy or the economy without exchange. The chain of thought which leads to this conclusion starts with the recognition that price formation is the specific economic characteristic of the economy—as distinct from all other social, historical, and technical characteristics—and that all specifically economic events can be comprehended within the framework of price formation. From a purely economic standpoint, the economic system is merely a system of dependent prices; all special problems, whatever they may be called, are nothing but special cases of one and the same constantly recurring process, and all specifically economic regularities are deduced from the laws of price formation. Already in the preface of Menger's work [*Principles*], we find this recognition as a self-evident assumption. His essential aim is to discover the law of price formation. As soon as he succeeded in basing the solution of the pricing problem, in both its "demand" and "supply" aspects, on an analysis of human needs and on what Wieser has called the principle of "marginal utility," the whole complex mechanism of economic life suddenly appeared to be unexpectedly and transparently simple.[77]

---

[76]Böhm-Bawerk, *Positive Theory*, pp. 248–56. For a discussion of Böhm-Bawerk's unduly neglected contribution in this area, see Joseph T. Salerno "Two Traditions in Modern Monetary Theory: John Law and A.R.J. Turgot," *Journal des Economistes et des Etudes Humaines* 2 (June/September 1991): 368–70.

[77]Schumpeter, "Carl Menger," p. 84.

Schumpeter concluded that, despite Menger's other substantial contributions, his "theory of value and price . . . is, so to speak, the expression of his real personality."[78] If this is so, Menger's personality lives on in the flourishing praxeological paradigm of contemporary Austrian economics.

## SELECTED READINGS


Caldwell, Bruce J., ed. 1990. *Carl Menger and his Legacy in Economics*. Durham, N.C.: Duke University Press.

Hayek, F.A. 1992. "Carl Menger (1840–1921)." In *The Fortunes of Liberalism: Essays on Austrian Economics and the Ideal of Freedom*. Vol. 4. *The Collected Works of F. A. Hayek*. Peter G. Klein, ed. Chicago: University of Chicago Press, 1992.

Jaffé, William. 1976. "Menger, Jevons, and Walras De-Homogenized." *Economic Inquiry* 14 (December): 511–24.

Kauder, Emil. 1965. *A History of Marginal Utility Theory*. Princeton, N.J.: Princeton University Press.

Menger, Carl. 1985. *Investigations into the Methods of the Social Sciences with Special Reference to Economics*. Louis Schneider, ed. Francis J. Nock, trans. New York: New York University Press.

——. 1976. *Principles of Economics*. James Dingwall and Bert F. Hoselitz, trans. New York: New York University Press.

Sennholz, Hans F. 1985. "The Monetary Writings of Carl Menger." In *The Gold Standard: Perspectives in the Austrian School*. Llewellyn H. Rockwell, Jr., ed., Auburn, Ala.: Ludwig von Mises Institute.

Streissler, Erich W., and Monika Streissler, eds. 1994. *Carl Menger's Lectures to Crown Prince Rudolf*. Cheltenham, U.K.: Edward Elgar.

Yagi, Kiichiro. 1993. "Menger's *Grundsätze* in the Making." *History of Political Economy* 25 (Winter).

# 7
# PHILIP WICKSTEED: THE BRITISH AUSTRIAN

ISRAEL M. KIRZNER

*Philip Wicksteed*
*1844–1927*

"WICKSTEED'S PLACE IN the history of economic thought is beside the place occupied by Jevons and the Austrians."[1] Ever since this profoundly insightful 1932 comment by Lionel Robbins, Philip Wicksteed has, at least doctrinally, been identified with the Austrian tradition. Perhaps for this very reason, however, we should, at the outset of a discussion of the Austrian character of Wicksteed's work, emphasize that, whatever the strength of Wicksteed's Austrian doctrinal credentials, he was not a member of the Austrian School in the usual sense. This British contemporary of Menger, Böhm-Bawerk, and Wieser appears to have had no direct contact or correspondence with any of them. His biography,[2] which provides detailed descriptions of Wicksteed's trips abroad, makes no mention of his ever having visited Vienna. His work seems to have made no direct impact on the work of his Austrian contemporaries.[3] He,

[1]Lionel Robbins, Introduction to Philip H. Wicksteed, *The Common Sense of Political Economy and Selected Papers and Reviews on Economic Theory*, Lionel Robbins, ed. (London: Routledge and Kegan Paul, [1910] 1933), p. xv.

[2]C.H. Herford, *Philip Wicksteed: His Life and Work* (London and Toronto: J.M. Dent, 1931).

[3]It is, however, of some interest that Joseph Schumpeter, then a twenty-three-year-old brilliant young Austrian economist, made a point of visiting for "an hour's chat" at Wicksteed's home in 1906. On that occasion, Schumpeter reports, Wicksteed's personality "radiated upon me," leaving an impression of "repose that owed nothing to callousness, . . . benevolence that was not weakness, . . . simplicity that

in turn, while certainly mentioning their work,[4] seems not to have drawn any of his main ideas from them.[5]

The elements in Wicksteed's work which we shall identify as "Austrian" were, it is well-recognized, the outcome of his own careful elaboration of the insights he discovered in the work of that other British "Austrian," William Stanley Jevons. Nor does Wicksteed's work seem to have had seminal impact on the second generation of Austrians, although it is to its economics that Wicksteed's own work is closest.[6] Late in his life Mises refers to Wicksteed's "great treatise"[7] but it would certainly be an exaggeration to contend that Mises's own system drew its central ideas from Wicksteed, rather than from Menger and Böhm-Bawerk.

Moreover, while, as we shall see, there is in Wicksteed's work a considerable affinity with the Austrians in regard to the scope, character, and content of economic analysis, this affinity hardly extends to the free-market ideological perspective often held to be inextricably linked with the Austrian tradition. Where the Austrians have fairly consistently been foremost among the economic critics of socialism, Wicksteed

went so well with . . . refinement, . . . unassuming modesty that did not lack dignity." Joseph A. Schumpeter, *History of Economic Analysis* (New York: Oxford University Press, 1954), p. 831. Robbins, in his Introduction to Wicksteed's *The Common Sense of Political Economy* (p. viii), credits Wicksteed, *The Alphabet of Economic Science* (London: Macmillan, 1888), with introducing the term "marginal utility" as a translation of the Austrian *Grenz-nutzen*.

[4]See, e.g., Wicksteed, *The Common Sense of Political Economy*, vol. 1, p. 2 and vol. 2, pp. 765, 808, 812.

[5]In a 1926 paper, Hayek apparently held that Wicksteed—who devoted much of his own work to the theory of distribution—had paid little if any attention to "the principles of imputation developed by the Austrian School." See F.A. Hayek, *Money, Capital, and Fluctuations: Early Essays*, Roy McCloughry, ed. (Chicago: University of Chicago Press, 1984), p. 43. At one point, Wicksteed credits the generation of economists who followed Jevons—mentioning particularly those "in Austria and in America"—with expanding on the "universal application of the theory of margins." The statement here in the text should, moreover, also be modified by noting that Robbins refers to "influences which shaped Wicksteed's thought" as including "Jevons and the earlier Austrians." See Wicksteed, *The Common Sense of Political Economy*, vol. 2, p. 812.

[6]An admittedly incomplete survey of Austrian work during the 1920s has revealed few references to Wicksteed. This absence was particularly noticeable in Hans Mayer's important 1932 paper, "The Cognitive Value of Functional Theories of Price," in *Classics in Austrian Economics: A Sampling in the History of a Tradition*, Israel M. Kirzner, ed. (London: William Pickering, 1994), vol. 2, pp. 55–168.

[7]Ludwig von Mises, *The Ultimate Foundation of Economic Science: An Essay on Method* (Princeton, N.J.: D. Van Nostrand, 1962), p. 78.

was deeply sympathetic to it.[8] If, despite all of this, Wicksteed is yet regarded by late-twentieth-century Austrians as a distinctly kindred spirit,[9] this must be attributed not to any strong personal links between Wicksteed and his Austrian contemporaries, nor to any shared political or ideological perspectives, but, far more narrowly, to a common set of doctrinal insights. These insights, contrary to the thrust of the Marshallian economics dominant at the time Wicksteed was writing, clearly and starkly recognized the profoundly *revolutionary* character of the marginal-utility emphasis introduced into economics during the 1870s. The story of Wicksteed as an Austrian must revolve around these doctrinal insights.

## THE WICKSTEED STORY

Born in 1844, the son of a Unitarian clergyman, Wicksteed was educated at University College, London, and Manchester New College, from 1861 to 1867, when he received his master's degree, with a gold medal in classics.[10] Following his father into the Unitarian ministry in 1867, Wicksteed embarked on an extraordinarily broad range of scholarly and theological explorations. His theological and ethical writings continued long after he left the pulpit (in 1897), and appear to have been the initial point of departure for a number of his other fields of scholarly inquiry. These included, in particular, his deep interest in Dante scholarship, an interest which not only produced a remarkable list of publications, but

---

[8]Ian Steedman concluded his article "Wicksteed, Philip Henry," in *The New Palgrave: A Dictionary of Economics*, John Eatwell, Murray Milgate, and Peter Newman, eds., 4 vols. (New York: Macmillan, 1987), p. 919, by stating that Wicksteed's *The Common Sense of Political Economy* is a "brilliant demonstration of a writer who . . . was friendly to the socialist and labor movements of his time, and who was sometimes a sharp critic of the market system, could yet be a purist of marginal theory." Robbins (Introduction to Wicksteed, *The Common Sense of Political Economy*, p. vi), reports that "all his life" Wicksteed "retained a sympathy for the idea of land nationalization." Despite all this, it must be emphasized that Wicksteed's message to the would-be social reformer was consistently that of the trained neoclassical economist. Referring to the "economic forces" which "are persistent and need no tending," Wicksteed reminds "the social reformer" that if "we can harness [these economic forces] they will pull for us without further trouble on our part, and if we undertake to oppose or control them we must count the cost" (p. 158).

[9]Murray Rothbard cites Wicksteed many times in *Man, Economy, and State: A Treatise on Economic Principles* (Auburn, Ala.: Ludwig von Mises Institute, 1993). When the present writer sought to present an Austrian restatement of price theory in the early 1960s, he found himself turning again and again to Wicksteed as a guiding source. See Israel M. Kirzner, *Market Theory and the Price System* (Princeton, N.J.: D. Van Nostrand, 1963).

[10]Herford, *Philip Wicksteed*, p. 25.

which built Wicksteed's reputation as one of the foremost medievalists of his time. It was Wicksteed's theologically-driven interest in and concern for the ethics of modern commercial society, with its disturbing inequalities of wealth and income, which appear to have led him into his economic studies, following on his reading of Henry George's 1879 *Progress and Poverty*.[11]

Perhaps it was the circumstance that economics entered into Wicksteed's field of scholarly vision in his mid-forties, and as only one of a number of areas of his interest—most of them to which he was committed for years before he began his economics—which led Schumpeter to remark that Wicksteed "stood somewhat outside of the economics profession."[12] Yet, within a few years, Wicksteed published a significant economic work of his own,[13] carefully expounding on the theory he learned from Jevons, and became a lecturer on economics for the University Extension Lectures.[14] In 1894, Wicksteed published his celebrated *An Essay on the Co-ordination of the Laws of Distribution*, in which he sought to prove mathematically that a distributive system which rewarded factory owners according to marginal productivity would exhaust the total product produced. But it was his 1910 *The Common Sense of Political Economy* which most comprehensively presents Wicksteed's economic system, and which expresses most clearly and emphatically those insights which today's Austrians find most congenial. Important elements of this Austrian side of Wicksteed's work were concisely presented in his well-known 1913 Presidential Address to Section F of the British Association, published in *Economic Journal*, March 1914, under the title "The Scope and Method of Political Economy in the Light of the 'Marginal' Theory of Value and Distribution." Apart from participation in a 1922 *Economica* symposium, Wicksteed published nothing further on economics during the last dozen years of his life, which ended in 1927. What was it in Wicksteed's economics which later Austrians have found most similar to their own tradition?

---

[11]See Herford, *Philip Wicksteed*, p. 197. George's book led Wicksteed to discover Jevons's book, a work which was to exercise the greatest influence on Wicksteed's own economic thought. See William Stanley Jevons, *The Theory of Political Economy* (London: Macmillan, 1871).

[12]Schumpeter, *History of Economic Analysis*, p. 831.

[13]Wicksteed, *The Alphabet of Economic Science*.

[14]This was a kind of adult-education program initiated in Great Britain in the 1870s to extend "the teaching of the universities, to serve up some of the crumbs from the university tables, in a portable and nutritious form, for some of the multitude who had no chance of sitting there." See Herford, *Philip Wicksteed*, p. 90.

WICKSTEED THE AUSTRIAN

Lionel Robbins's assessment of Wicksteed as an Austrian was not only insightful of Wicksteed's contribution to marginalist economics, it also expressed Robbins's own understanding of the history of modern economic thought. It was no accident that the Preface to Robbins's own enormously influential *An Essay on the Nature and Significance of Economic Science* (1932) concludes with an acknowledgment of his "especial indebtedness to the works of Professor Ludwig von Mises and to *The Common Sense of Political Economy* of the late Philip Wicksteed."[15] Robbins, at least in 1932, saw Wicksteed as a pioneer in that line of post-1879 economic writing, which clearly and cleanly directed economic thought in a direction differing drastically from that taken by classical economic thought. It was in this that Robbins identified Wicksteed's common ground with the Austrians (and particularly with Mises). It was an interpretation of modern economics which sharply disagreed with the perspective of Alfred Marshall, so dominant in British economics.

> The main stream of economic speculation in [Britain] in the last forty years has come *via* Marshall from the classics.... In intention at any rate Marshall's position was essentially revisionist. He came not to destroy, but—as he thought—to fulfil the work of the classics. Wicksteed, on the other hand, was one of those who, with Jevons and Menger, thought... that complete reconstruction was necessary. He was not a revisionist, but a revolutionary.[16]

In what follows, we shall identify several distinct components of Wicksteed's revolutionary approach to economic understanding.[17] Each of these components bears a strong Austrian flavor, and stems arguably from Wicksteed's subjectivist stance in economic thinking. We shall focus (a) on Wicksteed's emphasis on a subjectivist understanding of the concept of cost; (b) on Wicksteed's rejection of the classical view of economic analysis as concerned narrowly with the phenomena of material wealth

---

[15]Lionel C. Robbins, *An Essay on the Nature and Significance of Economic Science*, 2nd ed. (London: Macmillan, 1935), p. 16.

[16]Robbins, Introduction to Wicksteed, *The Common Sense of Political Economy*, pp. xvf). Stigler describes Wicksteed as one of the only two "important English economists of the period between 1870 and the World War who explicitly abandoned the classical tradition." See George J. Stigler, *Production and Distribution Theories: The Formative Period* (New York: Macmillan, 1941), pp. 38–39ff. The other economist to whom Stigler is here referring is William Smart, the translator of Böhm-Bawerk and Wieser.

[17]It should be noted that Wicksteed consistently refrained from claiming originality for his ideas. He saw himself as expounding and elaborating on the economics he learned from Jevons.

(and with a model of *homo oeconomicus* intent on nothing but the gain of material wealth); and (c) on Wicksteed's (admittedly limited but nonetheless significant) concern with the *process* of market equilibration (rather than exclusively with the attained equilibrium state itself). We may venture the conjecture that, in regard to these three aspects of Wicksteed's Austrianism, it was the first which seems to have most impressed Robbins, the second which perhaps most impressed Mises, and the third which may be of greatest interest to modern Austrians, the disciples of Mises and Hayek. Space constraints preclude any but an outline discussion of each of these three Austrian aspects of Wicksteed's work.

## WICKSTEED AND THE SUBJECTIVISM OF COST

It was in regard to the role of costs in the theory of economic value that Wicksteed saw himself as most clearly departing from the Marshallian orthodoxy of his British contemporaries. He saw that orthodoxy paying lip-service to the marginal utility theory introduced by Jevons, but refusing to recognize the full implications of this theory for the final rejection of the classical cost theory of value. "The school of economists of which Professor Marshall is the illustrious head," Wicksteed wrote in 1905,

> may be regarded from the point of view of the thorough-going Jevonian as a school of apologists. It accepts . . . the Jevonian *principles*, but declares that, so far from being revolutionary, they merely supplement, clarify, and elucidate the theories they profess to destroy. To scholars of this school, the admission into the science of the renovated study of consumption leaves the study of production comparatively unaffected. As a determining factor of normal prices, cost of production is coordinate with the schedule of demands.[18]

In other words, Wicksteed rebelled against a view of production activity which sees it as a matter of strictly technical relationships, entirely distinct from the marginal-utility considerations governing consumption activity.

It was the confusion arising from this Marshallian view which was responsible for the residual classical idea that market price is in some sense the outcome of a balancing of an (objective) cost of production with (subjective) marginal utility. In Wicksteed's own strongly-held opinion, the Jevonian view is an emphatically different one:

> In no case can the cost of production have any direct influence upon the price of a commodity, if the commodity has been produced and the cost

[18]Wicksteed, *The Common Sense of Political Economy*, vol. 2, p. 812.

> has been incurred; but in every case in which the cost of production has not yet been incurred, the manufacturer makes an estimate of the alternatives still open to him before determining whether, and in what quantities, the commodity shall be produced; and the stream of supply thus determined on fixes the marginal value and the price. *The only sense, then, in which cost of production can affect the value of one thing is the sense in which it is itself the value of another thing. Thus what has been variously termed utility, ophelemity, or desiredness, is the sole and ultimate determinant of all exchange values.*[19]

For Wicksteed, the only sense in which cost plays a role in the explanation of the market price is that in which cost is the anticipated value of a prospective alternative which is, at the moment of production decision, being rejected in favor of what it is decided to produce.

It is this view of Wicksteed which led Professor James Buchanan to write that the

> opportunity-cost conception was explicitly developed by the Austrians, by the American, H.J. Davenport, and the principle could scarcely have occupied a more central place than it assumed in P.H. Wicksteed's *Common Sense of Political Economy.*[20]

As Buchanan has emphasized,[21] Wicksteed's work "was a major formative influence on the cost theory that emerged in the late 1920s and early 1930s at the London School of Economics [LSE]." Certainly Robbins's own recognition of the Austrian School during these years, and his own intellectual leadership at the LSE at this time must have helped cement the perception of intellectual affinity linking Wicksteed with the Austrian School.

---

[19]Wicksteed, ibid., vol. 1, p. 391 (italics added). Wicksteed, in his celebrated 1913 paper ("The Scope and Method of Political Economy in Light of the 'Marginal' Theory of Value and Distribution," *Economic Journal*, 1914), pursued this insight so far as to establish one of his best-known and most provocative analytical insights, viz. that there is, in reality, no such thing as an independent "supply curve." The supply curve is merely part of what Wicksteed called the "total demand curve" which includes the schedule of quantities of a commodity which existing holders of that commodity will wish to hold for their own consumption, at different prices.

[20]James M. Buchanan, in *L.S.E. Essays on Cost*, James M. Buchanan and G.F. Thirlby, eds. (London: London School of Economics and Political Science, 1973), p. 14.

[21]See James M. Buchanan, *Cost and Choice: An Inquiry in Economic Theory* (Chicago: Markham Publishing, 1969), p. 17; also Buchanan and Thirlby, *L.S.E. Essays on Cost*, p. 14. For the extent to which Buchanan believes that Wicksteed attained Buchanan's own theoretical understanding of cost, see Buchanan, *Cost and Choice*, p. 17.

## WICKSTEED AND THE SCOPE OF ECONOMICS

Wicksteed devoted many pages of his *Common Sense* to the elucidation of the meaning of the adjective "economic." And his final major restatement of his overall perspective bore the title "The Scope and Method of Political Economy in the Light of the 'Marginal' Theory of Value and Distribution."[22] Here, again, we find Wicksteed pursuing the radical implications of the Jevonian revolution, and being led inevitably to the rejection of classical views on the scope of economics. It is utterly incoherent, Wicksteed insisted again and again, to view the pursuit of material wealth as constituting a uniquely distinct field for economic inquiry; it is both arbitrary and analytically unhelpful, to say the least, to see the conclusions of economic science as dependent upon the dominance of selfish motives (as identified with the classical *homo oeconomicus*).

It is here that we find Wicksteed treading the same path as the Austrians, and, in particular as Ludwig von Mises. Both Wicksteed and Mises insisted on the *universal* application of the conclusions which flow from our understanding of human purposefulness and rationality in the making of decisions. "We habitually talk," Wicksteed wrote,

> of a man gaining some object "at the price of honor"; or say to some one who contemplates an action which would alienate his friends, "Oh yes! Of course you can do it, if you choose to pay the price." "Price," then, in the narrower sense of "the money for which a material thing, a service, or a privilege can be obtained," is simply a special case of "price" in the wider sense of "the terms on which alternatives are offered to us."[23]

"Sensitive people," Mises wrote,

> may be pained to have to choose between the ideal and the material. But that . . . is in the nature of things. For even where we can make judgments of value without money computations, we cannot avoid this choice. Both isolated man and socialist communities would have to do likewise, and truly sensitive natures will never find it painful. Called upon to choose between bread and honor, they will never be at a loss how to act. If honor cannot be eaten, eating can at least be forgone for honor.[24]

---

[22]This was also part of his 1913 Presidential Address to Section F of the British Association.

[23]Wicksteed, 1933, p. 28. It is noteworthy that this page is cited approvingly by Ludwig von Mises, in *Epistemological Problems of Economics*, George Reisman, trans. (Princeton, N.J.: D. Van Nostrand, 1960), p. 34.

[24]Ludwig von Mises, *Socialism: An Economic and Sociological Analysis* (London: Jonathan Cape, 1936), p. 116. In this early (the original German edition was published in 1922) expression of Mises's rejection of any sharp line separating the economic from the non-economic, Mises does not cite Wicksteed.

It is no accident that when, in 1933, Mises first comprehensively laid out his view of economics as simply a branch of a "universally valid science of human action,"[25] and argued that the "laws of catallactics that economics expounds are valid for every exchange regardless of whether those involved in it have acted wisely or unwisely or whether they were actuated by economic or non-economic motives,"[26] he referred, in a footnote, to the page in Wicksteed from which we have cited the passage quoted above.

For Mises, the exclusion of altruistic motives from economics is arbitrary and based on misunderstanding. What drives human behavior is simply human purposefulness. "What a man does is always aimed at an improvement of his own state of satisfaction." Only in this sense can we accurately understand

> an action directly aiming at the improvement of other people's conditions. . . . The actor considers it as more satisfactory for himself to make other people eat than to eat himself. His uneasiness is caused by the awareness of the fact that other people are in want.[27]

Wicksteed elaborated on this same insight in his insistence that the "proposal to exclude 'benevolent' or 'altruistic' motives from consideration in the study of Economics is . . . wholly irrelevant and beside the mark." The common Austrian foundational tenet is the primacy of human *purposefulness*, seen far more broadly than as the expression of egoistic, selfish greed. As Robbins recognized,[28] it is considerations such as the dependency of economic phenomena upon "purposive action" which enables us adequately to dismiss the "oft-reiterated accusation that Economics assumes a world of economic men concerned only with money-making and self-interest." Clearly, what Wicksteed and the Austrians were doing was consistently and subjectivistically redirecting the focus of economic analysis away from the material *objects* of classical inquiry, to the implications of individual human choices and decisions.

---

[25]Mises, *Epistemological Problems*, p. 12.

[26]Ibid., p. 34.

[27]Ludwig von Mises, *Human Action: A Treatise on Economics*, The Scholar's Edition (Auburn, Ala.: Ludwig von Mises Institute, [1949] 1998), p. 243.

[28]Robbins, *Nature and Significance*, pp. 93ff. Robbins cites Mises in regard to the purposefulness of "rational" behavior. Robbins noted the parallelism between Wicksteed and Mises in this regard (see his Introduction to Wicksteed, *The Common Sense of Political Economy*, p. xxiii). Arguably it was this insight which inspired the central ideas in Robbins's first edition of *Nature and Significance*.

## WICKSTEED AND THE MARKET PROCESS

"A market," Wicksteed wrote,

> is the machinery by which those on whose scales of preference any commodity is relatively high are brought into communication with those on whose scale it is relatively low, in order that exchanges may take place to mutual satisfaction until equilibrium is established. But this process will always and necessarily occupy time.[29]

No doubt modern Austrians will be able to find a number of points on which to quibble with Wicksteed's careful and elaborate discussion[30] of how markets tend toward the equilibrium to which he is here referring. What is important, however, for our assessment of Wicksteed's Austrianism is his explicit recognition of the market as the framework within which a time-consuming equilibrating *process* is occurring—a process during which market participants are gradually "brought into communication" with each other—rather than as the social instrument in which initially assumed perfect mutual knowledge is instantaneously translated into an array of equilibrium prices and quantities.

Robbins perceptively drew attention to this aspect of Wicksteed's work.

> Wicksteed's approach is by no means the same as Pareto's. His analysis of the conditions of equilibrium is much less an end in it self, much more a tool with which to explain the tendencies of any given situation. He was much more concerned with economic phenomena as a process in time, much less with its momentary end-products.[31]

Admittedly, Wicksteed was not unique among the great neoclassical economists in seeing the market as a competitive *process*. Robbins's above-cited observation refers to a contrast with Pareto, from whom Wicksteed had otherwise learned a good deal. But outside the Walrasian school, an understanding of the competitive process was not as rare as late-twentieth-century portrayals of neoclassical economics may seem to imply.[32] Yet, one will surely find few early-twentieth-century discussions in which the details of the competitive market process (in the course of which errors come to be corrected, and mutual knowledge is *derived* rather than initially assumed) are as carefully worked out as they

---

[29]Wicksteed, *The Common Sense of Political Economy*, vol. 1, p. 236.

[30]Ibid., pp. 219–29.

[31]Robbins, Introduction to Wicksteed, *The Common Sense of Political Economy*, vol. 1, p. xix.

[32]On this, see the important work of Frank M. Machovec, *Perfect Competition and the Transformation of Economics* (London: Routledge, 1995).

are in Wicksteed. Here we see Wicksteed, in Austrian fashion, seeing the decisions of market participants not as the implications of equilibrium conditions somehow assumed already to exist, but as the initiating causes for (and stages in) the process of equilibration itself.

In conclusion, perhaps the sense in which Wicksteed can best be seen as Austrian is captured in Mises's remarks on the distinguishing features of the economist. "The economist," he wrote,

> deals with matters that are present and operative in every man. . . . What distinguishes [the economist] from other people is not the esoteric opportunity to deal with some special material not accessible to others, but the way he looks upon things and discovers in them aspects which other people fail to notice. It was this that Philip Wicksteed had in mind when he chose for his great treatise a motto from Goethe's *Faust*: Human life—everybody lives it, but only to a few is it known.[33]

## SELECTED READINGS

Buchanan, James M. 1969. *Cost and Choice: An Inquiry in Economic Theory*. Chicago: Markham Publishing.

Buchanan, James M., and G.F. Thirlby, eds. 1973. *L.S.E. Essays on Cost*. London: London School of Economics and Political Science.

Hayek, F.A. 1984. *Money, Capital, and Fluctuations: Early Essays*. Roy McCloughry, ed. Chicago: University of Chicago Press.

Herford, C.H. 1931. *Philip Wicksteed: His Life and Work*. London and Toronto: J.M. Dent.

Jevons, William Stanley. 1871. *The Theory of Political Economy*. London and New York: Macmillan.

Kirzner, Israel M. 1963. *Market Theory and the Price System*. Princeton, N.J.: D. Van Nostrand.

Machovec, Frank M. 1995. *Perfect Competition and the Transformation of Economics*. London and New York: Routledge.

Mayer, Hans. 1932. *The Cognitive Value of Functional Theories of Price*. ( German original in H. Mayer, ed. *Die Wirtschaftstheorie der Gegenwart*. Vienna. 1932. Vol. 2.) English translation in *Classics in Austrian Economics: A Sampling in the History of a Tradition*. Israel M. Kirzner, ed. London: William Pickering. 1994. vol. 2. pp. 55–168.

Mises, Ludwig von. 1962. *The Ultimate Foundation of Economic Science: An Essay on Method*. Princeton, N.J.: D. Van Nostrand.

---

[33]Ludwig von Mises, *The Ultimate Foundation of Economic Science: An Essay on Method* (Princeton, N.J.: D. Van Nostrand, 1962), p. 78.

——. [1933] 1960. *Epistemological Problems of Economics*. Translated from the German by George Reisman. Princeton: D. Van Nostrand.

——. [1949] 1998. *Human Action: A Treatise on Economics*, The Scholar's Edition. Auburn, Ala.: Ludwig von Mises Institute.

——. [1922 [1936. *Socialism: An Economic and Sociological Analysis*. London: Jonathan Cape. Translated from the second German edition, 1932.

Robbins, Lionel C. [1932] 1935. *An Essay on the Nature and Significance of Economic Science*. 2nd ed. London: Macmillan.

Rothbard, Murray N. 1962. *Man, Economy, and State: A Treatise on Economic Principles*. 2 Vols. Princeton, N.J.: D. Van Nostrand.

Schumpeter, Joseph A. 1954. *History of Economic Analysis*. New York: Oxford University Press.

Steedman, Ian. 1987. "Wicksteed, Philip Henry." *The New Palgrave: A Dictionary of Economics*. John Eatwell, Murray Milgate, and Peter Newman eds. 4 Vols. New York: Macmillan.

Stigler, George J. 1941. *Production and Distribution Theories: The Formative Period*. New York: Macmillan.

Wicksteed, Philip H. 1888. *The Alphabet of Economic Science*. London: Macmillan.

——. 1933. *The Common Sense of Political Economy and Selected Papers and Reviews on Economic Theory*. Lionel Robbins, Introduction and editor. London: Routledge and Kegan Paul.

# 8
# EUGEN VON BÖHM-BAWERK: CAPITAL, INTEREST, AND TIME

ROGER W. GARRISON

*Eugen von Böhm-Bawerk*
*1851–1914*

EUGEN VON BÖHM-BAWERK was in the right place at the right time to contribute importantly to the development of Austrian economics. Studying at the University of Vienna, he was twenty years old when Carl Menger's *Principles of Economics* appeared in print in 1871. His formal university training was in law (and thus he was not actually a student of Menger's), but after completing his doctorate in law in 1875, he began preparing himself both at home and abroad to teach economics in his native Austria. A parallel progression from law to economics characterized the career of his classmate (and, later, brother-in-law) Friedrich von Wieser, best known for his *Natural Value* published in 1893. The strong influence of Menger's writings on Böhm-Bawerk's thinking, together with a lifetime relationship with Wieser, made him a natural for expositing and developing the Austrian theory.[1]

---

[1]Böhm-Bawerk did receive formal training from Karl Knies of the older German Historical School, and from Albert Schäffle, who early on had written against socialist doctrine. These Viennese economists had a significant influence on Böhm-Bawerk's thinking, according to Klaus Hennings, in *The Austrian Theory of Value and Capital: Studies in the Life and Work of Eugen von Böhm-Bawerk* (Brookfield, Vt.: Edward Elgar, 1997), p. 54 and passim. In the judgment of Joseph Schumpeter, in his *History of Economic Analysis* (New York: Oxford University Press, 1954), p. 846, Böhm-Bawerk "was so completely the enthusiastic disciple of Menger that it is hardly necessary to look for other influences."

Böhm-Bawerk's career as a scholar, however, was an intermittent one. The most significant span of scholarly activity was his years at the University of Innsbruck (1881–1889). It was during the 1880s that he first published two of the three volumes of his *magnum opus, Capital and Interest*. His later years were dominated by his duties as the Austrian Minister of Finance, a position he held, though not continuously, throughout the 1890s and beyond—and for which he is fittingly honored by having his likeness on Austria's one hundred schilling note. After serving in this capacity and assuming other governmental duties, he returned to teaching in 1904. With a chair at the University of Vienna, he became a colleague of Wieser, successor to the retired Menger. Students who passed through the university during the last decade of Böhm-Bawerk's career (and life—he died in 1914) included Joseph Schumpeter and Ludwig von Mises.

In 1959, the twelve hundred pages of *Capital and Interest* were translated into English by Hans Sennholz and George Huncke and were published as a single volume. Reviewing this new translation, Mises described this "monumental work" as "the most eminent contribution to modern economic theory."[2] He indicated that no one could claim to be an economist unless he was perfectly familiar with the ideas advanced in this book, and he even went so far as to suggest—as only Mises could—that no citizen who takes his civic duties seriously should exercise his right to vote until he has read Böhm-Bawerk!

The first volume of *Capital and Interest*, titled *History and Critique of Interest Theories* (1884), is an exhaustive survey of the alternative treatments of the phenomenon of interest: use theories, productivity theories, abstinence theories, and many more. Most significant in this early work is his devastating critique of the exploitation theory, as embraced by Karl Marx and his forerunners: capitalists do not exploit workers; rather, they accommodate workers by providing them with income well in advance of the revenue from the output they helped to produce. More than a decade later, Böhm-Bawerk was to revisit the issues raised by the socialists. In *Karl Marx and the Close of His System*,[3] Böhm-Bawerk established that the question of how income is distributed among the factors of production is fundamentally an economic—rather than a political

---

[2]Ludwig von Mises, "Capital and Interest: Eugen von Böhm-Bawerk and the Discriminating Reader," *The Freeman* 9, no. 8 (August 1959): 52.

[3]Originally an 1896 contribution to a volume in honor of Karl Knies, this counter-offensive was translated into English and published as a book in 1898.

—question. And the Austrian answer effectively rebutted the labor theory of value as well as the so-called "iron law of wages."

Böhm-Bawerk's *Positive Theory of Capital* (1889) offered as the second volume of *Capital and Interest*, contains his most substantial and profound contribution to our understanding of the economy's time-consuming production processes and of the interest payments they entail. But this volume offers much more. Its treatment of "Value and Price" builds on Menger's *Principles* to present a distinctly Austrian version of marginalism. It is here that we find Böhm-Bawerk's celebrated discussion of the pioneer farmer faced with decisions about the allocation of his sacks of grain among the various uses—as basic feed for himself, his chickens, and his parrots, and as an ingredient for making brandy. The essence of Austrian marginalism is conveyed with his telling the story of what would happen (Parrots beware) if the farmer were to suffer the loss of one sack of grain. This story and many variations on it, told countless times by textbook writers over the decades since, stand in contrast to the twice-differentiable total-utility functions that evolved from William Stanley Jevons's marginalism and the general-equilibrium equations that dominate in Léon Walras's works.

Appendices to the third edition of the second volume (1909–1912) appeared as a separate third volume in 1921 with the title *Further Essays on Capital and Interest*. Here, Böhm-Bawerk offers clarifications, qualifications, and extensions to his theory, as well as responses to his critics. These essays, which contain much of substance, also reveal much about their author's scholarly and rhetorical methods. Böhm-Bawerk reasons like an economist and argues like a lawyer; his most critical remarks are directed towards those whose theories most closely resemble his own. For instance, Gustav Cassel's theory, in which the interest rate brings the supply and demand for "waiting" into balance, is flatly rejected. And despite the fact that the Austrian School is noted for its attention to methodological matters, Böhm-Bawerk took a no-holds-barred approach. Schumpeter articulates the implicit maxim: "Write little or nothing on method, and instead work the more energetically with all available methods."[4]

Modern economics is notorious for its inattention to capital in the sense of an intertemporal structure of intermediate goods. Production takes time, and the time that separates the formulation of multiperiod

[4]Joseph Schumpeter, *Ten Great Economists* (New York: Oxford University Press, 1951), p. 158.

production plans and the satisfaction of consumer demands is bridged by capital. If mentioned at all in modern textbooks, these aspects of economic reality are introduced as "the thorny issues of capital," a telltale phrase that portends a dismissive treatment of this critical subject area. Though a lacuna in mainstream economics, Austrian economics has, almost from its beginnings, given a special prominence to capital theory. With a full awareness of all the thorns, Böhm-Bawerk built his academic career around the goals of understanding the relationship between capital and interest and extending value theory to the context of intertemporal allocation.

Early in his career, Böhm-Bawerk took up a central question that was much discussed by his contemporaries and predecessors. "Is there any justification for the payment of interest to the owners of capital?"[5] The justification, in his view, rests on a simple fact of reality: people value present goods more highly than future goods of the same quantity and quality. Future goods trade at a discount, or alternatively, present goods trade at a premium. The payment of interest is a direct reflection of this intertemporal value differential. This interest, or agio, paid to capitalists allows workers to receive income on a more timely basis than would otherwise be possible. Böhm-Bawerk's "agio theory" and its implications for the alternative "exploitation theory" were undoubtedly enough to win him recognition by historians of economic thought. But with it he broke new ground and was able to parlay his refutation of socialist doctrine into a new understanding of the capitalist system. His *Positive Theory* culminates in a macroeconomic model of general equilibrium that serves to illuminate the classical issues of capital accumulation and technical progress, to resolve the neoclassical problem of the existence and the determination of the rate of interest, and to do still more.

He combined his agio theory of interest with Menger's theory of marginal value to show that given the wage rate that the market establishes, profit-maximizing capitalist-entrepreneurs will engage in production activities that not only employ the labor force to the fullest but also fully absorb the economy's subsistence fund.[6] Making use of the earliest

---

[5]In his chapter on "The Genesis of a Theory," Hennings establishes that this and similar questions were "in the air" at the time that Böhm-Bawerk began to write. See, *The Austrian Theory of Value and Capital*, pp. 53–73.

[6]Ibid., pp. 2 and 65; also see Schumpter, *Ten Great Economists*, p. 187. Böhm-Bawerk's own assessment in 1891 of the Austrian contribution is very much to the point. Citing primarily himself and Carl Menger, he remarks that the Austrian economists

and most foundational Austrian insights, and taking an economy-wide perspective, Böhm-Bawerk linked the intertemporal structure of production to the intertemporal preferences of workers and other income earners. Nearly a half-century before John Maynard Keynes made assertions to the contrary and offered them up as a *General Theory*, the *Positive Theory* showed that the market for labor and the market for loanable funds—or, more broadly, the market for subsistence—could simultaneously find their respective equilibria.

We have it, then, that Böhm-Bawerk was a macroeconomist—and a self-reflective one at that. The classical economists, especially Ricardo, could in retrospect be considered macroeconomists in an era that predates any hint of the modern distinction. The actual word "macroeconomics," of course, is a relatively modern one. Paul Samuelson, who reorganized the subject matter of economics on the basis of a first-order distinction between microeconomics and macroeconomics, traces the distinction itself to Ragnar Frisch and Jan Tinbergen, and dates the word's debut in print to Erik Lindahl in 1939.[7] But in his 1891 essay on "The Austrian Economists," Böhm-Bawerk wrote that "One cannot eschew studying the microcosm if one wants to understand properly the macrocosm of a developed economy."[8] Packed into this understated methodological maxim is both his desire to understand the macroeconomy and his recognition that microeconomic foundations are essential for a viable macroeconomics—a view that, in the mainstream, dates only to the mid-1960s.

To aid in his exposition of the macroeconomics of capital and interest, Böhm-Bawerk introduced his bull's-eye figure—a pattern of concentric rings intended to depict the time structure of production. Production begins in the center with the use of the original means (land and labor); the process emanates outward over time; and the final product emerges at the outermost ring to satisfy the consumers' ultimate

---

"have set forth a new and comprehensive theory of capital into which they have woven a new theory of wages, besides repeatedly working out the problems of the entrepreneur's profits and of rent." See Eugen von Böhm-Bawerk, "The Austrian Economists," *Shorter Classics of Böhm-Bawerk* (South Holland, Ill.:Libertarian Press, 1962).

[7]Paul A. Samuelson, "Credo of a Lucky Textbook Author," *Journal of Economic Perspectives* 11, no. 2 (Spring 1997): 157.

[8]Hennings, *The Austrian Theory of Value and Capital*, p. 74. The fact that Böhm-Bawerk issued so few methodological pronouncements makes this one all the more striking.

ends. Two bull's-eye figures appearing on consecutive pages are used to contrast a well-developed economy with a less-developed one.[9]

This idiosyncratic depiction can be seen as a forerunner of the more straightforward representation of the means-ends framework introduced by F.A. Hayek during the interwar period. The Hayekian triangle captures the essential linearity—not to deny that there are significant non-linearities—in the structure of production. The triangle, which is divided along the time axis into "stages of production," corresponds closely with the bull's eye figure, which is divided along the radius into "maturity classes."

Though static by its very construction, the bull's-eye figure, as well as the better known Hayekian triangle, is intended to facilitate the analysis of change. What is the nature of the market forces that govern the allocation of resources among the various rings? Böhm-Bawerk's formal analysis—and the simple graphics plus some arithmetic illustrations are the extent of the formalities—helps the reader in "getting the picture." For Böhm-Bawerk, however, "getting the picture" is but a prelude to "telling the story." His storytelling, his informal analysis of the nature of the process of change, breaks free of the static representation.

In the case of the stationary state, the concentric rings have two interpretations: (1) the production process can be seen as proceeding over time from earliest input to final output, and (2) the areas of the rings can represent the amounts of the different kinds of capital (goods in process) that exist at a given point in time.

But to depict the stationary state is only to establish a starting point for a discussion of change. Böhm-Bawerk briefly considered the question: "what is the procedure if we wish just to preserve the amount of capital in its previous magnitude?" His answer, given in short order, is followed by the more important question: "what must be done if there is to be an increase in capital?" The answer to this key question, which distinguishes Austrian macroeconomics from what would later become mainstream macroeconomics, involves a change in the configuration of the concentric rings. Several types of changes are suggested, each entailing the idea that real saving is achieved at the expense of consumption

[9]Though rarely reproduced or discussed in modern assessments of Böhm-Bawerk, these figures are central to his vision of a capital-using economy. They are featured in chapter 5, "The Theory of the Formation of Capital," of Book 2, "Capital as a Tool of Production," of vol. 2, *Positive Theory of Capital*. Bull's-eye figures appear on pp. 106 and 107. One of the figures is reproduced in Hennings, *The Austrian Theory of Value and Capital*, p. 131.

and of capital in the outer rings, and that the saving makes possible the expansion of capital in the inner rings. Böhm-Bawerk indicates that in a market economy it is the entrepreneurs who bring about such structural changes, and that their efforts are guided by changes in the relative prices of capital goods in the various rings.

Formal or informal, the message is clear: an expansion of the capital structure is not to be viewed as a simultaneous and equiproportional increase in capital in each of the maturity classes; it is to be viewed as a reallocation of capital among the maturity classes. Overlooked by his predecessors and largely ignored by the modern mainstream, this is the market mechanism that keeps the economy's intertemporal production plans in line with the intertemporal preferences of consumers. The significance of this market mechanism was at issue in his debate with John Bates Clark, who held that once capital is in place, the maintenance of capital is automatic, and that production and consumption are, in effect, simultaneous. Although a modern reader may conclude that Böhm-Bawerk won the debate, and that in later years Hayek was similarly victorious in his debate with Frank Knight, the development of mainstream macroeconomics reflects the implicit belief that it was Clark and Knight who won.[10]

It is easy for modern Austrian economists to see that Böhm-Bawerk was just a step away from articulating the Austrian theory of the business cycle. This step, which was actually taken by Mises and Hayek, would have involved a comparison of changes in the configuration of the rings on the basis of whether those changes were preference-induced or policy-induced. A change in intertemporal preferences in the direction of increased saving reallocates capital among the rings such that the economy experiences capital accumulation and sustainable growth; a policy-induced change in credit conditions, that is, a lowering of the interest rate achieved by the lending of newly created money, misallocates capital among the rings such that the economy experiences unsustainable growth and economic crisis.

Development of the theory in this direction was beyond Böhm-Bawerk for the simple reason that he would not allow himself to venture into monetary theory. His attitude toward this subject matter is revealed in

[10]Clark reviewed *Capital and Interest* in "The Genesis of Capital," *Yale Review* 11 (November 1893): 302–15. Böhm-Bawerk responded in "The Positive Theory of Capital and Its Critics," *Quarterly Journal of Economics* 9 (January 1895): 113–31. For a modern discussion of the Clark–Knight view of capital, see Israel M. Kirzner, *Essays on Capital and Interest: An Austrian Perspective* (Brookfield, Vt.: Edward Elgar, 1996), pp. 60–64 and 75–77.

the letters to Swedish economist, Knut Wicksell,[11] whose ideas about the divergence of the market rate of interest and the natural rate would become an important part of the Austrian theory. In 1907, Böhm-Bawerk wrote: "I have not myself given thought to or worked on the problem of money as a scholar, and therefore I am insecure *vis-à-vis* this subject" (p. 259). In 1912, he added: "You know that I do not really feel competent as regards the extremely difficult theory of money" (p. 268). Also in 1912, referring to *The Theory of Money and Credit*, in which Mises first articulates the Austrian theory of the business cycle, Böhm-Bawerk mentions to Wicksell,

> a book on the theory of money by a young Viennese scholar, Dr. von Mises. Mises is a student of myself and Prof. Wieser, which, however, does not mean that I would want to take responsibility for all his views. I have just begun to read his book myself, and am not yet familiar with its content. (p. 270)

And finally in 1913, a year before his death, "I have not yet included the theory of money in the subject-matter of my thinking, and I therefore hesitate to pass a judgment on the difficult questions it raises" (p. 272).

Schumpeter lists five general subject areas that Böhm-Bawerk excluded from his research agenda, one of which was money: Böhm-Bawerk endorsed the "indestructible core of truth" in the quantity theory, but accepted the idea that money is a veil. A second excluded area—in retrospect a clear corollary to the first—was business-cycle theory: Böhm-Bawerk took economic crises to be "neither an endogenous nor a uniform economic phenomenon, but rather the consequences of what are in principle accidental disturbances of the economic process." (The other three excluded subject areas are population, international trade, and applied price and distribution theory.)[12]

We can easily forgive Böhm-Bawerk for these sins of omission. When a profound thinker makes a great leap forward, we are not entitled to complain that the leap was not greater still. We should recognize instead that the successive advances by Mises, Hayek, and others have made Böhm-Bawerk's contributions look all the greater.

Early and modern literature on Böhm-Bawerk's economics has identified many supposed sins of commission as well. Much of the criticism comes from within the Austrian School: his theory was insufficiently

---

[11]Forty letters from Böhm-Bawerk to Wicksell (1893–1914) are included as an Appendix to Hennings, *The Austrian Theory of Value and Capital*.

[12]Schumpeter, *Ten Great Economists*, pp. 161–62.

subjectivist; his defense of the agio theory of interest relied needlessly on psychological considerations; his reckoning of production time was backward-looking rather than forward-looking.[13] Criticisms from outside the Austrian School stems largely from undue attention to Böhm-Bawerk's arithmetic illustrations and from attempts to restate his theory in the language of formal neoclassical theory: his conclusions about the relationship between the interest rate and the degree of roundaboutness in the production process apply less generally that he would have us believe; the economy's intertemporal structure of capital cannot be reduced to a single number; the definitional dependence of the average period of production on the rate of interest invalidates much of his theory. Fortunately, these and many other criticisms leave intact the essential ideas that were important to Böhm-Bawerk, and to the future development of Austrian theory.

As substantial an economist as Schumpeter could claim that interest is a disequilibrium phenomenon and could fantasize about a long-run equilibrium where market forces have pushed the interest rate to zero. John Maynard Keynes imagined interest to be a purely monetary phenomenon. Creating what Hayek called a "mythology of capital," Frank Knight, following Clark, held that production and consumption occur simultaneously, that the period of production is irrelevant, and that the interest rate is wholly determined by technological considerations. These and other twists and turns in twentieth-century views of capital and interest give increased significance to the enduring wisdom of Eugen von Böhm-Bawerk.

## SELECTED READINGS

Böhm-Bawerk, Eugen von. 1962. *Shorter Classics of Eugen von Böhm-Bawerk.* South Holland, Ill.: Libertarian Press.

——. 1959. *Capital and Interest* (3 vols. in one). George D. Huncke and Hans F. Sennholz, trans. South Holland, Ill.: Libertarian Press.

——. [1898] 1949. *Karl Marx and the Close of His System.* Alice McDonald, trans. London: T. Fisher Unwin.

——. 1895. "The Positive Theory of Capital and Its Critics." *Quarterly Journal of Economics* 9 (January): 113–31.

Garrison, Roger W. 1990. "Austrian Capital Theory: The Early Controversies." *History of Political Economy,* supplement to Vol. 22. Pp. 133–54. Published in *Carl Menger and His Legacy in Economics,* Bruce J. Caldwell, ed. Durham, N.C.: Duke University Press.

[13]These first three listed criticisms are the basis for Mises's dissatisfaction with Böhm-Bawerk's theory, according to Kirzner, *Essays on Capital and Interest,* pp. 125–28.

Hennings, Klaus H. 1997. *The Austrian Theory of Value and Capital: Studies in the Life and Work of Eugen von Böhm-Bawerk*. Brookfield, Vt.: Edward Elgar.

——. 1987. "Böhm-Bawerk, Eugen von." In *The New Palgrave Dictionary of Economics*. Vol. 2. John Eatwell, Murray Milgate, and Peter Newman, eds. London: Macmillan. Pp. 254–59.

Kirzner, Israel. 1996. *Essays on Capital and Interest: An Austrian Perspective*. Brookfield, Vt.: Edward Elgar.

Kuenne, Robert E. 1971. *Eugen von Böhm-Bawerk*. Vol. 2. *Columbia Essays on Great Economists*. New York: Columbia University Press.

Mises, Ludwig von. 1959. "*Capital and Interest*: Eugen von Böhm-Bawerk and the Discriminating Reader." *The Freeman* 9, no. 8 (August): 52–54.

Schumpeter, Joseph A. 1954. *History of Economic Analysis*. New York: Oxford University Press.

——. 1951. *Ten Great Economists*. New York: Oxford University Press.

# 9
# FRANK A. FETTER: A FORGOTTEN GIANT

JEFFREY M. HERBENER

*Frank A. Fetter*
*1863–1949*

IN THE PERIOD between the founders of the Austrian School (Menger, Böhm-Bawerk, and Wieser) and its next generation (led by Mises and Hayek), Frank Albert Fetter was the standard-bearer of Austrian economics. His 1904 treatise, *Principles of Economics,*[1] constructed a general theory of economics in the Austrian tradition that went unsurpassed until Ludwig von Mises's treatise of 1940, *Nationalökonomie.* Yet Fetter, an American Austrian long before the interwar migration from Austria, has not received due recognition for his many contributions to this school of thought.

Using the axiomatic–deductive method, Fetter traced economic laws to individual human action. In so doing, he demonstrated that just as the price of each consumer good is determined solely by subjective value, so is the interest rate determined solely by time preference. The rental price of each producer good is imputed to it by entrepreneurial demand, and is equal to its discounted marginal value product. The capital value of each durable good is equal to the discounted value of its future rents. Fetter showed how this uniform, subjective theory of value implies the demise of socialist theories of labor exploitation, Ricardian theories of rent, and productivity theories of interest.

---

[1]Frank A. Fetter, *The Principles of Economics* (New York: Century, 1904).

Building on the Austrian theories of capital, money, interest, and entrepreneurship, Fetter even developed a rudimentary theory of the trade cycle, arguing that the boom period is characterized by the artificial swelling of capital values as money and credit expand. The crisis follows when the inflation ceases which causes the mistaken capital values of the boom to suddenly correct downward and, in turn, results in the bankruptcy, unemployment, and retrenchment of the depression.

His work on capital and interest has yet to be surpassed or even fully appreciated, even by Austrians; much more than a correction of Eugen von Böhm-Bawerk's lapse into a productivity theory of interest, it is the foundation for all work on capitalization and the definitive refutation of the claim that productivity has any role in determining the interest rate.

## BACKGROUND

Born on March 8, 1863, in the farming community of Peru in north-central Indiana, Fetter enrolled at Indiana University at the age of sixteen. He left college after his junior year to operate the family's bookstore while his father was ill. During eight years as a successful entrepreneur, he read the books and periodicals provided to him on the job, including Henry George's *Progress and Poverty*, the book that influenced his decision to choose economics as a career.

He returned to Indiana University in 1890, and obtained his bachelor of arts degree in 1891. In this respect, too, his self-sacrificing delay in his formal studies proved momentous, for he finished his degree under the influence of Jeremiah W. Jenks. The following year, Jenks, who was then at Cornell University, obtained a fellowship for Fetter, who earned the degree of master of philosophy from Cornell that same year. Jenks then encouraged him to study under Johannes Conrad, as he himself had done, and, after attending lectures at the Sorbonne in Paris, Fetter earned a Ph.D. in 1894 under Conrad from the University of Halle in Heildelberg. He wrote his dissertation on population theory, which he saw as part of a larger theory of welfare, and devoted himself thereafter to the development of a general theory of value and welfare.[2]

---

[2]Fetter's dissertation was published as *Versuch einer Bevolkerungslehre ausgehend von einer Kritik des Malthus'schen Bevolkerungsprincips* (An essay on population doctrine based on a critique of the population principles of Malthus) (Jena: Gustav Fischer, 1894). After writing a few articles on population before the end of the century and one in 1907, he made it the topic of his Annual Address of the President of the American Economic Association; see his "Population and Prosperity," *American Economic Review*, supplement, 3 (March 1913): 5–19. His thesis was that civilizations are born and mature only by overcoming the Malthusian population problem. This is done by "volitional control" which includes institutional measures, like supplanting

Fetter returned from his formal studies to Cornell as instructor for one year, and then accepted a position as professor of economics and social sciences at Indiana University until 1898. For the next three years, he taught at Stanford University and, from 1901–1911, he became Jenks's colleague at Cornell University as professor of political economy and finance. In 1911, Fetter accepted the chairmanship of the interdisciplinary department incorporating history, politics, and economics at Princeton University and, beginning in 1913, he served as chairman of the newly configured economics department for eleven years. He attained emeritus status in 1931 under Princeton's forced retirement regulations, but his popularity and productivity were so great that he was kept on to teach graduate-level courses until he reached the age of seventy in 1933.

Fetter taught on a visiting or exchange basis at Harvard, Columbia, The Johns Hopkins and Northwestern Universities, the University of Illinois, and the Claremont Colleges. In every post, he was a revered professor and beloved mentor. He was awarded the honorary degree of doctorate of laws from Colgate University in 1909, Occidental College in 1930, and Indiana University in 1934. Intellectually active until his death in 1949, Fetter is the author of eight books, more than a hundred scholarly articles, and more than fifty book reviews. He gave a dozen major addresses, and testified before Congress and federal government agencies several times in his long and productive life.

## THEORY OF SUBJECTIVE VALUE

Prior to the advent of a mature Ludwig von Mises, Fetter was the world's leading subjective-value theorist. While Mises would bring the theory of money within a subjective-value, general theory of economics in 1912, Fetter had by 1904 already extended the principle of subjective value to bring factor prices and the rate of interest into a unified theory.[3]

---

communal property with private property, and "psychic" or "social" motives, like caring for offspring, and attaining a higher standard of living and a higher social class. See Fetter, *Principles*, pp. 184–94. His first writings on value theory were "Theories of Value in Their Application to the Question of the Standard of Deferred Payments," *American Economic Association Publications*, supplement, 10 (March 1895): 101–03; and "The Exploitation of Theories of Value in the Discussion of the Standard of Deferred Payments," *Annals of the American Academy of Political and Social Science* 5 (May 1895): 882–96.

[3]Ludwig von Mises, *The Theory of Money and Credit* (New Haven, Conn.: Yale University Press, [1912] 1953) and Frank A. Fetter, *The Principles of Economics*. As Fetter explains in the Preface, he "sought to give merely a summary of widely accepted economic theory." But, "his attempt to unify the statement of principles" led to "a new conception of the theory of distribution" which is "a consistently subjective analysis

The distinctiveness of his contribution was not lost on the profession at large, and it was widely recognized as an Austrian one. A twenty-page article assessing Fetter's treatise appeared in 1905 in the prominent *Quarterly Journal of Economics.* The author, Robert F. Hoxie, wrote that Fetter had removed "the lack of harmony . . . in the eclectic union of the Austrian doctrines with the older classical theory." Hoxie noted that Fetter had rejected the profession's "return towards the objective cost explanation" from the "purely psychic explanation of economic phenomena in terms of utility." Instead, Fetter held, according to Hoxie,

> that the Austrians were, after all, on the way towards a true and consistent interpretation of economic activity. They failed in this, not because they had departed too far from the classical preconceptions, but because they could not wholly emancipate themselves from the older economic notions.[4]

Hoxie claimed that Fetter had taken up again "the initial conceptions of the Austrians" and attempted "to push their characteristic line of thought to its just and ultimate conclusions." Fetter saw "economics as essentially the study of value, and has viewed all economic phenomena as the concrete expression, under varied circumstances, of one uniform theory of value."[5]

Fetter himself was so adamant about the subjective nature of value in economic theory that he disdained referring to the watershed of economic thought in the 1870s as the Marginalist Revolution, preferring the adjectives "subjective" or "psychological" to describe the new theory. He even rejected Léon Walras in the standard trilogy of revolutionaries because he thought Walras, unlike the other mathematical marginalist William Stanley Jevons, did not agree that the essence of the revolution was the reintroduction of subjective value into value theory. In Fetter's

---

of the relations of goods to wants, in place of the admixture of objective and subjective distinctions found in the traditional conceptions of rent, interest, and price. . . . The hope has long been entertained by economists that a conception of the whole problem of value would be attained that would coordinate and unify the various 'laws,'—those of rent, wages, interest, etc." Both men extended subject value beyond the point that Eugen von Böhm-Bawerk was willing to go. Böhm-Bawerk, who was Mises's mentor, rejected much of Mises's analysis during his extended treatment of *The Theory of Money and Credit* in his famous seminar. Neither could Fetter, who became Böhm-Bawerk's friend during a long visit to Europe in 1910 and corresponded frequently with him until his untimely death in 1914, convince Böhm-Bawerk of his insights about time preference and interest.

[4]Robert H. Hoxie, "Fetter's Theory of Value," *Quarterly Journal of Economics* 19 (February 1905): 210–11.

[5]Ibid.

revisionist account, the correct trilogy is Carl Menger (whose "unusual vigor, independence, and originality of his mind seem to have been felt and esteemed by all those who came in contact with him"), Jevons (whose "versatility, originality, and vigor of thought are evident on every page"), and J.B. Clark (who "is classed by his friendly American critics in the list of the six ablest Anglo-American economists [and] is apparently conceded by all foreign critics the deanship of American theorists").[6]

### THEORY OF WAGES

Fetter also recognized the larger significance of a subjective-value theory's replacing an objective one in the history of economic thought. He said that, "the labor theory of value had been adopted by Adam Smith after only the most superficial discussion," which led him to "his confusion of ideas regarding labor embodied and labor commanded, labor as the source and as the measure of value, rent and profits now forming a part and now not a part of price." Fetter concluded that "the resulting confusion was felt by all of the next generation of economists."[7]

In particular, David Ricardo, because he accepted Smith's concept of embodied labor, exerted

> a tremendous and evil influence in ways then all unforeseen. Labor is the source of value; . . . labor is the cause of value; labor produces all wealth. Naturally follows the ethical and political conclusion: if labor produces all wealth then labor should receive all wealth.[8]

This was a conclusion "the Ricardian socialists" were all too eager to embrace, and which Karl Marx later used to great effect.

The Ricardo–Mill theory put a potent weapon in the hands of Marxists who, by basing their theory of exploitation on the labor theory of value, paralyzed bourgeois economists whose own cherished theories

---

[6]About the marginalists, Fetter wrote, "The names of Jevons, Menger, and J.B. Clark are most fully representative of the three creative sources of the marginal theory, though Böhm-Bawerk and Wieser have outstanding importance in some respects fully as great." See Fetter, "Value and the Larger Economics I: Rise of the Marginal Doctrine," *Journal of Political Economy* 31 (October 1923): 594. It was the combination of adherence to logic and concern for mankind that Fetter claimed led to the Marginalist Revolution. "When both intellectual power and humanitarian interest are united in one person as in Jevons, or Menger, or J.B. Clark," said Fetter, "it is not surprising that something noteworthy happens in the history of economic thought" (p. 600). Fetter strove to emulate these men both in rigor of thought and depth of concern.

[7]Ibid., p. 596.

[8]Ibid., pp. 596–97. See also Frank Fetter, "Price Economics versus Welfare Economics," *American Economic Review* 10 (September 1920): 483–86.

were founded on the same conception of value. Fetter knew this by personal experience:

> Well I remember the confidence and gusto with which this demonstration of the truth of Marxism was still presented by socialist speakers in the nineties, as I listened to it from Berlin to San Francisco, when it was generally though mistakenly assumed that all bourgeois economists were still orthodox Ricardians.[9]

It was not, however, solely Marxism that inspired the marginalists to strike a blow for reason and welfare. "Henry George's semi-communistic doctrine of land confiscation, based on the labor theory, or rent feature of it," argued Fetter, "impelled [economists of the 1860s] to re-examine the theory of value." Fetter knew that "the evasive and self-contradictory labor-theory as left by J.S. Mill . . . was a broken reed against the surplus-value attack upon the system of private industry and private property."[10] The subjective-value rejoinder to the Marxist and Georgist attack was to be found, said Fetter, in the capital value concept of John Bates Clark, and "more prominently and explicitly" in Wieser's *Natural Value* and in Böhm-Bawerk's *Karl Marx and the Close of His System*.[11] A demonstration of this process of value imputation from products back to labor formed the first part of Fetter's *Principles of Economics*.

Fetter's method of explaining these principles was Misesian. He wrote:

> The aim . . . has been to proceed by gradual steps, as in a series of geometrical propositions, from the simple and familiar acts and experiences of the individual's every-day life, through the more complex relations, to the most complex, practical, economic problems of the day.[12]

In addition to employing successive approximation, he was, like Mises, a strict logician in method. As Fetter saw it, "Every theory must ultimately

---

[9]Fetter, "Value and the Larger Economies I: Rise of the Marginal Doctrine," *Journal of Political Economy* 31 (October 1923): 601.

[10] Ibid. Though "deeply moved" by Henry George's *Progress and Poverty*, Fetter was a stern critic of George's theories and policies. See, Joseph Dorfman, *The Economic Mind in American Civilization* (New York: Viking Press, 1959), vol. 3, p. 360.

[11]Fetter, "Value and the Larger Economies I," p. 604.

[12]In another place, Fetter said his method "begins with introspection and pursues the analysis of man's nature and wants by observing and comparing the impressions, the hopes, and the motives that determine acts in relation to gratification." Cited in Dorfman, *The Economic Mind*, vol. 3, p. 361. These statements are akin to Mises's on method. See Ludwig von Mises, *Human Action: A Treatise on Economics*, 3rd rev. ed. (Chicago: Henry Regnery, 1966).

meet two tests: one, that of internal consistency, the other that of consistency with reality." And the latter referred not to empiricism, but the "Rude contact with the world of events [which] is often what tests or betrays theory, and forces thought out of the conventional ruts."[13] Hoxie, writing about *Principles*, said of Fetter,

> he has presented to economic students a system which, for logical consistency, is without precedent; a system which from the first fundamental conception advances without a break to the end. . . . The logical sequence and harmonious symmetry of this work affords, at least, a strong presumption of its essential truth.[14]

Fetter began with the "simple" and "almost self-evident" proposition that "the motive force in economics is found in the feelings of men." It is man's wants that urge him to action, first in primitive pursuits, but eventually "wants develop and transform the world" by propelling man to accumulate wealth and upon wealth to build civilization. Moreover, wants are not limited to the narrow self-interest of man or to desires for merely material attainments, but span the full range of man's "social and spiritual" desires.[15]

When studying the problem of value, Fetter saw that one must "recognize any motive that leads men to attach importance to acts and things" because "value is in the closest relation with wants," and "from

---

[13]Fetter, "Value and the Larger Economics I," pp. 601–02. Of the two tests, he wrote:

> Each of these is impersonal, logical, non-partisan, and not simply an adjustment of beliefs to preconceived ends. And it will hardly be disputed even by its severest critics that the subjective school in much of its work reached the highest level yet attained in economics in critical methods and impersonal reasoning. (Ibid. p. 602)

About his own, more strictly praxeological, view of the relationship between experience and logic Mises said, in *Human Action*,

> The end of science is to know reality. . . . Therefore, praxeology restricts its inquiries to the study of acting under those conditions and presuppositions which are given in reality. . . . However, this reference to experience does not impair the aprioristic character of praxeology and economics. Experience merely directs our curiosity toward certain problems and diverts it from other problems. It tells us what we should explore, but it does not tell us how we could proceed in our search for knowledge. (p. 65)

For Fetter, experience was an *ex post* "reality check" for a poorly thought out theory that would force the economist back to the drawing board of logical construction. For Mises, experience established assumptions which constrained logical construction so that the resulting theory conformed to reality.

[14]Hoxie, "Fetter's Theory of Value," p. 230.

[15]Fetter, *Principles*, pp. 9–14.

the meeting and comparison of the estimates [of value] of individuals, arise market values or prices."[16] A man's demand for a consumer good is formed from the law of diminishing utility (a proposition whose truth is found "in the very nature of man"), which refers to the "marginal utility" or "gratification afforded by the added portion of the good."[17] Since the term "marginal utility" expresses "by a single phrase the idea both of demand and supply," prices "are built up on subjective valuations" alone and "correspond closely with the subjective estimates" of the marginal buyer and seller, i.e., "the least eager buyer and the least eager seller."[18]

Fetter divided the value of production goods into two categories: the problem of rent (which explains the value of temporary use) and the problem of capitalization (which explains the value of permanent control and ownership).[19] The rent of a factor of production depends on the universal principle of diminishing returns.[20] Like the law of diminishing marginal utility, "the concept of diminishing returns is one aspect of the great law of proportionality" which is the "fundamental, axiomatic truth, that there is a best or proper adjustment of means and ends" in man's action. "Out of it grow the important economic theories of rent and capitalization."[21]

Since gratification is the basis of all values, what is implied about the prices of consumer goods must be true of factor prices as well. The price of a unit of "a group of consumption goods, all of the same quality" is dictated solely by diminishing marginal utility given the "quantity of an article capable of ministering to man's wants." Although, units of a good of the same quality will have the same price, a series of consumption goods of different qualities will differ in price. If a good has no marginal

---

[16]Ibid., pp. 17–20.

[17]Ibid., pp. 22–23. The similarity with Rothbard's view on "ordinal marginal utility" is striking. See Murray N. Rothbard, "Toward a Reconstruction of Utility and Welfare Economics," in *The Logic of Action One: Method, Money, and the Austrian School* (Cheltenham, U.K.: Edward Elgar). Also Fetter makes the same distinction as Rothbard between consumption of "immediate" goods—"those things which are immediately at the point of gratifying man's desires"—and production of "intermediate" goods—"those things which are not yet ready to gratify desires." Fetter, *Principles*, p. 20; and Murray N. Rothbard, *Man, Economy, and State* (Auburn, Ala.: Ludwig von Mises Institute 1993), pp. 6–7.

[18]Fetter, *Principles*, pp. 32–35.

[19]Ibid., pp. 53–60.

[20]Ibid., pp. 62–64.

[21]Ibid., pp. 71–72.

utility, it will be a "free" good, and goods of similar kind but higher quality will have prices "measured from zero upward." The extent to which the "lower grades acquire value" and come into use depends on "scarcity of the higher grades."[22]

The rent of productive factors "varies with the quality of the products yielded" and with "the quantities of goods yielded by them." The concept of "differential advantage" is no more efficacious for explaining factor prices than it is for explaining prices of consumer goods. And as with the latter, the use of a factor is extended to satisfy the degree of scarcity of the factor, i.e., its value relative to its stock. Finally, the problem of pricing complementary factors which "are necessary to secure a product" is solved "according to the principle of marginal utility at every moment in every market" as "the different uses . . . bid for an agent and thus, its marginal utility is determined just as is the price of a good by the bidding of buyers."[23]

Competitive bidding for labor results in the law of wages; that is, that any labor or class of labor is equal to the marginal value of its products. "Each agent in industry, whether it be a horse, a plough, or a man, is valued in connection with other agents." Thus, "it is not the total service any one of them performs" that determines its pay, but the value attributed to the last unit of supply. For Fetter, their marginal contribution determines their importance, and thus, their rental prices. This "law of wages is but the general law of value, working itself out amid the special conditions accompanying the gratification of wants by human effort."[24]

Fetter went further than marginal value product theory, arguing that the rental price of a factor would be equal to its discounted marginal value product. Since the application of labor services to different tasks has "much diversity in their nearness to the gratification for which they are destined," very different intervals of time must elapse before the gratification matures. The expected value of all products but those immediately available is discounted in advance, Fetter argued, since all gratifications disparate in time "are compared at one and the same moment"; that is, in the present.

In the market, "labor is distributed according to the prevailing rate of time-value, which . . . is approximately expressed by the rate of interest." "Hence, all wages paid for help on products that are remote," Fetter

[22]Ibid., pp. 73–75.

[23]Ibid., pp. 75–78.

[24]Ibid., pp. 213–14.

concluded, "are based on the present worth, or discounted value, of the future gratification to which the labor contributes." While noting the implication of the theory for the socialist doctrine of exploitation, Fetter extended the theory to all factors. Time-value is a different genus of the general value problem: "it must be found in connection with every use that is not immediate. . . . Its application to rent is more frequent and obvious, as only the uses of material agents are capitalized; that is, sold in perpetuity."[25]

THEORY OF CAPITALIZATION

Turning to the theory of capitalization, Fetter defined capital as "economic wealth expressed in terms of the general unit of value." And while capital, at any moment in time, includes all economic goods in existence, Fetter said that most capital is "composed of things durable." For this reason, "when interest is defined as the payment for the use of capital, it is connected with all wealth that is expressed in the capital form."[26]

For Fetter, interest permeated all time-consuming action, and the determination of its rate was a prerequisite to, not a result of, the calculation of capital value. To make a rational account of the market value of anything, including a durable good, "its importance must be traced back to 'gratification.'" The buyer of durable wealth pays a "definite sum in return for the right to enjoy a series of future rents." It then becomes impossible that capital value could precede income, and therefore, "the mere mention of a capital sum implies the interest problem, and assumes the interest rate."[27]

Interest, no matter how it is manifested, is fundamentally based on time-value, which is omnipresent. Time-value is "the premium rate on present goods," and its manifestation as a rate of interest is "unlike the ordinary market price of goods only in the special nature of the utilities exchanged" which derive from "present and future goods." Capitalization (that is, "the discounting of future rents in goods") is necessary because of scarcity of present gratifications; it implies the emergence of a surplus, or "a net yield, over and above the value of the capital." Because their future uses have been discounted, newly-produced agents will have a price "less than they will be when realized as actual rents." Not

[25]Ibid., pp. 219–22. As with ordinal marginal utility, it is Rothbard who accepts and develops Fetter's concept of discounted marginal value product. See Rothbard, *Man, Economy, and State*, pp. 387–409.

[26]Fetter, *Principles*, p. 115.

[27]Ibid., pp. 122–24.

only does this rebut the socialist exploitation theory, it also shows that "to explain the rate of interest as due to the process of 'producing' capital agents out of other materials, is to beg the question" of interest rate determination.[28]

No one has appreciated Fetter's performance on capital, rent, and interest more than Murray N. Rothbard. Fetter, according to Rothbard, filled in the "great many lacunae in the [Austrian] theories of capital, rent, and interest." His "imaginative contribution to rent theory was to seize upon the businessman's commonsense definition of rent as the price per unit of service of any factor." "For Fetter," as Rothbard said, "the marginal productivity theory of distribution becomes the marginal productivity theory of rent determination for every factor of production." Then "Fetter demonstrated that the [net return to an investor in capital goods] can only be found by separating the concept of marginal productivity from that of interest" because "marginal productivity explains the height of a factor's rental price, but another principle is needed to explain why and on what basis these rents are *discounted* to get the present capitalized value of the factor." That other principle is time preference, prompting Rothbard to claim that Fetter "was the first economist to explain interest rates solely by time-preference.[29] But Fetter's contributions to a subjective-value, general theory of economics did not end with capital and interest.

## THEORIES OF GROWTH, MONEY, AND CYCLES

Based on his view that "the rate of interest" is "a ratio of exchange between present and future," Fetter argued that time-preference affects the accumulation of wealth because of "a close relation between saving and the rate of time-discount." Savers put aside present wants only when the future good has at least the value of the present good. By converting savings into durable indirect agents, man achieves accumulation of wealth, a process that depends on "the successful competition of forethought with present desire." "Savings," according to Fetter, "lifts society from poverty to wealth by the progressive enlargement of the sources of future utilities." In modern industry, saving often takes the form of money, which is then loaned to productive borrowers who are

[28]Ibid., pp. 141–51.

[29]So impressed was Rothbard with Fetter's contributions to capital and interest that he collected Fetter's scattered articles on the subjects, and edited the resulting book, *Capital, Interest, and Rent: Essays in the Theory of Distribution* (Kansas City: Sheed Andrews and McMeel, 1977). Rothbard's claims, quoted above, are in his Introduction to the collection, pp. 2–4.

"thus empowered to increase [their] stock of productive agents in the measure that the lender has limited his consumption." A lower rate of interest means a higher capitalization of all incomes which stimulates the production of capital goods. A lower rate also makes it "advantageous to apply newly formed capital to uses which before did not justify the investment," which include expansion of present investments and "putting new links into the chain of technical production." The benefits of saving not only accrue "to the owner of the wealth saved," but are "diffused throughout society" because they raise the efficiency of production.[30]

Although Fetter did not extend the concept of subjective value as completely as Mises did to the topic of money, his views foreshadow the latter's subjective-value analysis. Fetter saw money's value as part of the general problem of value. After distinguishing between "primary money," which was gold and silver coin, and "money substitutes," which were bank notes ("redeemable in gold on demand"), and government money or "political money" (founded on "legal tender" laws and "political power"), Fetter argued that under a system of free coinage, money presents no special problem of value. "The value of gold as bullion and money is fixed by marginal demand" among "the several uses of gold [that] are constantly competing for it."

The exchange value of a dollar (for Fetter, the term dollar is "a convenient name applied to twenty-three and twenty-two hundredths grains of fine gold") will vary in different times and places. Money "is a valuable good kept on hand as the best possible provision against emergency" whose "use is subject to the law of diminishing utility." For this reason, "other things being equal, the value of money falls as its quantity increases, and vice versa." Any time increasing gold supplies brings about larger stocks of money the optimal proportion between money incomes and money is altered. Individuals respond to the "surplus money" by buying goods to reduce their stock of money; this will bid up prices until the optimal proportion is restored.[31]

Fetter also worked out a rudimentary theory of the business cycle. Noting first that "a crisis is a decisive moment or turning point; hence, in industry, a collapse of prosperity," he divided the trade cycle into three phases: prosperity, crisis, and depression. Every crisis is financial at its root, and "a jolt to prices which shatters the credit of some banks, brokers, merchants, and manufacturers." The phase of prosperity is characterized by

---

[30]Fetter, *Principles*, pp. 160–69.

[31]Ibid., pp. 431–42.

increasing money, confidence, and credit which cause "old enterprises [to be] resumed and new ones [to be] undertaken." During prosperity, "profits are apparently great" but "partly illusory" since they "exist only on paper." Greater profits stimulate the purchase of materials in larger quantities which "causes a rise in prices and an increase in costs" and the "surplus labor on the margin of efficiency gets employment, and wages begin to rise." A reversal of monetary and credit expansion caused by a "large and continued exportation of specie" is inevitable "when foreign prices [calculated in dollars] do not rise in as great a proportion as domestic prices." Monetary deflation and credit contraction bring on the crisis which reduces "the specie reserves of banks" and "the value of many stocks and securities held by the banks." Banks become cautious, and brokers and speculators are forced to convert resources into cash. The falling prices, the shattered credit, and the financial losses cause bankruptcy, unemployment, and retrenchment.

For Fetter "crises must be explained essentially as the forcible and sudden movement of readjustment in the mistaken capitalization of productive agents." That "capitalization runs through all industry" coupled with the enormous extension of investment in "new machinery and processes" implies a disturbance of "the equilibrium of prices both in time and space." "When the balance between the capitalization of various industries and between the rents of the various periods proves to be false," Fetter concluded, "the inevitable readjustment causes suffering and loss to many, but particularly in the inflated industries."[32]

### ENTREPRENEURSHIP

Fetter recognized the importance of the "enterpriser" as the organizer of the division of labor. The enterpriser's main skill was judgment, which referred to accurate predictions about future events. Everyone possesses and exhibits this skill to some degree, but "as men differ in judgment," the market will establish a division of labor in enterprisers by "the ceaseless working of competition," which ensures that "the higher places are taken by those most capable of filling them, and the efficiency both of the employers and of the workmen is increased."[33]

In like manner, the enterprisers arrange the division of labor and establish "methods of organization" which are "tested by their results." For their services of "foresight" and "judgment" enterprisers earn profit. Profit is not "contract wages, not being paid by agreement . . . but economic wages or earning of services," which are uncertain. The enterpriser

[32]Ibid., pp. 345–55.

[33]Ibid., pp. 265–72.

guarantees to the capitalist-lender a fixed return, and likewise he gives to workers a definite amount for services applied to distant ends while he "risks his own services and accepts an indefinite chance instead of a definite amount for them." The enterpriser is "the specialized risk-taker, he is the spring or buffer, which takes up and distributes the strain of industry" and his "profits are due not to risks, but to superior skill in taking risks. They are not subtracted from the gains of labor but are earned, in the same sense in which the wages of skilled labor are earned."[34]

## THE THEORY OF WELFARE AND THE STATE

Fetter recognized that just as resources differ in their capacity to gratify wants, so do men differ in their powers of labor. Because the "variety and inequality of human talent" is biological, Fetter chided Adam Smith for "discussing wages on the assumption that all men had equal natural ability," and criticized "radical social reformers" who thought that "all the differences in success result from political injustice." He concluded that "to those who ignore the inequality of men, the whole problem of industrial remuneration must remain a mystery. A crude socialism is possible only to those who are blind to the enormous differences in human capacity."[35] The division of labor "beginning because of such natural differences" among individuals will extend to "trades, territories, and nations" causing "increases [in] efficiency" in a host of ways and giving opportunity for "the individual worker to attain his highest economic efficiency" by selecting the occupation "for which his talents are best fitted" in the division of labor. "It is of importance to society as well as to the individual," according to Fetter, "that each member of society should attain to his highest efficiency."[36]

Fetter also recognized that "the organization of industry where some men, owning and directing capital, buy at their competitive value the services of men without capital" relieves the worker of "the risk as to the future selling price of the product" and puts it on the employer. "Wage payment, therefore, is a form of insurance to the workingman" for Fetter and "a form of credit" to him "whose labor has not yet produced the distant gratification." Also, the worker "gets the competitive value of his services" which, Fetter claimed, is "much more than a bare subsistence" in most cases and the market system by "insuring a higher return" to increasing efficiency "appeal[s] to the ambition of each man"

[34]Ibid., pp. 282–91.

[35]Ibid., pp. 177–82.

[36]Ibid., pp. 202–04.

and his desire for a rising standard of living. Most importantly, "the present wage system is the freest condition for the mass of men ever has existed" and has driven "real wages . . . [higher] than ever before" debunking the claim that "with the wage system, there must go a steady depression in the welfare of workingman." The rise in standards of living are accompanied by an "increased proportion of workers in the higher occupations" implying "a further rise in the average condition of the masses" proving that "the diffused advantages of progress mean relatively more to the masses than to the rich.[37]

Fetter's admiration for capitalism was tempered by his theory of welfare. In contrast to wealth, "the collective term for those things which are felt to be related to the gratification of wants," Fetter saw welfare as "the abiding condition of well-being." This distinction is "very much like that often made between pleasure and happiness" by philosophers and refers to the difference between "momentary gratification" and "ultimate, or abiding, welfare." It is the difference between "the thoughtlessness and impulsiveness of a child or savage" and "the more rational life of those with foresight and patience." Although Fetter did not deny an overlap between the two concepts in human action, he asserted that wealth was the appropriate concept in value theory while "the question of social prosperity" can be answered only by taking "the standpoint of the social philosopher" and considering "the more abiding effects of wealth."[38] Based on this distinction Fetter argued that private property, which he defined as individual "ownership" or "control" of "the sources of economic income" and saw as a prerequisite for value theory, must be judged in welfare theory by this test: "Does it further the welfare of society better than would any alternative plan for the control of economic wealth?" And although it "furthers the progress of society" generally speaking, "social expediency implies the need of a readjustment of the institution of private property."[39]

---

[37]Ibid., pp. 229–34.

[38]Ibid., pp. 17–18.

[39]Ibid. pp. 360–66. Fetter was charting a different course in welfare theory than would be taken by pioneers of the Pareto Rule approach. Both the Austrian and "new" welfare theorists accepted the Pareto Rule on the impossibility of objective interpersonal utility comparisons, a position that defines social welfare in terms of the subjective valuations of individuals, and developed their welfare theories with this constraint. In contrast, Fetter defined welfare by an objective standard which is an approach more akin to Mises's use of the concept of "rightly understood interests" which he used to justify laissez-faire as the best social system and education as the means of achieving it. See Mises, *Human Action,* pp. 673–82. Fetter's "abiding

Fetter thought that "the belief that the economic interests of all men are in harmony," i.e., "if men are left entirely free to do as their interest dictates the highest and best efficiency for all will follow," and the resulting social order gave men "the benefits of competition and the virtues of economic freedom" was an "exaggerated expression" of a "truth in political philosophy." To the contrary, "experience shows that the economic interests of men are only partly, not wholly, in harmony." From which Fetter concluded that "wherever economic interests are not in harmony and it is possible to further the social welfare" society is "justified in acting." "The state regulates and limits," according to Fetter, with "its aim to preserve the benefits of competition without its evils, to lift the competition to a higher plane, and . . . to give a higher and truer economic freedom.[40]

In the 1920s, Fetter believed that welfare theory was transcending value theory in economics, presumably giving greater impetus to his project of "rational" interventionism.[41] "The larger, truer political economy," he wrote, "is a theory of welfare and not a theory of value." Far from implying that "value theory is to be scrapped," instead "it takes its place within the larger conception" of economics as a theory of "human welfare." Only in the "many cases where the result of private competition is not demonstrably an increase of wealth and welfare," do the "value- and price-rules lose their justification as social policy." This failure can occur when "competition . . . as a method" is faulty, or when the "bidders for goods" are "ignorant," i.e., "their foolish desires are out of accord with their own true welfare and that of the nation," or when "the motive of private gain" increases scarcity "instead of . . . production and plenty." For Fetter, "whenever the value rule and the welfare (utility) rule diverge, it is value that must give way, and utility that must dominate in true political economy."[42]

The sufficient requisite for designing the optimal social system, for Fetter, was the scientific, impartial mind. "The scientific spirit" can be acquired only "by prolonged effort and training" and is "essential to social progress and to the preservation of civilization." He lamented that

welfare" led him to justify interventionism as the optimal system and social custom and government coercion as appropriate methods of attaining it.

[40]Ibid., pp. 426–30.

[41]Fetter, "Value and the Larger Economics II: Value Giving Way to Welfare," *Journal of Political Economy* 31 (December 1923): 790–803, and Fetter, "Price Economics versus Welfare Economics," *American Economic Review* 10 (December 1920): 719–37.

[42]Fetter "Value and the Larger Economics II," p. 801.

such economists were not held in high enough esteem among the public for only they could dictate policy without "partisan feelings" and with a "fair and judicial spirit." Fetter claimed, in 1925, that "the danger that threatens the world can be averted only by drafting all the powers of science, and all the finer possibilities of human nature, into the service of a new statesmanship." The role of the scientifically-spirited economists was to supply "wisdom in the art of using wealth toward rational aims," which would "make economics not the slave of industry" but "industry the servitor of mankind."[43]

Twenty years after offering this vision of political economy, he reiterated his admiration for capitalism in a highly favorable review of Mises's *Bureaucracy* in which he also discussed F.A. Hayek's *The Road to Serfdom*. In contrasting the German Historical School led by Gustav Schmoller with the Austrian Theoretical School of Carl Menger, Fetter noted that the former "pointed the way to the totalitarian state" while the latter led "to a greater and better liberalism in economic and political affairs." He called Mises and Hayek "two of the most effective contemporary critics of socialism and most valiant defenders of free enterprise" and claimed that their books are "essentially harmonious formulations of the present issue between freedom (political as well as economic) and the trend toward totalitarianism." Of *Bureaucracy* he wrote, "the case for free enterprise versus socialism has nowhere been more ably and readably stated in brief compass."[44]

---

[43]Fetter, "The Economists and the Public," *American Economic Review* 15 (March 1925): 24–26. Fetter's concrete contribution to this effort was in anti-monopoly theory. He played a prominent role, with John R. Commons of the University of Wisconsin and William Z. Ripley of Harvard University, in the "Pittsburgh-plus" or base-point pricing-system antitrust case. His two major theoretical works on this issue are "The Economic Law of Market Areas," *Quarterly Journal of Economics* 38 (May 1924): 520–29, and "Exit Basing Point Pricing," *American Economic Review* 38 (December 1948): 815–27. The role he suggested for the state in curbing monopoly was strictly limited. "The remedies at hand" for the ills of monopoly are laws requiring "a posted price" to prevent "discriminatory" pricing and uneconomical "dumping" of goods across regional territories and enforcement of antitrust statutes to prevent mergers that "stifle competition." The goal of these measures "is the fostering and creating of open markets where traders in each line of products could and would meet to buy and sell goods fairly in free competition." He likened this role for the state to "the well-grounded public purpose of the medieval fairs and markets with their 'merchant law.'" See Frank Fetter, *The Masquerade of Monopoly* (New York: Harcourt, Brace, 1931), pp. 410–25.

[44]Frank A. Fetter, "Economic Systems: Post-War Planning," *American Economic Review* 35 (June 1945): 445–46. In this review, Fetter also wrote of John Maynard Keynes that it was no "mystery or chance that [he] . . . found it necessary when he

## CONCLUSION

Deservedly, Fetter rose to the top of the American economics profession. His work was routinely published in the major journals: *American Economic Review*, *Quarterly Journal of Economics*, *Journal of Political Economy*. He held professorships at several prestigious colleges and universities, was invited to speak at major events held by prominent economic associations, wrote commentary for the *Encyclopedia of the Social Sciences* on the discipline, and wrote for European scholars on American economic thought.[45] He was an officer and eventually president of the American Economic Association, and was a member of the American Philosophical Society.[46] In a rare tribute, he received a note commemorating his eightieth birthday in the *American Economic Review* and a Memorial, in the same publication, upon his death.[47]

At the turn of the century, Frank A. Fetter was elevating the Austrian banner to greater heights than any other scholar. He constructed a uniform general theory of economics based on the principle of subjective

---

became an advocate of national planning, to abandon the 'classical' doctrines, and to make the state the arbiter of prices."

[45]Fetter gave the Annual Address of the President of the American Economic Association in 1912, "Population or Prosperity," and the address at the unveiling of Richard T. Ely's portrait at the University of Wisconsin in 1924, "The Economists and the Public." He also delivered a speech in honor of J.B. Clark, "Tribute to Professor John Bates Clark at Dinner in His Honor," *American Economic Review,* supplement, vol. 17 (June 1927): 11–13, and addressed a gathering of the American Philosophical Society, "The Early History of Political Economy in the United States of America," *American Philosophical Society Proceedings* 87 (July 14, 1943): 51–60. Fetter wrote three entries for the *Encyclopedia of the Social Sciences* (New York: MacMillan, 1930–1935): "John Elliot Cairnes," vol. 3, p. 140; "Capital," vol. 3, pp. 187–190; and "Rent," vol. 13, pp. 289–92. He visited Europe for extended periods in 1910, 1914, 1931, and 1932 and was invited to contributed a long article on the state of America economic thought for the Wieser Festschrift in 1927, "Amerika," *Die Wirtschaftstheorie der Gegen-wart, Friedrich Wieser in Memoriam, in Gestembild der Forschung in den einselnen Landern* (Vienna: Julius Springer, 1927), pp. 31–60 and on his concept of economic theory in 1930, "The New Conceptual Basis of Economics," *Economia Politica contemporanea, saggi di economia efinanza in onore del Prof Camillo Supino* 1 (Padova: A. Milani, 1930), pp. 93–102.

[46]Fetter served as Secretary–Treasurer for the American Economic Association from 1901–1906, on the Executive Committee from 1906–1911 and 1944–1945, and as President in 1912. He joined the American Philosophical Society in 1935 and was a member of its Council and Committee on Research. Fetter was also a member of the American Academy of Arts and Sciences and was awarded the Carl Menger Medal of the Austrian Economics Society in 1927.

[47]Stanley E. Howard and E.W. Kemmerer, "Frank Albert Fetter, A Birthday Note," *American Economic Review* 33 (March 1943): 233–34, and J. Douglas Brown, "Memorial: Frank Albert Fetter, 1863–1949," *American Economic Review* 39 (1949): 979.

value and his work on capital and interest fully-integrated these difficult subjects into his general theory. Frank A. Fetter was one of the brightest stars in the golden era of Austrian economics.

## SELECTED READINGS

Fetter, Frank A. 1977. *Capital, Interest, and Rent: Essays in the Theory of Distribution*. Murray N. Rothbard, ed. Kansas City: Sheed Andrews and McMeel.

——. 1945. "Economic Systems: Post-War Planning." *American Economic Review* 35 (June): 445–46.

——. 1923. "Value and the Larger Economics I: Rise of the Marginal Doctrine." *Journal of Political Economy* 31 (October): 594.

——. 1920. "Price Economics versus Welfare Economics." *American Economic Review* 10 (September): 483–86.

——. 1913. "Population and Prosperity." *American Economic Review*, Supplement 3 (March): 5–19.

——. 1904. *Principles of Economics*. New York: Century.

——. 1895. "Theories of Value in Their Application to the Question of the Standard of Deferred Payments." *American Economic Association Publications*, Supplement 10 (March): 101–03.

Hoxie, Robert F. 1905. "Fetter's Theory of Value." *Quarterly Journal of Economics* 19 (February): 210–11.

# 10

# LUDWIG VON MISES: THE DEAN OF THE AUSTRIAN SCHOOL[1]

MURRAY N. ROTHBARD

*Ludwig von Mises*
*1881–1973*

THOUGH THE PREEMINENT theorist of our time, Mises's interest, as a teenager, centered in history, particularly economic and administrative history. But even while still in high school, he reacted against the relativism and historicism rampant in the German-speaking countries, dominated by the Historical School. In his early historical work, he was frustrated to find historical studies virtually consisting of paraphrases from official government reports. Instead, he yearned to write genuine economic history. He early disliked the State orientation of historical studies. Thus, in his memoirs, Mises writes:

> It was my intense interest in historical knowledge that enabled me to perceive readily the inadequacy of German historicism. It did not deal with scientific problems, but with the glorification and justification of Prussian policies and Prussian authoritarian government. The German universities were state institutions and the instructors were civil servants. The professors were aware of this civil-service status, that is, they saw themselves as servants of the Prussian king.[2]

---

[1]This article is an edited version of Rothbard's *Ludwig von Mises: Scholar, Creator, Hero* (Auburn, Ala.: Ludwig von Mises Institute, 1988).

[2]Ludwig von Mises, *Notes and Recollections* (South Holland, Ill.: Libertarian Press, 1978), p. 7.

Ludwig von Mises entered the University of Vienna at the turn of the twentieth century, and his major professor was the economic historian Karl Grünberg, a member of the German Historical School and a statist who was interested in labor history, agricultural history, and Marxism. Grünberg was a follower of the German economic historian Georg Friedrich Knapp, the author of the major work claiming that money was in its origin and its essence a pure creature of the State. At his center for economic history at the University of Strasbourg, Knapp was having his students work on the liberation of the peasantry from serfdom in the various German provinces. Hoping to create a similar center at Vienna, Professor Grünberg set his students to do research on the elimination of serfdom in the various parts of Austria. Young Ludwig Mises was assigned the task of studying the disappearance of serfdom in his native Galicia. Mises later lamented that his book on this subject, published in 1902, was, because of the Knapp–Grünberg methodology, "more a history of government measures than economic history."[3] The same problems beset his second historical work published three years later, a study of early child labor laws in Austria, which proved to be "not much better."[4]

Despite his chafing at the statism and Prussianism of the Historical School, Mises had not yet discovered economic theory, the Austrian School, and the economic liberalism of the free market. In his early years at the university, he was a left-liberal and interventionist, although he quickly rejected Marxism. He joined the university-affiliated Association for Education in the Social Sciences, and plunged into applied economic reform. In his third year at the university, Mises did research on housing conditions under Professor Eugene von Philippovich, and the following semester, for a seminar on criminal law, did research on changes in the law on domestic servants. From his detailed studies, Mises began to realize that reform laws only succeeded in being counterproductive, and that all improvements in the conditions of the workers had come about through the operations of capitalism.

Around Christmas, 1903, Mises discovered the Austrian School of economics by reading Carl Menger's great *Principles of Economics*, and thus began to see that there was a world of positive economic theory and

---

[3]Mises, *Notes and Recollections*, p. 6. Nonetheless, about forty years ago, Edith Murr Link, then at work on a doctoral dissertation on a closely related subject, told me that Mises's work was still considered definitive. On Grünberg, also see Earlene Craver, "The Emigration of Austrian Economists," *History of Political Economy* 18 (Spring 1987): 2.

[4]The book was entitled *A Contribution to Austrian Factory Legislation*. Mises, *Notes and Recollections*, p. 6.

free-market liberalism that complemented his empirical discoveries on the weaknesses of interventionist reform.

On the publication of his two books in economic history, and on the receipt of his doctorate in 1906, Mises ran into a problem that would plague him the rest of his life: the refusal of academia to grant him a full-time, paid position. It boggles the mind what this extraordinarily productive and creative man was able to accomplish in economic theory and philosophy, when down to his mid-50s, his full-time energies were devoted to applied political-economic work. Until middle-age, in short, he could only pursue economic theory and write his extraordinary and influential books and articles as an overtime leisure activity. What could he have done, and what would the world have gained, if he had enjoyed the leisure that most academics fritter away? As it is, Mises writes that his plans for extensive research in economic and social history were thwarted for lack of available time. He states wistfully that "I never found opportunity to do this work. After completing my university education, I never again had the time for work in archives and libraries."[5]

Mises's doctorate was in the Faculty of Law at the University of Vienna, and so for several years after 1906 he clerked at a series of civil, commercial, and criminal courts, and became an associate at a law firm. In addition, preparing himself for a teaching career, Mises began to teach economics, constitutional law, and administration to the senior class of the Vienna Commercial Academy for Women, a position which he held until the completion of his first great book in 1912.[6]

Mises's major post, from 1909 until he left Austria twenty-five years later, was his full-time job as economist at the Vienna Chamber of Commerce.[7] In Austria, the Chambers of Commerce were akin to "Economic Parliaments," created by the government, with delegates elected by businessmen and financed by taxation. The Chambers were formed to give economic advice to the government, and the center of power was its General Assembly, consisting of delegates from the various local and provincial Chambers, and with the committees of that Assembly. The experts advising the Chambers and the General Assembly were

---

[5]Mises, *Notes and Recollections*, pp. 6–7.

[6]Margit von Mises, *My Years with Ludwig von Mises*, 2nd ed. (Cedar Falls, Iowa: Center for Futures Education, 1984), p. 200.

[7]The name of the organization, upon Mises's joining it in 1909, was the Lower Austrian Chamber of Commerce and Industry. In 1920, it changed its name to the Vienna Chamber of Commerce, Handicrafts, and Industry.

gathered in the offices of the secretaries to the various Chambers. By the turn of the twentieth century, economists working in the secretary's office of the Vienna Chamber (the preeminent of the various Chambers) had become important economic advisers to the government. By the end of World War I, Mises, operating from his quasi-independent position at the Chamber, became the principal economic adviser to the government, and won a number of battles on behalf of free markets and sound money.

## *The Theory of Money and Credit*

In 1903, the influential monetary economist Karl Helfferich, in his work on money, laid down a challenge to the Austrian School. He pointed out correctly that the great Austrians, Menger, Böhm-Bawerk, and their followers, despite their prowess in analyzing the market and the value of goods and services (what we would now call "microeconomics"), had not managed to solve the problem of money. Marginal utility theory had not been extended to the value of money, which had continued, as under the English classical economists, to be kept in a "macro" box strictly separate from utility, value, and relative prices. Even the best monetary analyses, as in Ricardo, the Currency School, and Irving Fisher in the United States, had been developed in terms of "price levels," "velocities," and other aggregates completely ungrounded in any micro analysis of the actions of individuals.

In particular, the extension of Austrian analysis to money faced a seemingly insuperable obstacle, the "problem of the Austrian circle." The problem was this: for directly consumable goods, the utility and therefore the demand for a product can be arrived at clearly. The consumer sees the product, evaluates it, and ranks it on his value scale. These utilities to consumers interact to form a market demand. Market supply is determined by the expected demand, and the two interact to determine market price. But a particular problem is posed by the utility of, and the demand for, money. For money is demanded on the market, and held in one's cash balance, not for its own sake but solely for present or future purchases of other goods. The distinctive nature of money is that it is not consumed, but only used as a medium of exchange to facilitate exchanges on the market. Money, therefore, is only demanded on the market because it has a preexisting purchasing-power, or value or price on the market. For all consumer goods and services, therefore, value and demand logically precede and determine price. But the value of money, while determined by demand, also precedes it; in fact, a demand for money presupposes that money already has a value and price.

A causal explanation of the value of money seems to founder in unavoidable circular reasoning.

In 1906, his doctorate out of the way, Mises determined to take up the Helfferich challenge, apply marginal utility theory to money, and solve the problem of the Austrian circle. He devoted a great deal of effort to both empirical and theoretical studies of monetary problems. The first fruits of this study were three scholarly articles, two in German journals and one in the English *Economic Journal* in 1908–09, on foreign exchange controls and the gold standard in Austria-Hungary. In the course of writing the articles, Mises became convinced that, contrary to prevailing opinion, monetary inflation was the cause of balance-of-payments deficits instead of the other way around, and that bank credit should not be "elastic" to fulfill the alleged needs of trade.

Mises's article on the gold standard proved highly controversial. He called for a *de jure* return in Austria-Hungary to gold redemption as a logical conclusion of the existing *de facto* policy of redeemability. In addition to running up against advocates of inflation, lower interest rates, and lower exchange rates, Mises was surprised to face ferocious opposition by the central bank, the Austro-Hungarian Bank. In fact, the bank's vice president hinted at a bribe to soften Mises's position. A few years later, Mises was informed by Böhm-Bawerk, the Minster of Finance, of the reason for the vehemence of the bank's opposition to his proposal for a legal gold standard. Legal redemption in gold would probably deprive the bank of the rights to invest funds in foreign currencies. But the bank had long used proceeds from these investments to amass a secret and illegal slush fund from which to pay subventions to its own officials, as well as to influential journalists and politicians. The bank was keen on retaining the slush fund, and so it was fitting that Mises's most militant opponent was the publisher of an economic periodical who was himself a recipient of bank subsidies.

Mises came to a decision, which he pursued for the rest of his career in Austria, not to reveal such corruption on the part of his enemies, and to confine himself to rebutting fallacious doctrine without revealing their sources. But in taking this noble and self-abnegating position, by acting as if his opponents were all objective scholars, it might be argued that Mises was legitimating them and granting them far higher stature in the public debate than they deserved. Perhaps, if the public had been informed of the corruption that almost always accompanies government intervention, the activities of statists and inflationists might have been desanctified, and Mises's heroic and lifelong struggle against statism might have been more successful. In short, perhaps a one-two punch was needed: refuting the economic fallacies of Mises's statist enemies, and also showing the public their self-interested stake in government privilege.[8]

His preliminary research out of the way, Mises embarked, in 1909, on his first monumental work, published in 1912 as *Theories des Geldes and der Umlaufsmittel* [The theory of money and credit]. It was a remarkable achievement, because for the first time, the micro–macro split that had begun in English classical economics with Ricardo was healed. At long last, economics was whole, an integral science based on a logical, step-by-step analysis of individual human action. Money was fully integrated into an analysis of individual action and the market economy.

By basing his analysis on individual action, Mises was able to show the deep fallacies of the orthodox mechanistic Anglo-American quantity theory and of Irving Fisher's "equation of exchange." An increase in the quantity of money does not mechanically yield a proportional increase in a nonexistent "price level," without affecting relative utilities or prices. Instead, an increase lowers the purchasing power of the money unit, but does so by inevitably changing relative incomes and prices. Micro and macro are inextricably comingled. Hence, by focusing on individual action, on choice and demand for money, Mises not only was able to integrate the theory of money with the Austrian theory of value and price; he transformed monetary theory from an unrealistic and distorted concentration on mechanistic relations between aggregates, to one consistent with the theory of individual choice.[9]

Moreover, Mises revived the critical monetary insight of Ricardo and the British Currency School of the first half of the nineteenth century: that while money is a commodity subject to the supply-and-demand determination for value of any other commodity, it differs in one crucial aspect. Other things being equal, an increase in the supply of consumer goods confers a social benefit by raising living standards. But money, in contrast, has only one function: to exchange, now or at some

---

[8]On Mises's articles on gold and foreign exchange, on Böhm-Bawerk's revelations, and on Mises's decision, see Mises, *Notes and Recollections*, pp. 43–53.

[9]Mises's stress on the utility of, and demand for, cash balances anticipated a seemingly similar emphasis by Alfred Marshall and his Cambridge School disciples, Pigou and Robertson. The difference, however, is that the Marshallian k, the demand for cash balances, was aggregative and mechanistic as the Fisherine V, or "velocity of circulation," so that the Cambridge k could easily be trivialized as the mathematical inverse of the Fisherine V. Mises's demand for cash balances, grounded as it is in each individual's demand, cannot be mathematically reduced in this way.

time in the future, for capital or consumer goods. Money is not eaten or used as are consumer goods, nor used up in production as are capital goods. An increase in the quantity of money only serves to dilute the exchange effectiveness of each franc or dollar; it confers no social benefit whatever. In fact, the reason why the government and its controlled banking system tend to keep inflating the money supply is precisely *because* the increase is not granted to everyone equally. Instead, the nodal point of initial increase is the government itself and its central bank; other early receivers of the new money are favored new borrowers from the banks, contractors to the government, and government bureaucrats themselves. The early receivers of the new money, Mises pointed out, benefit at the expense of those down the line of the chain who get the new money last, or of people on fixed incomes who never receive the new influx of money. In a profound sense, then, monetary inflation is a hidden form of taxation or redistribution of wealth, to the government and its favored groups and from the rest of the population. Mises's conclusion, then, is that once there is enough for a supply of a commodity to be established on the market as money, there is no need ever to increase the supply of money. This means that any supply of money whatever is "optimal," and every change in the supply of money stimulated by government can only be pernicious.[10]

In the course of refuting the Fisherine notion of money as some sort of "measure of value," Mises made an important contribution to utility theory in general, a contribution that corrected an important flaw with Austrian utility analysis of Menger and Böhm-Bawerk. Although the older Austrians did not stress this flaw as much as Jevons or Walras, there were indications that they believed utility to be measurable, and that there is sense in talking of a "total utility" of the supply of a good that would be an integral of its "marginal utilities." Mises built on an important insight of the Czech economist Franz Čuhel, a student at Böhm-Bawerk's graduate seminar, that since marginal utility was strictly subjective to each individual, it was purely an ordinal ranking, and could in no sense be added, subtracted, or measured, and *a fortiori* could not be compared between persons. Mises developed this theme to demonstrate that therefore the very concept of "total utility" makes no

---

[10]When gold or some other useful commodity is money, an increase in the stock of gold does confer a social benefit in its non-monetary uses, for now there is more gold available for jewelry, for industrial and dental uses, etc. Only in its monetary uses is any supply of gold optimal. When fiat paper is the monetary standard, in contrast, there are no non-monetary uses to render palatable an increase in its supply.

sense at all, particularly as an integral of marginal utilities. Instead, the utility of a larger batch of a good is simply another marginal utility of a large unit. Thus, if we take the utility to the consumer of a carton of a dozen eggs, it is impermissible to make this utility some sort of a "total utility," in some mathematical relation to the "marginal utility of one egg." Instead, we are merely dealing with marginal utilities of different-sized units, in one case a dozen-egg package, in the other case one egg. The only thing we can say about the two marginal utilities is that the marginal utility of a dozen eggs is worth more than the marginal utility of one egg. Period. Mises's correction of his mentors was consistent with the fundamental Austrian methodology of focusing always on the real actions of individuals, and allowing no drift into relying on mechanistic aggregates.[11]

If the Čuhel–Mises insight had been absorbed into the mainstream of utility theory, economics would have been spared, on the one hand, the tossing out of marginal utility altogether in the late 1930s as hopelessly cardinal, in favor of indifference curves and marginal rates of substitution; and, on the other, the current absurd micro-textbook discussions of "utilities," nonexistent entities subject to measurement and mathematical manipulation.

What of the famous problem of the Austrian circle? Mises solved that in one of his most important, and yet most neglected, contributions to economics: the regression theorem. Mises built on Menger's logical-historical account of the origin of money out of barter, and demonstrated logically that money can only originate in that way. In doing so, he solved the problem of the circular explanation of the utility of money. Specifically, the problem of the circle is that, at any given time, say $\text{day}_N$, the value [purchasing-power] of money on that day is determined by two entities: the supply of $\text{money}_N$ and the demand for $\text{money}_N$, which itself depends on a preexisting purchasing power on $\text{day}_{N-1}$. Mises broke out of this circle precisely by understanding and grasping the time dimension of the problem. For the circle on any given day is broken by the fact that the demand for money on that day is dependent on a previous day's purchasing power, and hence on a previous day's demand for money. But haven't we broken out of the circle only to land ourselves

[11]For a discussion of this point, see Murray N. Rothbard, "Toward a Reconstruction of Utility and Welfare Economics" (New York: Center for Libertarian Studies, 1977), pp. 9–15. Franz Čuhel's contribution is in his *Zur Lehre von den bedurfnissen* (Innsbruck, 1906), pp. 186ff. Böhm-Bawerk's attempt to refute Čuhel can be found in Eugen von Böhm-Bawerk, *Capital and Interest* (South Holland, Ill.: Libertarian Press, 1959), vol. 3, pp. 124–36.

in an infinite regress backwards in time, with each day's purchasing power resting on today's demand for money, in turn dependent on the previous day's purchasing power, in turn determined by the previous day's demand, etc.? It is no help to escape circular reasoning only to land in a regress of causes that can never be closed.

But the brilliance of Mises's solution is that the logical regress backward in time is not infinite: it closes precisely at the point in time when money is a useful non-monetary commodity in a system of barter. In short, say that $day_1$ is the first moment that a commodity is used as a medium of indirect exchange (to simplify: as a "money"), while the previous day is the last day that commodity, say gold, was used only as a direct good in a system of barter. In that case, the causal chain of any day's value of money, say $day_N$, goes back locally in time, to $day_1$, and then goes back to $day_0$. In short, the demand for gold on $day_1$ depends on the purchasing power of gold on $day_0$. But then the regress backward stops, since the demand for gold on $day_0$ consists only of its direct value in consumption, and hence does not include a historical component, i.e., the existence of prices for gold on the previous day, $day_1$.

In addition to closing the determinants of the value or purchasing power of money, and thereby solving the Austrian circle, Mises's demonstration showed that, unlike other goods, the determinants of the value of money include an important historical dimension. The regression theorem also shows that money, in any society, can only become established by a market process emerging from barter. Money cannot be established by a social contract, by government imposition, or by artificial schemes proposed by economists. Money can only emerge, "organically" so to speak, out of the market.[12]

Comprehension of Mises's regression theorem would spare us numerous impossible schemes, some proffered by Austrians or quasi-Austrians, to create new moneys or currency units out of thin air, such as F.A.

---

[12]The presentation of the regression theorem is in Ludwig von Mises, *The Theory of Money and Credit*, 3rd ed. (New Haven, Conn.: Yale University Press, 1953), pp. 108–23. Mises later answered critics of the theorem in his *Human Action* (New Haven, Conn.: Yale University Press, 1949), pp. 405–13. For a reply to more recent critics, Gilbert and Patinkin, see Rothbard, "Toward a Reconstruction of Utility and Welfare Economics," p. 13, and Rothbard, *Man, Economy, and State* (Princeton, N.J.: Van Nostrand, 1962), vol. 1, pp. 231–37, and esp. p. 448. Also see Rothbard, "The Austrian Theory of Money," in *The Foundations of Modern Austrian Economics*, Edwin Dolan, ed. (Kansas City: Sheed and Ward, 1976), p. 170. For the most recent discussion of the regression theorem, including a reply to Moss's critique of Mises, see James Rolph Edwards, *The Economist of the Country: Ludwig von Mises in the History of Monetary Thought* (New York: Carlton Press, 1985), pp. 49–67.

Hayek's proposed "ducat," or plans to separate units of account from media of exchange.

In addition to his feat in integrating the theory of money with general economics and placing it on the micro foundations of individual action, Mises, in *The Theory of Money and Credit*, transformed the existing analysis of banking. Returning to the Ricardian Currency School tradition, he demonstrated that it was correct in wishing to abolish inflationary fractional-reserve credit. Mises distinguished two separate kinds of function undertaken by banks: channeling savings into productive credit ("commodity credit"), and acting as a money warehouse in holding cash for safekeeping. Both are legitimate and non-inflationary functions; the trouble comes when the money warehouses issue and lend out phony warehouse receipts (banknotes or demand deposits) to cash that does not exist in the banks' vaults ("fiduciary credit"). These "uncovered" demand liabilities issued by the banks expand the money supply and generate the problems of inflation. Mises therefore favored the Currency School approach of one-hundred-percent specie reserves to demand liabilities. He pointed out that Peel's Act of 1844, established in England on Currency School principles, failed and discredited its authors by applying one-hundred-percent reserves only to bank notes. They failed to realize that demand deposits were also surrogates for cash, and therefore functioned as part of the money supply. Mises wrote his book at a time when much of the economics profession was still not sure that demand deposits constituted part of the money supply.

Not wishing to trust government to enforce one-hundred-percent reserves, however, Mises advocated totally free banking as a means of approaching that ideal. *The Theory of Money and Credit* demonstrated that the major force coordinating and promoting bank credit inflation was each nation's central bank, which centralized reserves, bailed out banks in trouble, and made sure that all banks inflated together. *The Theory of Money and Credit* showed that an individual bank enjoyed very little room to expand credit.

But this is not all. For Mises began, on the foundations of his theory of money and banking, to develop what was to become his famous theory of the business cycle—the only such theory integrated with general microeconomics and built on the foundations of the analysis of action. These rudiments were further developed in the second edition of *The Theory of Money and Credit* in 1924.

In the first place, Mises was brilliantly able to identify the process as essentially the same: (a) one bank's expanding credit, soon leading to a contraction and demand for redemption; and (b) all banks in the nation, guided by a central bank, expanding money and credit together and thereby gaining more time for a Hume–Ricardo specie-flow price mechanism to develop. Thus, credit and the money supply expand, incomes and prices rise, gold flows out of the country (i.e., a balance-of-payments deficit), and a resulting collapse of credit and the banks, forces a contraction of money and prices, and reverses specie flow into the country. Not only did Mises see that these two processes were basically the same, he was also the first to see that there was a rudimentary model of a boom-bust cycle, created and driven by monetary factors, specifically expansion and later contraction of "created" bank credit.

During the 1920s, Mises formulated his business cycle theory out of three pre-existing elements; the Currency School boom-bust model of the business cycle; the Swedish "Austrian" Knut Wicksell's differentiation between the "natural" and the bank interest rates; and Böhm-Bawerkian capital and interest theory. Mises's remarkable integration of these previously totally separate analyses showed that any inflationary or created bank credit, by pumping more money into the economy and by lowering interest rates on business loans below the free-market, time-preference level, inevitably caused an excess of malinvestment in capital goods industries remote from the consumer. The longer the boom of inflationary bank credit continues, the greater the scope of malinvestment in capital goods, and the greater the need for liquidation of these unsound investments. When the credit expansion stops, reverses, or even significantly slows down, the malinvestments are revealed. Mises demonstrated that the recession, far from being a strange, unexplainable aberration to be combated, is really a necessary process by which the market economy liquidates the unsound investments of the boom, and returns to the right consumption–investment proportions to satisfy consumers in the most efficient way.

Thus, in contrast to interventionists and statists who believe that the government must intervene to combat the recession process caused by the inner workings of free-market capitalism, Mises demonstrated precisely the opposite: that the government must keep its hands off the recession, so that the recession process can quickly eliminate the distortions imposed by the government-generated inflationary boom.

Mises's career, along with many others, was interrupted for the four years of World War I. After three years at the front as an artillery officer, Mises spent the last year of the war in the economics division of the War Department, where he was able to write journal articles on foreign trade, and in opposition to inflation, and to publish *Nation, Staat, und Wirtschaft*

[Nation, state, and economy] (1919) on behalf of ethnic and cultural freedom for all minorities.

The question of academic posts was then faced fully after the end of the war. The University of Vienna conferred three paid professorships in economics; before the war, they were filled by Böhm-Bawerk, his brother-in-law Friedrich von Wieser, and Eugen von Philippovich. Böhm-Bawerk died tragically shortly after the outbreak of the war, Philippovich retired before the war, and Wieser followed soon after the war was over. The first vacancy went to Mises's old teacher, Carl Grünberg, but Grünberg went off to a chair at Frankfurt in the early 1920s. This left three vacancies at Vienna, and it was generally assumed that Mises would get one of them. Certainly, by any academic standards, he richly deserved it.

But Mises was never chosen for a paid academic post; indeed he was passed over four times. Instead, the two theoretical chairs went (a) to Othmar Spann, a German-trained Austrian organicist sociologist, barely cognizant of economics, who was to become one of Austria's most prominent fascist theoreticians and (b) to Hans Mayer, Wieser's handpicked successor, who, despite his contributions to Austrian utility theory, was scarcely in the same league as Mises.

After interviewing Mises's friends and former students, Earlene Craver indicates that Mises was not appointed to a professorial chair because he had three strikes against him: (1) he was an unreconstructed laissez-faire liberal in a world of opinion that was rapidly being captured by socialism of either the Marxian left or of the corporatist–fascist right; (2) he was Jewish, in a country that was becoming increasingly anti-Semitic; and (3) he was personally intransigent and unwilling ever to compromise his principles. Mises's former students F.A. Hayek and Fritz Machlup concluded that "Mises's accomplishments were such that two of these defects might have been overlooked—but never three."[13]

While Mises's ideas, reputation, and writing—if not his academic post—enjoyed a growing influence in Austria and the rest of Europe in the 1920s, his influence in the English-speaking world was greatly limited by the fact that *The Theory of Money and Credit* was not translated until 1934. American economist Benjamin M. Anderson, Jr., in his *The Value of Money* (1917), was the first English-speaking writer to appreciate Mises's work. The remainder of Mises's Anglo-American influence had to wait for the early 1930s. *The Theory of Money and Credit* could have been far more

---

[13]Craver, "The Emigration of Austrian Economists," p. 5.

influential had it not received a belittling and totally uncomprehending review from the brilliant young economist John Maynard Keynes, then an editor of the leading British scholarly economic periodical, the *Economic Journal*. Keynes wrote that the book had "considerable merit," that it was "enlightened in the highest degree possible" [whatever that may mean], that the author was "widely read," but that in the end Keynes was disappointed because it was not "constructive" or "original." Now, whatever may be thought about *The Theory of Money and Credit*, it was highly constructive and systematic, and almost blazingly original, and so Keynes's reaction is puzzling indeed. The puzzle was cleared up, however, a decade and half later, when, in his *Treatise on Money*, Keynes wrote that "In German, I can only clearly understand what I already know—so that new ideas are apt to be veiled from me by the difficulties of the language." The breathtaking arrogance, the sheer gall of reviewing a book in a language in which he could not grasp new ideas, and then denouncing the book for containing nothing new, was all too characteristic of Keynes.[14]

## MISES IN THE 1920S: SCHOLAR AND CREATOR

The Bolshevik Revolution, as well as the growth of corporatist sentiment during and after World War I, transformed socialism from a utopian vision and goal into a spreading reality. Before Mises turned his great searchlight of a mind on the problem, criticisms of socialism had been strictly moral or political, stressing its use of massive coercion. Or, if economic, they had focused on the grave disincentive effects on communal or collective ownership (often expressed in the gibe, "Under socialism, who will take out the garbage?"). But Mises, addressing the problem in a paper delivered to the Nationalökonomisch Gesellschaft (Economic Society) in 1919, came up with the most devastating possible demolition: the impossibility of economic calculation under in the socialist commonwealth"). It was a verifiable shock to thoughtful socialists, for it demonstrated that, since the socialist planning board

[14]Keynes's review is in the *Economic Journal* 24 (September 1914): 417–19. His damaging admissions are in his *A Treatise on Money* (New York: Harcourt, Brace, 1930), vol. 1, p. 199, n. 2. Hayek's account of this study characteristically misses the arrogance and gall, and treats the episode as merely a learning defect, concluding that "the world might have been saved much suffering if Lord Keynes's German had been a little better." The trouble with Keynes was hardly confined to his defective knowledge of German! See Hayek, "A Tribute to Ludwig von Mises," in Mises, *My Years with Ludwig von Mises*, p. 219.

would be shorn of a genuine price system for the means of production, the planners would be unable to actually calculate the costs, the profitability, or the productivity of these resources, and hence would be unable to allocate resources rationally in a modern complex economy.

The stunning impact of Mises's argument came from its demolishing socialism on its own terms. A crucial objective of socialism was for central planners to allocate resources to fulfill the planner's goals. But Mises showed that, even if we set aside the vexing question of whether the planner's goals coincide with the public good, socialism would not permit the planners to achieve their own goals rationally, let alone those of consumers or of the public interest. For rational planning and allocation of resources require the ability to engage in economic calculation, and such calculation in turn requires resource prices to be set in free markets where titles of ownership are exchanged by owners of private property. But since the very hallmark of socialism is government or collective ownership (or, at the very least, control) of all non-human means of production—land and capital—this means that socialism will not be able to calculate or rationally plan a modern economic system.

Mises's profound article had a blockbuster impact on European socialists, particularly in German-speaking countries, over the next two decades, as one socialist after another tried to solve the Mises problem. By the late 1930s, the socialists were confident that they had solved it by using mathematical economics, wildly unrealistic neoclassical perfect competition and general equilibrium assumptions, and—particularly in the schemes of Oskar Lange and Abba P. Lerner—by the central planning board's ordering the various manners of socialist firms to "play at" markets and market prices. Mises expanded his arguments in journal articles and in his comprehensive critique, *Die Gemeinwirtschaft* [Socialism] in 1922. The seminal article was finally translated into English in 1935, and his *Socialism* a year later, and F.A. Hayek also weighed in with elaboration and development. Finally, Mises gave the final rebuttal to the socialists in is monumental *Human Action* in 1949.

While the official textbook line by the 1940s—when socialism had triumphed among intellectuals—decreed that Lange and Lerner had solved the crucial question posed by Mises, Mises and the free market have had the last laugh. It is now generally acknowledged, especially in Communist countries, that Mises and Hayek were right, and that the enormous defects of socialist planning in practice have confirmed their views.

Mises's earliest research had taught him that government intervention almost invariably proved to be counterproductive; and his explorations into money and business cycles amply confirmed and reinforced this insight. In a series of articles in the 1920s, Mises investigated various forms of government intervention, and showed them all to be ineffective and counterproductive. (The essays were published in book form as *Kritik des Interventionismus* in 1919.) In fact, Mises arrived at a general law that, whenever the government intervened in the economy to solve a problem, it invariably ended not only in *not* solving the original problem, but also *creating* one or two others, each of which then seemed to cry out for further government intervention. In this way, he showed government interventionism, or a "mixed economy," to be unstable. Each intervention only creates new problems, which then face the government with a choice: either repeal the original intervention, or go on to new ones. In this way, government intervention is an unstable system, leading logically either back to laissez-faire or on to full socialism.

But Mises knew from his study into socialism that a socialist system was "impossible" for the modern world; that is, it was lacking the price system necessary to economic calculation, and therefore for running a modern industrial economy. But if interventionism is unstable, and socialism is impossible, then the only logical economic policy for a modern industrial system was laissez-faire liberalism. Mises therefore took the rather vague commitment to the market economy of his Austrian predecessors and hammered it into a logical, consistent, and uncompromising adherence to laissez-faire. In keeping with this insight, Mises published his comprehensive work, *Liberalismus*, on "classical," or laissez-faire, liberalism, in 1927.

Remarkably, we have by no means exhausted the extent of Ludwig von Mises's profound contributions to scholarship and to economics during the 1920s. From his earliest days, Mises had confronted and challenged the Historical School of economics dominant in Germany. The Historical School was marked by its insistence that there can be no economic laws transcending mere description of the circumstances of individual time and place, and that the only legitimate economics therefore is not theory but a mere examination of history. Politically, this meant that there were no inconvenient economic laws for government to violate, and to cause counterproductive consequences of governmental measures.

The logical positivists presented their own grave challenge to economic theory, charging that economic law could only be established tentatively and hesitantly, and then only by "testing" the consequences of such laws by empirical (in practice, statistical) fact. Based on their own interpretation of the methods of the physical sciences, the positivists tried to hack away at methodologies they saw as "unscientific."

The onslaughts of the institutionalists and especially the positivists on economic theory forced Mises to think deeply about the methodology of economics, and also about the basic epistemology of the sciences of human action. He arrived at the first philosophically self-conscious defense of the economic method used by the earlier Austrians and some of the classicists. Furthermore, he was able to demonstrate the truly "scientific" nature of this correct method, and to show that the developing positivist methodology of much neoclassical economics was itself profoundly mistaken and unscientific. In brief, Mises demonstrated that all knowledge of human action rests on methodological dualism, on a profound difference between the study of human beings on the one hand, and of stones, molecules, or atoms, on the other. The difference is that individual human beings are conscious, that they adopt values and make choices—act—on the basis of trying to attain those values and goals. He pointed out that this axiom of action is self-evident; that is (a) evident to the self once pointed out, and (b) cannot be refuted without self-contradiction; that is, without using the axiom in any attempt to refute it. Since the axiom of action is self-evidently true, any logical deductions or implications from that action must be absolutely, uncompromisingly, "apodictically," true as well. Since this body of economic theory is absolutely true, any talk of testing its truth is absurd and meaningless, since the axioms are self-evident and no testing could occur without employing the axiom. Moreover, no testing can take place since historical events are not, as are natural events in the laboratory, homogeneous, replicable, and controllable. Instead, all historical events are heterogeneous, not replicable, and the result of complex causes. The role of economic history, past and contemporary, then, is not to test theory but to illustrate theory in action, and to use it to explain historical events.

Mises also saw that economic theory was the formal logic of the inescapable fact of human action, and that such theory was therefore not concerned with the content of such action, or with psychological explanations of values and motives. Economic theory was the implication of the formal fact of action. Hence, Mises, in later years, would name it "praxeology," the logic of action.

Mises began publishing his series of epistemological articles in 1928, and then collected and published them in his seminal philosophical and methodological work, *Grundprobleme der Nationalökonomie* [Epistemological problems of economics] in 1933.

## MISES IN THE 1920S: TEACHER AND MENTOR

Since Mises was under severe restrictions in his teaching post at the University of Vienna, as noted above, his influence at university teaching was severely limited. While such outstanding Misesians of the 1920s as F.A. Hayek, Gottfried von Haberler, and Oskar Morgenstern studied under Mises at the university, Fritz Machlup was his only doctoral student. And Machlup was prevented from acquiring his Habilitation degree, which would have permitted him to teach as a *privatdozent*, by anti-Semitism among the economics professors.[15]

Mises's enormous influence, as teacher and mentor, arose instead from the private seminar that he founded in his office at the Chamber of Commerce. From 1920 until he left for Geneva in 1934, Mises held the seminar every other Friday from seven to approximately ten o'clock (accounts of participants differ slightly) after which they repaired to the Italian restaurant Anchora Verde for supper, and then, around midnight, the seminar stalwarts, invariably including Mises, went on to the Cafe Künstler, the favorite Vienna coffeehouse for economists, until one in the morning or after. The Mises seminar gave no grades, and had no official function of any kind, either at the university or at the Chamber of Commerce. And yet, such were Mises's remarkable qualities as scholar and teacher that, very quickly, his *Privatseminar* became the outstanding seminar and forum in all of Europe for discussion and research in economics and the social sciences. An invitation to attend and participate was considered a great honor, and the seminar soon became an informal but crucially important center for postdoctoral studies. The list of later-to-be eminent names of *Miseskreis* participants, from England and the United States as well as from Austria, is truly staggering.

While most Viennese, including Mises's friends and students, basked in the Pollyanna view that Nazism could never happen in Austria, Mises, in the early 1930s, foresaw disaster and urged his friends to emigrate as soon as possible.

More alert than any of his colleagues to the ever-encroaching Nazi threat in Austria, Mises accepted a chair in 1934 as professor of International Economic Relations at the Graduate Institute of International

---

[15]Karl Popper remembers of Vienna in the 1920s that "It became impossible for anyone of Jewish origin to become a University teacher." Fritz Machlup, a distinguished student and disciple of Mises, who was Jewish, was prevented from receiving his Habilitation degree, the equivalent of the second half of a doctorate, which was needed to permit one to teach at the University of Vienna as a *privatdozent*. This contrasted to the receipt of their Habilitations by the three other leading students of Mises, who were not Jewish: Hayek, Haberler, and Morgenstern.

Studies at the University of Geneva. Since the initial contract at Geneva was only for one year, Mises retained a parttime post at the Chamber of Commerce, on one-third salary. Mises's contract was to be renewed until he left Geneva in 1940. While it saddened him to leave his beloved Vienna, Mises was happy during his six years in Geneva. Established at his first (and last) paid academic post, he was surrounded by friends and like-minded colleagues.

Teaching only one weekly seminar on Saturday mornings, and divested of his political and administrative duties at the Chamber, Mises finally enjoyed the leisure to embark upon, and finish, his great masterpiece integrating micro and macroeconomics, the analysis of the market and of interventions into that market, all constructed on the praxeological method that he had set forth in the 1920s and early 1930s. This treatise was published as *Nationalökonomie* (Economics) in Geneva, in 1940.

The onset of World War II put an enormous amount of pressure on Mises. In addition to depriving the Institute of its non-Swiss students, the war meant that refugees, such as Mises, were increasingly made to feel unwelcome in Switzerland. Finally, when the Germans conquered France in the spring of 1940, Ludwig, prodded by his wife, decided to leave a country now surrounded by the Axis Powers, and flee to the Mecca for victims of tyranny, the United States.

The couple arrived in New York City in August 1940 and, lacking any prospect of employment, lived off meager savings, moving repeatedly in and out of hotel rooms and furnished apartments. It was the lowest point of Mises's life, and shortly after he landed he began writing a despairing, searing intellectual memoir, which he finished in December, and which was translated and published after his death as *Notes and Recollections* (1978).[16] A major theme in this poignant work is the pessimism and despair that so many classical liberals, friends, and mentors of Mises had suffered from the accelerating statism and destructive wars of the twentieth century. Menger, Böhm-Bawerk, Max Weber, Archduke Rudolf of Austria-Hungary, Mises's friend and colleague Wilhelm

[16]A decade or so later, after Mises had launched his graduate seminar at New York University, some of us, during a post-seminar snack at Childs's Restaurant, reacted to some of the marvelous anecdotes Mises told us about the old days in Vienna by suggesting that he write his autobiography. Mises drew himself up, in a rare moment of severity, and declared "Please! I am not yet old enough to write my autobiography." It was a tone that brooked no further discussion. But since Mises was then in his seventies—a very advanced age to the rest of us—and since this is a country where twerps of twenty are publishing their "autobiographies," we naturally, though silently, disagreed with the master.

Rosenberg—all had been broken in spirit or driven to death by the intensifying gloom of the politics of their time. Mises, throughout his life, resolved to meet these grave setbacks by fighting on, even though the battle might seem hopeless. In discussing how fellow classical liberals had succumbed to the despair of World War I, Mises then recounts his own response:

> I thus had arrived at this hopeless pessimism that for a long time had burdened at the best minds of Europe. . . . This pessimism had broken the strength of Carl Menger, and it over shadowed the life of Max Weber.
>
> It is a matter of temperament how we shape our lives in the knowledge of an inescapable catastrophe. In high school I had chosen the verse by Virgil as my motto: *Tu ne cede malis sed contra audentio ito* ("Do not yield to the bad, but always oppose it with courage"). In the darkest hours of the war, I recalled the dictum. Again and again I faced situations from which rational deliberations could find no escape. But then something unexpected occurred that brought deliverance. I could not lose courage even now. I would do everything an economist could do. I would not tire in professing what I knew to be right.[17]

Every other terrible situation faced by Mises in his life was met by the same magnificent courage: in the battle against inflation, the struggle against the Nazis, the flight during World War II. In every case, no matter how desperate the circumstances, Ludwig von Mises carried the fight forward, and deepened and expanded his great contributions to economics and to all the disciplines of human action.

Life began to improve for Mises when his old connection with John Van Sickle and the Rockefeller Foundation led to a small annual grant via the National Bureau of Economic Research, a grant which began in January 1941 and was renewed through 1944. From these grants emerged two important works, the first books of Mises written in English, both published by the Yale University Press in 1944. One was *Omnipotent Government: The Rise of the Total State and Total War*. The dominant interpretation of Nazism in that era was the Marxist view of Columbia University Professor and German refugee Franz Neumann: that Nazism was the last desperate gasp of German big business, anxious to crush the rising power of the proletariat. That view, now thoroughly discredited, was first challenged by *Omnipotent Government*, which pointed out the statism and totalitarianism that underlay all forms of leftwing and rightwing collectivism. The other Mises book,

---

[17]Mises, *Notes and Recollections*, pp. 69–70.

*Bureaucracy*, was a marvelous little classic which delineated, as never before, the necessary differences between profit-seeking enterprise, the bureaucratic operation of nonprofit organizations, and the far worse bureaucracy of government.

Yale University Press published Mises's first English works in the teeth of an overwhelming dedication to socialism and statism by the major book publishers of that era. The press was secured for publishing Mises by his first new friend in the United States, the prominent economic journalist, Henry Hazlitt, then the lucid editorial writer and economist for the *New York Times*.

Harold Luhnow, of the William Volker Fund, took up the crusade of finding Mises a suitable full-time academic post. Since obtaining a paid position seemed out of the question, the Volker Fund was prepared to pay Mises's entire salary. Even under the subsidized conditions, however, the task was difficult, and finally New York University Graduate School of Business agreed to accept Mises as a permanent "Visiting Professor," teaching, once again, his beloved graduate seminar on economic theory.[18] Mises began teaching his seminar every Thursday night in 1949, and continued to teach the seminar until he retired, still spry and active twenty years later, at the age of eighty-seven, the oldest active professor in the United States.

As early as 1942, Mises, dismayed but undaunted by the sad fate of *Nationalökonomie*, began work on an English-language version of the book. The new book was not simply an English translation of *Nationalökonomie*. It was revised, better written, and greatly expanded, so much so as to be virtually a new book.[19] It was the great work of Mises's life. Under the care and aegis of Eugene Davidson, the Yale University Press published the new treatise in 1949 as *Human Action: A Treatise on Economics*.[20]

---

[18]Harold W. Luhnow was head of the William Volker Company, a furniture distributing warehouse in Kansas City, and of the William Volker Fund, which played a vitally important but still unsung role in supporting libertarian and conservative scholarship from the late 1940s until the early 1960s.

For a while, Mises continued to teach his socialism course as well as conduct his seminar. After a few years, the seminar was his only course at NYU.

[19]I have been so informed by my German–American colleague, Professor Hans-Hermann Hoppe of the economics department of the University of Nevada, Las Vegas, a knowledgeable and creative praxeologist and Misesian.

[20]A particularly valuable assessment of the importance of publishing an English version of *Nationalökonomie* was sent to Davidson in January 1945 by Dr. Benjamin Anderson, monetary economist, economic historian, and friend of Mises, and formerly economist for the Chase National Bank.

Happily, the opening of Mises's seminar coincided with the publication of *Human Action,* which came out on September 14, 1949. *Human Action* is: Mises's greatest achievement and one of the finest products of the human mind in our century. It is economics made whole, based on the methodology of praxeology that Mises himself had developed, and grounded in the ineluctable and fundamental axiom that human beings exist, and that they *act* in the world, using means to try to achieve their most valued goals. Mises constructs the entire edifice of correct economic theory as the logical implications of the primordial fact of individual human action. It was a remarkable achievement, and provided a way out for the discipline of economics, which had fragmented into uncoordinated and clashing sub-specialties. It is remarkable that *Human Action* was the first integrated treatise on economics since Taussig and Fetter had written theirs before World War I. In addition to providing this comprehensive and integrated economic theory, *Human Action* defended sound, Austrian economics against all its methodological opponents, against historicists, positivists, and neoclassical practitioners of mathematical economics and econometrics. He also updated his critique of socialism and interventionism.

In addition, Mises provided important theoretical corrections of his predecessors. Thus, he incorporated the American Austrian Frank Fetter's pure time-preference theory of interest into economics, at long last rectifying Böhm-Bawerk's muddying of the waters by bringing back the fallacious productivity theory of interest after he had disposed of it in the first volume of his *Capital and Interest.*

Yale University Press was so impressed with the popularity as well as the quality of Mises's book that it served for the next decade as the publisher of his work. The press published a new, expanded edition of *Socialism* in 1951, and a similarly expanded edition of *The Theory of Money and Credit* in 1953. Remarkably, too, Mises did not rest on his laurels after the publication of *Human Action.* His essay on "Profit and Loss" is perhaps the best discussion ever written of the function of the entrepreneur and of the profit-and-loss system of the market.[21] In 1957, the press published Mises's

---

> *Nationalökonomie* is von Mises's first book on general economic principles. It is the central trunk, so to speak, of which the subject discussed in his book on money and his book on socialism are merely the branches. It is the fundamental theory of which the conclusions in the books on socialism and money are the corollaries. (Mises, *My Years with Ludwig von Mises,* p. 103)

[21]"Profit and Loss" was written as a paper for the meeting of the Mont Pèlerin Society, held in Beauvallon, France, in September 1951. The essay was published as a booklet the same year by Libertarian Press, and is now available as a chapter in the

last great work, the profound *Theory and History*, his philosophical masterpiece that explains the true relation between praxeology, or economic theory, and human history, and engages in a critique of Marxism, historicism, and various forms of scientism. *Theory and History* was, understandably, Mises's favorite next to *Human Action*.[22] However, after the departure in 1959 of Eugene Davidson to be founding editor of the conservative quarterly, *Modern Age*, Yale University Press no longer served as a friendly home for Mises's works.[23] In its final years, the publishing program of the William Volker Fund took up the slack, and provided the world with an English edition of *Liberalismus* (The free and prosperous commonwealth), and of *Grundprobleme der Nationalökonomie* (Epistemological problems of economics), both published in 1962. Also, in the same last year of Volker Fund existence, the Fund published Mises's final book *The Ultimate Foundation of Economic Science: An Essay on Method*, a critique of logical positivism in economics.[24]

During his post-World War II American years, Mises experienced ups and downs from observing the actions and influence of his former students, friends, and followers. On the one hand, he was happy to be one of the founding members in 1947 of the Mont Pèlerin Society, an international society of free-market economists and scholars. He was also delighted to see such friends as Luigi Einaudi as President of Italy, Jacques Rueff as monetary adviser to general Charles De Gaulle, and Röpke and Alfred Müller-Armack as influential advisers of Ludwig Erhard, play a

---

selected essays of Mises, in Ludwig von Mises, *Planning for Freedom*, 5th ed. (South Holland, Ill.: Libertarian Press, 1980), pp. 108–50.

[22]Mises, *My Years with Ludwig von Mises*, p. 106. Unfortunately, *Theory and History* has been grievously neglected by much of the post-1974 Austrian School revival. See Murray N. Rothbard, "Preface," in Ludwig von Mises, *Theory and History: An Interpretation of Social and Economic Evolution*, 2nd ed. (Auburn, Ala.: Ludwig von Mises Institute, 1985).

[23] The grisly story of the botched—seemingly deliberately—second edition of *Human Action* in 1963 can be found in Mises, *My Years with Ludwig von Mises*, pp. 106–11. The Yale University Press settled Mises's lawsuit on this horrendous printing job out of court, giving in to virtually all his demands. The rights to publish were transferred to Henry Regnery and Co., which published the third edition of *Human Action* in 1966, but the Yale University Press continues to take its cut to this day. The worst aspect of the affair was the torment inflicted on this 82-year-old intellectual giant, distressed at the mangling of his life's masterwork.

[24]All three works were published by D. Van Nostrand, whose chairman was a Mises sympathizer, and who had a publishing arrangement with the Volker Fund. *Grundprobleme* was translated by George Reisman, and *Liberalismus* by Ralph Raico, both of whom started attending Mises's seminar while still in high school in 1953. On Raico and Reisman, see Mises, *My Years with Ludwig von Mises*, pp. 136–37.

major role in shifting their respective nations during the 1950s in the direction of free markets and hard money. Mises played a leading part in the Mont Pèlerin Society in its early years, but after a while became disillusioned with its accelerating statism and mushy views on economic policy. And even though Mises and Hayek maintained cordial relations until the end, and Mises never spoke a bad word about his long-time friend and protégé, Mises was clearly unhappy about the developing shift in Hayek after World War II away from Misesian praxeology and methodological individualism, and toward the logical empiricism and neo-positivism of Hayek's old Viennese friend Karl Popper. Mises pronounced himself "astonished" when Hayek, in a lecture in New York on "Nomos and Taxis" in the 1960s, clearly if implicitly repudiated the praxeological methodology of his own *Counter-Revolution of Science*. And Mises, while generally admiring Hayek's 1960 work on political philosophy and political economy, *The Constitution of Liberty*, took Hayek gently but firmly to task for holding that the welfare state is "compatible with liberty."[25]

After being in failing health for the last two years of his life, the great and noble Ludwig von Mises, one of the giants of our century, died on October 10, 1973, at the age of ninety-two.

Since 1974, the revival of Austrian economics and of interest in Mises and his ideas has accelerated greatly. Scorned for the last four decades of Mises's life, Austrian economics in general, and Mises in particular, are now generally considered, at the very least, a worthy ingredient amidst the current potpourri and confusion of economic thought and opinion.

SELECTED READINGS

Mises, Ludwig von. [1949] 1998. *Human Action*, The Scholar's Edition. Auburn, Ala.: Ludwig von Mises Institute.

——. 1960. *Epistemological Problems of Economics*. New York: New York University Press.

——. 1978. *Notes and Recollections*. South Holland, Ill.: Libertarian Press.

——. 1978. *On the Manipulation of Money and Credit*. Dobbs Ferry, N.Y.: Free Market Books.

——. 1985. *Theory and History*. Auburn, Ala.: Ludwig von Mises Institute.

——. 1980. *The Theory of Money and Credit*. Indianapolis, Ind.: Liberty Classics.

——. 1981. *Socialism: An Economic and Sociological Analysis*. Indianapolis, Ind.: Liberty Classics.

——. 1984. Mises, Margit von. *My Years with Ludwig von Mises*. Cedar Falls, Iowa: Center for Futures Education.

[25]Mises, *Planning for Freedom*, p. 219.

# 11
# Henry Hazlitt: The People's Austrian

JEFFREY TUCKER

HENRY HAZLITT MADE a distinctive contribution to the history of the Austrian School through his ability to write well and explain economic theory and policy to a broad audience outside academia. He did this in his capacity as a free-market journalist, editorialist, and public intellectual, primarily working to restate Ludwig von Mises's own theories in popular venues.[1] Hazlitt displayed a tremendous analytical competence in making the subtleties and complexities of such a profound thinker as Mises accessible to everyone, and he did so without compromising the theoretical integrity of Mises's argument.

*Henry Hazlitt*
*1894–1993*

---

Paul Cwik, Roger Garrison, Llewellyn H. Rockwell, Jr., and Joseph Salerno provided very helpful comments. The author alone is responsible for errors.

[1]On Hazlitt's crucial role as an Austrian publicist, commentator, and organizer, see John L. Kelley, *Bringing the Market Back In: The Political Revitalization of Market Liberalism* (New York: New York University Press, 1997), pp. 33, 35, 53, 60, 64; and George H. Nash, *The Conservative Intellectual Movement in America* (Wilmington, Del.,: Intercollegiate Studies Institute, [1976] 1996), pp. 5, 9, 10, 14, 18–19, 22–25. Murray N. Rothbard, in *The Free Market* (December, 1987): 4, writes,

> In my own case, I was a Hazlittian years before I was a Misesian. In fact, before I had heard of von Mises I knew about Henry Hazlitt. When I was first getting interested in free-market economics, during and just after World War II, Henry was all over the place—in *Newsweek*, on radio and later television—lucid, sound, brilliant, and decisive, carrying the free-market message. And he was the only one.

That alone would have been sufficient to earn Hazlitt's space in the pantheon of great Austrian economists. But, in fact, Hazlitt also made scholarly contributions of his own to Austrian literature, particularly with his detailed response to John Maynard Keynes's *General Theory*, published at the height of Keynesian dominance of the profession. Without Hazlitt's hard work and his sacrifice of professional status for fixed principles, the history of the Austrian School in America would have been very different indeed.

Hazlitt was born in Philadelphia in 1894. His father died when Hazlitt was only two years old. His schooling began at Girard College, established to provide a good education for boys without fathers. When Hazlitt was nine, his mother remarried, and the family moved to Brooklyn.[2] He attended the Boys High School in Brooklyn, where his "great gods" became Herbert Spencer and William James. He studied for a year at the College of the City of New York, but when he ran out of money, Hazlitt had to quit school and seek employment.

After a series of quick jobs, he found a position at the *Wall Street Journal* as a stenographer.[3] He began working on his first book, *Thinking as a Science*, and, in an impressive accomplishment for a twenty-year-old, found a major publisher for it.[4] After a brief stint in the Army Air Corps, he wrote *The Way to Will Power*, a critique of psychoanalysis, in 1915.[5] Next, he became a full-time editorialist with the *New York Evening Post* (1916–18), the financial letter of the Mechanics & Metals National Bank (1919–20), the *New York Evening Mail* (1921–23), and the *New York Sun* (1924–29). It was this last position that established his reputation as a literary critic, and attracted the interest of *The Nation* magazine, where he served as literary

---

[2]Hazlitt was adopted by his stepfather; he took the name "Piebes," and changed it back again when he was sixteen, after his stepfather died.

[3]In an interview with *Reason* (December 1984): 37, Hazlitt said:

> I remember I had no skills whatever. So I would get a job, and I would last two or three days and be fired. It never surprised me nor upset me, because I read the *Times* early in the morning, went through the ads, and I'd practically have a job that day. This shows what happens when you have a free market. There was no such thing as minimum wage at the time. There was no such thing as relief, except maybe there were places where you could get a soup handout or something, but there was no systematic welfare. You had a free market. And so I usually found myself at a job the next day, and I'd get fired about three or four days after that. But each time I kept learning something, and finally I was getting about $3 or $4 a week.

[4]Henry Hazlitt, *Thinking as a Science* (New York: Nash Publishing, [1915] 1969).

[5]Henry Hazlitt, *The Way to Will Power* (New York: E.P. Dutton, 1922).

editor from 1930–1933, in addition to writing chapters on literary topics in a number of important books appearing at the time.[6]

In these years, he met economist Benjamin Anderson. "I used to go to see him about once a week to talk about economic developments," Hazlitt said. "I read his magnificent book, *The Value of Money*, which is one of the classics of American economic writing and world monetary literature."[7] Hazlitt continued to write on these two fronts—economics and literary criticism—while working for *The Nation*, but his anti-New Deal positions were increasingly at odds with the dominant editorial view of the magazine.[8]

Rather than simply fire Hazlitt, the magazine scheduled a full-blown debate between socialist Louis Fischer and Hazlitt, which ran in the May 24, 1939 issue. Fischer argued the Marxian view that workers were being exploited by owners during the 1920s, and therefore didn't have the means to consume what they needed; meanwhile the owners of capital, hoarding all the wealth, would not consume the products of industry. Fischer's solution was to divide the wealth. Hazlitt refuted that theory by pointing to the growing returns to labor during the 1920s. Instead, he offered a version of the Austrian business cycle as explanation. The World War and credit expansion in the 1920s artificially inflated prices and encouraged "colossal real-estate and stock-market speculation." The 1929 stock-market crash was merely a correction, but the adjustment was impeded by economic controls. Hazlitt recommended complete economic decontrol as the only way out.

---

[6]Among them, "Humanism and Value," in *The Critique of Humanism*, Clinton Hartley Grattan, ed. (Freeport N.Y.: Books for Libraries Press, [1930] 1968); "Emerson," in *American Writers on American Literature*, Jon Albert Macy, ed. (Westport, Conn.: Greenwood Press, 1931); "Introduction," to Stephen Crane, *Maggie and Other Stories* (New York: Alfred A. Knopf, 1931); "Our Greatest Authors (How Great Are They?)," in *Essays and Addresses Toward a Liberal Education*, A.C. Baird, ed. (Boston: Ginn, 1934); "Literature as Propaganda," in *The Practice of Book Selection*, Louis Round Wilson, ed. (Chicago: University of Chicago Press, 1940); and, with Dorothy Thompson and Mark van Doren, "Nietzsche: Beyond Good and Evil," in *New Invitation to Learning*, Mark van Doren, ed. (New York: Random House, 1942).

[7]Henry Hazlitt, "Reflections at 70," *Henry Hazlitt: An Appreciation* (Irvington-on-Hudson, N.Y.: Foundation for Economic Education, 1989), p. 9. Also during these years, he was commissioned by W.W. Norton to do a biography of Bertrand Russell. "I spent a good deal of time with him, in New York and London, in the period of 1928–1929, until one day, while reminiscing for my benefit, he suddenly said, 'You know, I have had a very interesting life; I think I'd like to do my own autobiography.'"

[8]For the full story of this split with *The Nation*, see Jeffrey Tucker, "Hazlitt and the Great Depression," *The Free Market* (September 1993): 2–4.

*The Nation* weighed in against Hazlitt and the free-market policies he advocated, and Hazlitt left the magazine. In the meantime, Hazlitt had come to admire and even idolize H.L. Mencken, the legendary editor of *American Mercury*. As two of the only anti-New Deal intellectuals with high public profiles, they shared a common political and literary bond. Mencken asked Hazlitt to take over as editor, saying Hazlitt was "the only competent critic of the arts that I have heard of who was at the same time a competent economist, of practical as well as theoretical training." And, Mencken added, "he is one of the few economists in human history who could really write."[9] During the year he spent with the *American Mercury*—attacking the New Deal at every turn—he also wrote what is surely his least known work, *The Anatomy of Criticism*. Set in the form of a trialogue, Hazlitt defends the role and function of literary criticism, but also deals directly with a number of theoretical problems in economics. He attempts a reconciliation between the subjective economic value of arts and literature and the objective worth of the work of artists and writers.[10]

That same year, he published a short monograph called *Instead of Dictatorship*, in which he argued, somewhat naively, that a council of businessmen should be assigned to restrain executive tyranny, which was then being rubberstamped by a complacent Congress.[11] Hazlitt's independent Council would turn over problems of economics to "5 or 7 trained monetary and banking economists" who would then draft legislation. Later, his interest in political reform led to *A New Constitution Now*, in which he argued for the U.S. to be transformed into a European-style parliamentary system.[12] As Murray N. Rothbard has written,

> whether or not one agrees fully with Hazlitt, he made an extremely important point which has taken on far more importance in these days of unbridled executive power. For he argued that the great defect of the

---

[9]The quotation appears on the book jacket of the first edition of *Economics in One Lesson*, which may or not have been its first appearance.

[10]Henry Hazlitt, *The Anatomy of Criticism* (New York: Simon and Schuster, 1933). Hazlitt takes the position that we can gain an approximate understanding of artistic and literary worth by reflecting on the "social mind," which is the source of the intellectual's reputation. By using the concept of the Social Mind, we avoid falling into radical subjectivism of the deconstructionist variety (Hazlitt provides a full-blown critique of Marxist deconstructionism as an appendix) and excessive objectivism that denies the role of taste and preference in assessing artistic merit.

[11]Henry Hazlitt, *Instead of Dictatorship* (New York: John Day, 1933).

[12]Henry Hazlitt, *A New Constitution Now* (New York: McGraw, 1942).

> American Constitution is that it permits runaway executive power, unchecked by Congress or the public.[13]

Leaving the *American Mercury*, Hazlitt was hired by the *New York Times* as an editorialist, and also as a book reviewer for its influential Sunday book review section. For the daily edition of the newspaper, he wrote against the National Industrial Recovery Administration, union privileges, stock market regulation, inflation, protectionism, industrial planning of all sorts, economic nationalism, curbs in the work week, unemployment insurance, welfare and relief, social security, higher taxes, all inheritance taxes, government spending, and other forms of growing government power.[14]

Two book reviews in particular had profound significance in the history of the Austrian School. First, there was Hazlitt's featured review of Mises's *Socialism*, written while Mises was still teaching in Geneva. This book, Hazlitt writes,

> examines socialism from almost every possible aspect—its doctrine of violence as well as that of the collective ownership of the means of production; its ideal of equality; its relation to problems of sex and the family; its proposed solution for the problem of production as well as of distribution; its probable operation under both static and dynamic conditions; its national and international consequences. . . . [It] must rank as the most devastating analysis of socialism yet penned. Doubtless even some anti-Socialist readers will feel that he occasionally overstates his cases. On the other hand, even confirmed socialists will not be able to withhold admiration from the masterly fashion in which he conducts his argument. He has written an economic classic in our time.[15]

Hazlitt sent a copy of his review to Mises in Geneva, the two men exchanged letters, and when Mises came to the U.S. two years later, he called Hazlitt, thus beginning a friendship that would last a lifetime. "Hazlitt was one of the first people Lu met in New York," writes Margit von Mises, "and one of the first to take an active interest in getting Lu

---

[13]Murray N. Rothbard, "Henry Hazlitt Celebrates 80th Birthday," *Human Events* (November 30, 1974).

[14]In the book review section at the very same time, he was reviewing books by and about Bertrand Russell, John Dewey, H.G. Wells, George Santayana, and Stuart Chase. His reputation and writing skill meant that he was often featured on the front page of the section.

[15]*New York Times Book Review* (January 9, 1938). Excerpt reprinted in Bettina Bien Greaves, *Mises: An Annotated Bibliography* (Irvington-on-Hudson, N.Y.: Foundation for Economic Education, 1993), p. 159.

established in America. . . . The Hazlitts, well aware of Lu's situation [no academic position; no savings], were extremely hospitable and kind."[16] A gracious and charitable man, Hazlitt worked to get Margit's daughter, Gitta Sereny, out of occupied France, by using connections he had with Assistant Secretary of State Breckinridge Long. "Only the mother of a young daughter will understand what this meant to me," Margit writes. "Hazlitt himself may long have forgotten about this incident; I haven't and I never will."[17]

The second important book review was of F.A. Hayek's *The Road to Serfdom*, appearing on the front page of the September 24, 1944 edition of the *Times Book Review*. Hazlitt described it as "one of the most important books of our generation." To understand the crucial importance of this review for the huge status this book would eventually achieve, we need only recall that the University of Chicago had only printed up three thousand copies of the book on its first print run. But after Hazlitt's review, sales boomed, eventually leading to a *Reader's Digest* version of the book, which brought the thesis (of the connections between brown, red, and U.S.-style socialism) to millions.

In 1946, while still working at the *Times*, Hazlitt wrote *Economics in One Lesson*,[18] the book for which he is most well-known. He did so without the slightest expectation that it would become a bestseller.[19] Yet, sales would eventually top one million, causing it to rank among the most popular economics books ever written. This is especially ironic considering its orientation is entirely Austrian, and was even refereed by Ludwig von Mises himself, whom Hazlitt thanks in the preface to the first edition.[20] It turned out to serve as a key educational tool for several

---

[16]Margit von Mises, *My Years with Ludwig von Mises* (Cedar Falls, Iowa: Center for Futures Education, 1984), p. 57–58.

[17]Ibid., p. 70.

[18]Henry Hazlitt, *Economics in One Lesson* (New York: Harper and Brothers, 1946).

[19]Interview with the author, October 1987.

[20]"I am grateful to Professor von Mises for reading the manuscript and for helpful suggestions." Mises is the only person so thanked. For intellectual influence, Hazlitt names Frédéric Bastiat, Philip Wicksteed, and Mises. See *Economics in One Lesson*, pp. ix–xi. On Wicksteed in particular, Hazlitt says that upon his first reading *The Common Sense of Political Economy*, "I caught my first glimpse of the fact—which Ludwig von Mises was later to make much more explicit—that the world of economics is almost coextensive with the whole world of human action and of human decision." See *The Wisdom of Henry Hazlitt* (Irvington-on-Hudson, N.Y.: Foundation for Economic Education, 1983).

generations of students and businessmen, inoculating them against then-popular Keynesian fallacies.

The book drives home two crucial points about sound economic thinking. First, economics "consists in looking not merely at the immediate but at the longer effects of any act or policy." Second, "it consists in tracing the consequences of that policy not merely for one group but for all groups."[21] These principles are applied first through retelling Frédéric Bastiat's "Broken Window Fallacy" (the destruction is fallaciously celebrated by Keynesian-like spectators because it will make business for the glazier), and then applied to a host of economic issues, from taxes and credit expansion to price supports and tariffs. In case after case, he shows that coercive government intervention to help one group is against the interests of most every other group, particularly consumers. And while that intervention may appear to succeed in the short run, it only brings about inefficiencies and lower living standards in the long run.

The publication of *Economics in One Lesson,* his first solely on economics, marks the beginning of his full-time association with Austrian and free-market causes. He had been working as a highly influential editorialist for the *New York Times* since June, 1934, but two events conspired to cause him to leave the *Times*. First, he was being identified more openly with free-market causes at a time when this was an unpopular position to hold, and the authorship of his articles—usually anonymous[22]—was increasingly obvious to readers, not all of whom approved. Second, Hazlitt had been editorializing against the pseudo-gold standard of the proposed Bretton Woods monetary agreement. "I found myself almost alone, particularly in the journalistic world, in calling attention to" the dangers of the agreement.[23] After the monetary pact was signed, editor Arthur Sulzberger called him in and said, "Now, look, Henry. I've let you write these editorials. But now that forty-three nations have signed this, we can't continue to oppose it." Hazlitt refused

---

[21]Hazlitt, *Economics in One Lesson*, p. 5.

[22]The question of which editorials were his remained a mystery until 1994 with the publication of a nearly complete bibliography of his writings, listing some three thousand unsigned articles. See *Henry Hazlitt: A Giant of Liberty,* compiled by the present author from archives mainly held by the George Arents Research Library at Syracuse University.

[23]Henry Hazlitt, *From Bretton Woods to World Inflation: A Study of the Causes and Consequences* (Chicago: Regnery Gateway, 1984) p. 10. In his magnanimous introduction to this volume, he does not mention that his anti-Bretton Woods essays led to his dismissal.

to endorse the pact, so he just stopped writing about the issue altogether. "This made for sort of strained relations," Hazlitt told an interviewer, "but they didn't fire me."[24]

Two years later, with *Economics in One Lesson* in print, and Hazlitt still in conflict with the editorial board over Bretton Woods, he departed the *New York Times*. His departure should also be considered in light of the explosion of fury the social democratic left exhibited toward his column, and the sudden crystallization of the fact that Hazlitt was the actual source. "Like a Sunday-school teacher in a slum," wrote George Soule of *Economics in One Lesson*,

> Henry Hazlitt bids us return to the economic gospel. The world is all but lost; not a nation in it with the possible exception of the United States clings to the faith, and even here false prophets have led us astray. But to Hazlitt the truth is clear and whole. . . . For years newspapers like the *New York Times* have maddened progressives by bland opposition to economic reforms, and Hazlitt has been the mainstay of the *Times* in economic opinion.[25]

Ironically, it appears that Hazlitt himself might have been unaware of how out-of-the-mainstream his ideas were; his last experiences with the left had been with an ideologically-oriented journal, not the mainstream profession as a whole.

> When I wrote my *Economics in One Lesson* in 1946, I didn't quite realize how socialistic most economic writing had already become. This was a fortunate thing for me because my book was not angry at all; it just spoofed the controllers and the price-fixers. I think that's one of the things that attracted readers—there was little anger in the book. It just treated the interventionists as if they didn't really know what they were talking about.[26]

Having left the *Times*, his greatest work on behalf of the Austrian School was just beginning. His new role as *Newsweek's* "Business Tides" columnist gave him a weekly venue to articulate his positions, and the time and opportunity to devote the remainder of his efforts to Austrian scholarship and journalism. He began with a series of articles on two major postwar economic issues: price control (and the related attempt to "stabilize" the economy through other forms of control), and the growing

---

[24] "An Interview with Henry Hazlitt," *Austrian Economics Newsletter* (Spring 1984); "Henry Hazlitt," *Reason* (December 1984): 38.

[25] George Soule, "The Gospel According to Hazlitt," *The New Republic* (August 19, 1946): 202–05.

[26] "An Interview with Henry Hazlitt."

problem of labor strikes. He argued for an immediate repeal of all price controls, pointing out precisely how they are the very source of economic instability, and for an immediate end to all labor-union privileges, which were preventing wages from adjusting to a new postwar level. His theme was that prices are essential signaling devices that permit businessmen and consumers to assess the value of resources and services. Without freely floating prices, even a nominally capitalist country would experience the bottlenecks, inefficiencies, and economic chaos that afflicted planned economies. He explained, too, how union strikes are not something we would expect to see in a free market; rather they are a consequence of special privilege. Moreover, union strikes were being encouraged by the Truman administration as a political tool.

In 1949, the Truman administration pushed for domestic spending programs to match its international ones. But Hazlitt attacked the growth in the American welfare state in the forms of student aid and Social Security, and the rise of inflationist ideology which purported to solve all macroeconomic troubles through credit expansion. Hazlitt recommended a return to a nineteenth-century convertible gold standard. In a series of landmark columns on isolationism and internationalism, Hazlitt was nearly alone in debunking the Truman administration's attempt to paint opponents of foreign aid as head-in-the-sand isolationists (an effort that continues to this day). In Hazlitt's view, true internationalism is not characterized by international bureaucracies and loans, but unfettered world trade (of which neither the Truman nor Eisenhower administrations were true friends). Hazlitt also editorialized against deficit spending, against regarding supposed tax loopholes as subsidies, against the moon shot and agricultural aid, and against soak-the-rich and anti-business policies.

In the same period, and in relatively rapid succession, Hazlitt brought out a series of highly creative books that explain Austrian theory, and use it as the basis for critical analysis of competitive doctrines and interventionist policies. *Will Dollars Save the World?* and *The Illusions of Point Four* attack the Marshall Plan and development aid on grounds that they both misconstrue the nature of wealth creation and overlook the importance of market-driven capital investment in laying the foundations for economic development.[27] Hazlitt's criticism of the Marshall Plan, in particular, was cited in later years by the defenders of Marshall

[27]Henry Hazlitt, *Will Dollars Save the World?* (New York: Appleton Century, 1947); and idem, *The Illusions of Point Four* (Irvington-on-Hudson, N.Y.: Foundation for Economic Education, 1950).

as a particularly irritating source of naysayism. In 1951, Hazlitt offered a fictional account of the process of desocialization that would transpire if a benign dictator of a world socialist system began to disassemble the interventionist apparatus piece by piece.[28] Murray Rothbard called it "the only novel ever written that exemplifies and explains the Misesian doctrine of the impossibility of calculation under socialism."[29] The novel garnered new attention after the collapse of socialist states in Eastern Europe in 1989, and debate ensued about whether the politics of transition should be gradual or rapid. And in 1956, Hazlitt wrote *The Free Man's Library*, a deeply annotated bibliography of works on the libertarian idea, arranged alphabetically. It exhibits the wide reading in philosophy and economics Hazlitt had done, and became a standard reference book for the burgeoning free-market movement.[30]

His next project was a page-by-page refutation of Keynes's *General Theory*, something never before attempted by any economist.[31] In fact, as Hazlitt noted, in the vast Keynesian literature, there were precious few commentators on Keynes's book itself. Most Keynesians wrote what they regarded as elaborations on the great master, while curiously neglecting the master himself. The few who did examine the *General Theory* began with the assumption that the book is both coherent and deeply insightful, and saw their job as merely discovering precisely what it was that made it so. Hazlitt took the opposite approach. He came at the project with the intention of discovering whether *in fact* the book is coherent, much less insightful. In area after area, he found mangled theoretical constructs, inconsistencies, failures in logic, incomplete argumentation, syllogisms masquerading as explanations, and untenable policy recommendations. The final product was *The Failure of the "New Economics"* a four-hundred-and-fifty-eight-page book shredding Keynes, the great economist of that age. As Mises said, "Hazlitt has entirely demolished the Keynesian misconceptions."[32]

---

[28]Henry Hazlitt, *The Great Idea* (New York: Appleton, 1951); reprinted as *Time Will Run Back* (New Rochelle, N.Y: Arlington House, 1966).

[29]Annotation in *Henry Hazlitt: Giant of Liberty*, p. 24.

[30]Henry Hazlitt, *The Free Man's Library* (Princeton, N.J.: D. Van Nostrand, 1956). At one-hundred-and-seventy-six pages, it ironically highlights the dearth of contemporary literature available in 1956. A similar volume today would have to be impossibly huge.

[31]Henry Hazlitt, *The Failure of the "New Economics": An Analysis of the Keynesian Fallacies* (Princeton, N.J.: D. Van Nostrand, 1959).

[32]Book jacket to *The Failure of the "New Economics."*

From the standpoint of the Austrian School, it is this book, more than any other, that has to be considered Hazlitt's unique contribution to the history of thought. Hazlitt had anticipated criticisms that would emerge in later Austrian literature on macroeconomics. In particular, Hazlitt points out that Keynes discusses the relationship between savings and investment in two contradictory contexts. In the first, he argues for definitional identity between the two. In the second, he argues they are always out of kilter and need to be corrected through some sort of interventionism.[33]

Rothbard called Hazlitt's book on Keynes his *magnum opus*, but Hazlitt himself regarded his book on social ethics to be his greatest work.[34] It is an elaboration on Mises's theory of social cooperation as a normative standard for evaluating public policy (and less so, personal ethics), sometimes called rule utilitarianism. Whereas many authors in the Austrian tradition have followed the path of Rothbard (and even Ayn Rand) in integrating economic theory with a rights-based moral framework, Mises himself insisted that rights claims cannot be rationally established.[35] The Misesian alternative postulates the long-run harmony of interests between individuals and society and the ethical obligation of people to evaluate social systems and individual behavior in light of that harmony of interests. Societies should pursue paths that lead to cooperation, prosperity, and peace, and not tread upon those that lead to conflict, poverty, and war. Hazlitt named this view "cooperatism," and defended it against alternatives.[36]

---

[33]See *The Failure of the "New Economics,"* pp. 217–35. In addition, Hazlitt published a companion volume, *The Critics of Keynesian Economics* (Princeton, N.J.: D. Van Nostrand, 1960), which included the work of J.B. Say, John Stuart Mill, Jacob Viner, Frank Knight, Etienne Mantoux, F.A. Hayek, Franco Modigliani, Benjamin Anderson, Philip Cortney, R. Gordon Wasson, Garet Garrett, Jacques Rueff, John H. Williams, L. Albert Hahn, Ludwig von Mises, Joseph Stagg Lawrence, Wilhelm Röpke, W.H. Hutt, Arthur F. Burns, Melchior Palyi, and David McCord Wright. In doing so, he provided the anti-Keynesian remnant a crucial source for arguments against the Keyensian view, as well as subtly illustrated that Keynesian fallacies on the inherent flaws of the price system predate *The General Theory*.

[34]Henry Hazlitt, *Foundations of Morality* (Princeton, N.J.: D. Van Nostrand, 1964). One of Hazlitt's final projects was to put together a compilation of the writings of the Stoic philosophers. Idem, *The Wisdom of the Stoics: Selections from Seneca, Epictetus, and Marcus Aurelius* (Lanham, Maryland: University Press of America, 1983).

[35]Ludwig von Mises, *Human Action*, The Scholar's Edition (Auburn, Ala.: Ludwig von Mises Institute, 1998), pp. 174–75.

[36]Leland Yeager, in an interview in *The Austrian Economics Newsletter* (Summer 1991): 6, cites the Hazlitt book as an inspiration in his own work on social ethics.

From 1964 to the mid-1970s, Hazlitt contributed a number of studies that exploded the myth of the welfare state on economic grounds, and forecast the problems now so well documented in the literature. *Man vs. The Welfare State* criticized plans for curbing the welfare state that were gradual in nature, especially the negative income tax proposed by Milton Friedman (which eventually became the Earned Income Tax Credit).[37] He saw all proposals that curb welfarism as merely introducing new perverse incentives to become and remain poor while imposing artificial disincentives for earning money. Hazlitt favored all-out abolition of the welfare state, the only position he regarded as being consistent with sound economics. *The Conquest of Poverty* demonstrated that enormous gains in living standards have followed the introduction of free markets throughout history. In contrast, the problem of poverty and economic dislocation has been the result of interventionism throughout human history.

While he concentrated primarily on writing books during these years, he never let up in his journalistic efforts in periodicals. He served as co-editor of *The Freeman* (1950–53), wrote a nationally syndicated weekly column for the *Los Angeles Times* (1966–69), and continued through the 1970s and early 1980s to write for *The Freeman*, *Human Events*, and *National Review*. His last printed article appeared in the inaugural issue of *The Review of Austrian Economics*.

As a brilliant stylist and an indefatigable defender of individualism and the capitalist economy, he accepted the personal sacrifices that were required to take positions that were highly unpopular at that time. Before the war, Hazlitt held high positions in publishing circles, an especially remarkable accomplishment considering his lack of credentials or advanced formal education. Yet, he took the path where he believed truth led him, and that was with deeply unpopular causes. Today, he appears to be far more a mainstream thinker than in his day, partially due to the educational efforts of the free-market movement he helped pioneer.

"When I look back on my own career," he told an audience in 1964,

> I can find plenty of reasons for discouragement, personal discouragement. I have not lacked for industry. I have written a dozen books. For most of 50 years, from the age of 20, I have been writing practically every weekday: news items, editorials, columns, articles. I figure I must have written in total some 10,000 editorials, articles, and columns; some

[37] Henry Hazlitt, *Man vs. The Welfare State* (New Rochelle, N.Y.: Arlington House, 1969); idem, *The Conquest of Poverty* (Los Angeles: Nash Publishing, 1973).

10,000,000 words! And in print! The verbal equivalent of about 150 average-length books!

And yet, what have I accomplished? . . . The world is enormously more socialized than when I began. . . . Yet in spite of this, I am hopeful. After all, I'm still in good health, I'm still free to write, I'm still free to write unpopular opinions, and I'm keeping at it. And so are many of you. So I bring you this message: be of good cheer; be of good spirit. If the battle is not yet won, it is not yet lost either. . . . Even those of us who have reached and passed our seventieth birthdays cannot afford to rest on our oars and spend the rest of our lives dozing in the Florida sun. The times call for courage. The times call for hard work. But if the demands are high, it is because the stakes are even higher. They are nothing less than the future of human liberty, which means the future of civilization.[38]

## SELECTED READINGS

Hazlitt, Henry. 1984. *From Bretton Woods to World Inflation: A Study of Causes and Consequences*. Chicago: Regnery Gateway.

——. [1946] 1979. *Economics in One Lesson*. New York: Crown Trade Paperbacks.

——. 1973. *The Conquest of Poverty*. Los Angeles: Nash Publishing.

——. 1969. *Man vs. The Welfare State*. New Rochelle, N.Y: Arlington House.

——. 1964. *The Foundations of Morality*. Princeton, N.J.: D. Van Nostrand.

——. 1959. *The Failure of the "New Economics": An Analysis of the Keynesian Fallacies*. Princeton, N.J.: D. Van Nostrand.

——. 1951. *The Great Idea*. New York: Appleton; reprinted as *Time Will Run Back. London: Ernest Benn.*

——. 1942. *A New Constitution Now.* New York: McGraw.

——. 1933. *The Wisdom of Henry Hazlitt*. Irvington-on-Hudson, N.Y.: Foundation for Economic Education.

——. 1933. *The Anatomy of Criticism: A Trialogue*. New York: Simon and Schuster.

——. 1916. *Thinking as a Science*. New York: E.P. Dutton.

*Henry Hazlitt: An Appreciation*. 1989. Irvington-on-Hudson, N.Y.: Foundation for Economic Education.

Tucker, Jeffrey, comp. Murray Rothbard, annot. 1994. *Henry Hazlitt: A Giant of Liberty*. Auburn, Ala: Ludwig von Mises Institute.

[38]Hazlitt, "Reflections at 70," pp. 14–15.

# 12
# F.A. HAYEK: AUSTRIAN ECONOMIST AND SOCIAL THEORIST

PETER G. KLEIN

FRIEDRICH AUGUST VON HAYEK ranks among the most eminent of the modern Austrian economists. Student of Friedrich von Wieser, protégé and colleague of Ludwig von Mises, and foremost among an outstanding generation of Austrian School theorists, Hayek was perhaps more successful than anyone else in spreading Austrian ideas throughout the English-speaking world. "When the definitive history of economic analysis during the 1930s comes to be written," said John Hicks in 1967, "a leading character in the drama will be Professor Hayek. . . . [I]t is hardly remembered that there was a time when the new theories of Hayek were the principal rival of the new theories of Keynes."[1] Unfortunately, Hayek's theory of the business cycle was eventually swept aside by the Keynesian revolution. Ultimately, however, this work was again recognized when Hayek received, along with the Swede Gunnar Myrdal, the 1974 Nobel Memorial Prize in Economic Science.

*F. A. Hayek*
*1899–1992*

## LIFE AND WORK

Hayek's life spanned the twentieth century, and he made his home in some of the great intellectual communities of the period. Born in 1899 to

[1]Sir John Hicks, *Critical Essays in Monetary Theory* (Oxford: Clarendon Press, 1967), p. 203.

a distinguished family of Viennese intellectuals (one grandfather, a statistician, was a friend of Eugen von Böhm-Bawerk; the philosopher Ludwig Wittgenstein was a second cousin), Hayek attended the University of Vienna, earning doctorates in 1921 and 1923. Hayek came to the University at age nineteen, just after World War I, when it was one of the three best places in the world to study economics (the others being Stockholm and Cambridge). Though he was enrolled as a law student, his primary interests were economics and psychology, the latter due to the influence of Mach's theory of perception on Wieser and Wieser's colleague Othmar Spann, and the former stemming from the reformist ideal of Fabian socialism so typical of Hayek's generation.

Like many students of economics then and since, Hayek chose the subject not for its own sake, but because he wanted to improve social conditions—the poverty of postwar Vienna serving as a daily reminder of such a need. Socialism seemed to provide a solution. Then, in 1922, Mises published his *Die Gemeinwirtschaft*, later translated as *Socialism*. "To none of us young men who read the book when it appeared," Hayek recalled, "the world was ever the same again."[2] *Socialism*, an elaboration of Mises's pioneering article from two years before, argued that economic calculation requires a market for the means of production; without such a market there is no way to establish the values of those means and, consequently, no way to find their proper uses in production. Mises's devastating attack on central planning converted Hayek to laissez-faire, along with contemporaries like Wilhelm Röpke, Lionel Robbins, and Bertil Ohlin.

It was around this time that Hayek began attending Mises's famed *Privatseminar*. For several years, the *Privatseminar* was the center of the economics community in Vienna. Later, Hayek became the first of this group to leave Vienna; most of the others, along with Mises himself, were also gone by the start of World War II.

Mises had done earlier work on monetary and banking theory, successfully applying the Austrian marginal-utility principle to the value of money, and then sketching a theory of industrial fluctuations based on the doctrines of the British Currency School and the ideas of the Swedish economist Knut Wicksell. Hayek used this last as a starting point for his own research on fluctuations, explaining the origin of the business cycle in terms of bank-credit expansion, and its transmission in terms of capital

---

[2]F.A. Hayek, "In Honor of Professor Mises," in idem, *The Fortunes of Liberalism*, vol. 4, *The Collected Works of F.A. Hayek*, Peter G. Klein, ed. (Chicago: University of Chicago Press, 1992), p. 133.

malinvestments. His work in this area eventually earned him an invitation to lecture at the London School of Economics and Political Science (LSE), and then to occupy its Tooke Chair in Economics and Statistics, which he accepted in 1931. There he found himself among a vibrant and exciting group: Robbins, J.R. Hicks, Arnold Plant, Dennis Robertson, T.E. Gregory, Abba Lerner, Kenneth Boulding, and George Shackle, to name only the most prominent. Hayek brought his (to them) unfamiliar views, and gradually, the Austrian theory of the business cycle became known and accepted. At the LSE, Hayek lectured on Mises's business-cycle theory, which he was refining and which, until Keynes's *General Theory* came out in 1936, was rapidly gaining adherents in Britain and the United States, and was becoming the preferred explanation of the Depression.

Hayek and Keynes had sparred in the early 1930s in the pages of the *Economic Journal* over Keynes's *Treatise on Money*. As one of Keynes's leading professional adversaries, Hayek was well situated to provide a full refutation of the *General Theory*, but he never did. Part of the explanation for this no doubt lies with Keynes's personal charm and legendary rhetorical skill, along with Hayek's general reluctance to engage in direct confrontation with his colleagues. Hayek also considered Keynes an ally in the fight against wartime inflation and did not want to detract from that issue. Furthermore, as Hayek later explained, Keynes was constantly changing his theoretical framework, and Hayek saw no point in working out a detailed critique of the *General Theory*, if Keynes might change his mind again. Hayek thought a better course would be to produce a fuller elaboration of Böhm-Bawerk's capital theory, and he began to devote his energies to this project. Unfortunately, *The Pure Theory of Capital* was not completed until 1941, and by then the Keynesian macro model had become firmly established.[3]

Within a very few years, the fortunes of the Austrian School suffered a dramatic reversal. First, the Austrian theory of capital, an integral part of the business-cycle theory, came under attack from Italian-born

---

[3]Hayek also believed that an effective refutation of Keynes would have to begin with a thorough critique of aggregate, or "macro" economics more generally. See F.A. Hayek, "The Economics of the 1930s as Seen from London," in idem, *Contra Keynes and Cambridge: Essays, Correspondence*, vol. 9, *The Collected Works of F.A. Hayek*, Bruce Caldwell, ed. (Chicago: University of Chicago Press, 1995), pp. 49–73. Brian McCormick and Mark Blaug propose an entirely different reason: Hayek couldn't respond because the Austrian capital theory, on which the cycle theory was built, was simply wrong. See Brian J. McCormick, *Hayek and the Keynesian Avalanche* (New York: St. Martin's Press, 1992), pp. 99–134; and Mark Blaug, "Hayek Revisited," *Critical Review* 7, no. 1 (1993): 51–60.

Cambridge economist Piero Sraffa and American Frank Knight, while the cycle theory itself was forgotten amid the enthusiasm for the *General Theory*. Second, beginning with Hayek's move to London and continuing until the early 1940s, the Austrian economists left Vienna, for personal and then for political reasons, so that a school ceased to exist there as such.[4] Mises left Vienna in 1934 for Geneva and then New York, where he continued to work in isolation; Hayek remained at the LSE until 1950, when he joined the Committee on Social Thought at the University of Chicago. Other Austrians of Hayek's generation became prominent in the United States—Gottfried Haberler at Harvard, Fritz Machlup and Oskar Morgenstern at Princeton, Paul Rosenstein-Rodan at MIT—but their work no longer seemed to show distinct traces of the tradition founded by Carl Menger.

At Chicago, Hayek again found himself among a dazzling group: the economics department, led by Knight, Milton Friedman, and later George Stigler, was one of the best anywhere, and Aaron Director at the law school soon set up the first law-and-economics program.[5] But economic theory, in particular its style of reasoning, was rapidly changing: Paul Samuelson's *Foundations* had appeared in 1947, establishing physics as the science for economics to imitate, and Friedman's 1953 essay on "positive economics" set a new standard for economic method. In addition, Hayek had ceased to work on economic theory, concentrating instead on psychology, philosophy, and politics. Austrian economics entered a prolonged eclipse. Important work in the Austrian tradition was done during this period by Rothbard, Kirzner, and Lachmann, but, at least publicly, the Austrian tradition lay mostly dormant.

When the 1974 Nobel Prize in economics went to Hayek, interest in the Austrian School was suddenly and unexpectedly revived. While this was not the first event of the so-called Austrian revival, the memorable South Royalton, Vermont conference having taken place earlier the same year, the rediscovery of Hayek by the economics profession was nonetheless a decisive event in the renaissance of Austrian economics.[6] Hayek's

---

[4]See Earlene Craver, "The Emigration of the Austrian Economists," *History of Political Economy* 18, no. 1 (1986): 1–32.

[5]However, at Chicago, Hayek was considered something of an outsider; his post was with the Committee on Social Thought, not the economics department, and his salary was paid by a private foundation, the William Volker Fund (the same organization that paid Mises's salary as a visiting professor at New York University).

[6]The proceedings of the South Royalton conference were published as *The Foundations of Modern Austrian Economics*, Edwin G. Dolan, ed. (Kansas City: Sheed and Ward, 1976).

writings were taught to new generations, and Hayek himself appeared at the early Institute for Humane Studies conferences in the mid-1970s. He continued to write, producing *The Fatal Conceit* in 1988, at the age of 89.[7] Hayek died in 1992 in Freiburg, Germany, where he had lived since leaving Chicago in 1961.[8]

Hayek's legacy in economics is complex. Among mainstream economists, he is mainly known for his popular *The Road to Serfdom*[9] and for his work on knowledge in the 1930s and 1940s. Specialists in business-cycle theory recognize his early work on industrial fluctuations, and modern information theorists often acknowledge Hayek's work on prices as signals, although his conclusions are typically disputed. Hayek's work is also known in political philosophy, legal theory, and psychology.

Within the Austrian School of economics, Hayek's influence, while undeniably immense, has very recently become the subject of some controversy. His emphasis on spontaneous order and his work on complex systems have been widely influential among many Austrians. Others have preferred to stress Hayek's work in technical economics, particularly on capital and the business cycle, citing a tension between some of Hayek's and Mises's views on the social order. (While Mises was a rationalist and a utilitarian, Hayek focused on the limits to reason, basing his defense of capitalism on its ability to use limited knowledge and learning by trial and error.)

### BUSINESS-CYCLE THEORY

Hayek's writings on capital, money, and the business cycle are generally regarded as his most important contributions to economics. Building on Mises's *Theory of Money and Credit*,[10] Hayek showed how fluctuations in economy-wide output and employment are related to the economy's capital structure. In *Prices and Production*,[11] he introduced the famous "Hayekian triangles" to illustrate the relationship between the value of

---

[7]F.A. Hayek, *The Fatal Conceit: The Errors of Socialism*, vol. 1, *The Collected Works of F.A. Hayek*, W.W. Bartley III, ed. (Chicago: University of Chicago Press, 1988).

[8]For a fuller biographical account, see F.A. Hayek, *Hayek on Hayek: An Autobiographical Dialogue*, Stephen Kresge and Leif Wenar, eds. (Chicago: University of Chicago Press, 1994).

[9]F.A. Hayek, *The Road to Serfdom* (Chicago: University of Chicago Press, 1944).

[10]Ludwig von Mises, *The Theory of Money and Credit*, H.E. Batson, trans. (Indianapolis, Ind.: Liberty Classics, [1912] 1980).

[11]F.A. Hayek, *Prices and Production* (London: Routledge and Kegan Paul, [1931] 1935).

capital goods and their place in the temporal sequence of production. Because production takes time, factors of production must be committed in the present for making final goods that will have value only in the future after they are sold. However, capital is heterogeneous; as capital goods are used in particular production processes, they become increasingly specific to those processes, so they cannot be easily redeployed as demands for final goods change. The central macroeconomic problem in a modern capital-using economy is, thus, one of intertemporal coordination: how can the allocation of resources between capital and consumer goods be aligned with consumers' preferences between present and future consumption? In *The Pure Theory of Capital*,[12] perhaps his most ambitious work, Hayek describes how the economy's structure of production depends on the characteristics of capital goods—durability, complementarity, substitutability, specificity, and so on. This structure can be described by the various "investment periods" of inputs, an extension of Böhm-Bawerk's notion of "roundaboutness," the degree to which production takes up resources over time.[13]

In *Prices and Production* and *Monetary Theory and the Trade Cycle*,[14] Hayek showed how monetary injections, by lowering the rate of interest below what Mises (following Wicksell) called its "natural rate," distort the economy's intertemporal structure of production.[15] Most theories of the effects of money on prices and output (then and since) consider only the effects of the total money supply on the price level and aggregate output or investment. The Austrian theory, as developed by Mises and Hayek, focuses on the way money enters the economy ("injection effects"), and how this affects relative prices and investment in particular sectors. In Hayek's framework, investments in some stages of production are "malinvestments" if they do not help to align the structure of production to consumers' intertemporal preferences. The reduction in interest rates caused by credit expansion directs resources toward

[12]F.A. Hayek, *The Pure Theory of Capital* (Chicago: University of Chicago Press, 1941).

[13]Hayek ultimately rejected Böhm-Bawerk's "average period of production" as a useful concept, though Hayek had used it earlier in *Prices and Production*. See Hayek, *Hayek on Hayek*, p. 141.

[14]F.A. Hayek, *Monetary Theory and the Trade Cycle*, N. Kaldor and H.M. Croome, trans. (New York: Harcourt, Brace, 1933).

[15]Hayek thought the more important case was when the market interest rate was kept constant despite a rise in the natural interest rate. In his writings, however, he focused on the expositionally easier case when credit expansion lowers the market interest rate below an unchanged natural rate.

capital-intensive processes and early stages of production (whose investment demands are more interest-rate elastic), thus "lengthening" the period of production. If interest rates had fallen because consumers had changed their preferences to favor future over present consumption, then the longer time structure of production would have been an appropriate, coordinating response. A fall in interest rates caused by credit expansion, however, would have been a "false signal," causing changes in the structure of production that do not accord with consumers' intertemporal preferences.[16] The boom generated by the increase in investment is artificial. Eventually, market participants come to realize that there are not enough savings to complete all the new projects; the boom becomes a bust as these malinvestments are discovered and liquidated.[17] Every artificial boom induced by credit expansion, then, is self-reversing. Recovery consists of liquidating the malinvestments induced by the lowering of interest rates below their natural levels, thus restoring the time structure of production so that it accords with consumers' intertemporal preferences.

### KNOWLEDGE, PRICES, AND COMPETITION AS A DISCOVERY PROCEDURE

Hayek's writings on dispersed knowledge and spontaneous order are also widely known, but more controversial. In "Economics and Knowledge"[18] and "The Use of Knowledge in Society,"[19] Hayek argued that the central economic problem facing society is not, as is commonly expressed in textbooks, the allocation of given resources among competing ends.

---

[16]For most of his career, Hayek viewed a system of fractional-reserve banking as inherently unstable, endorsing a role (in principle) for government stabilization of the money supply. In later writings, beginning with *The Constitution of Liberty* (Chicago: University of Chicago Press, 1960), and culminating in *Denationalization of Money: An Analysis of the Theory and Practice of Concurrent Currencies* (London: Institute of Economic Affairs, 1976), he argued in favor of competition among private issuers of fiat money.

[17]Anticipating modern cycle theories Hayek recognized that the behavior of the cycle depends on expectations about future price and interest-rate movements. But Hayek did not believe agents could know the real structure of the economy, to correctly distinguish movements in interest rates generated by changes in consumers' intertemporal preferences from those generated by changes in the money supply. See F.A. Hayek, "Price Expectations, Monetary Disturbances, and Malinvestments," in idem, *Profits, Interest, and Investment* (London: Routledge, 1939).

[18]F.A. Hayek, "Economics and Knowledge," *Economica* 4 (1937): 33–54.

[19]F.A. Hayek, "The Use of Knowledge in Society," *American Economic Review* 35 (September 1945): 519–30.

> It is rather a problem of how to secure the best use of resources known to any of the members of society, for ends whose relative importance only those individuals know. Or, to put it briefly, it is a problem of the utilization of knowledge not given to anyone in its totality.[20]

Much of the knowledge necessary for running the economic system, Hayek contended, is in the form not of "scientific" or technical knowledge—the conscious awareness of the rules governing natural and social phenomena—but of "tacit" knowledge, the idiosyncratic, dispersed bits of understanding of "circumstances of time and place." This tacit knowledge is often not consciously known even to those who possess it, and can never be communicated to a central authority. The market tends to use this tacit knowledge through a type of "discovery procedure"[21] by which this information is unknowingly transmitted throughout the economy as an unintended consequence of individuals pursuing their own ends.[22] Indeed, Hayek's distinction between the neoclassical notion of "competition," identified as a set of equilibrium conditions (number of market participants, characteristics of the product, and so on), and the older notion of competition as a rivalrous process, has been widely influential in Austrian economics.[23]

For Hayek, market competition generates a particular kind of order —an order that is the product "of human action but not of human design" (a phrase Hayek borrowed from Adam Ferguson). This "spontaneous order" is a system that comes about through the independent actions of many individuals, and produces overall benefits unintended and mostly unforeseen by those whose actions bring it about. To distinguish between this kind of order and that of a deliberate, planned system, Hayek used the Greek terms *cosmos* for a spontaneous order, and

---

[20]Ibid., p. 520.

[21]F.A. Hayek, "Competition as a Discovery Procedure," in idem, *New Studies in Philosophy, Politics, and Economics* (Chicago: University of Chicago Press, 1978), pp. 179–90.

[22]Hayek's use of an argument from ignorance as a defense of the market is unusual. Modern economists typically require assumptions of hyperrationality—complete and perfect information, rational expectations, perfect markets, and so on—to justify market allocations as "efficient." In the new microeconomics literature on information and incentives, theorists like Joseph Stiglitz have used deviations from these assumptions of perfection to reach a verdict of market *failure* and to provide a rationale for government intervention. For Hayek, by contrast, the fact that agents are not hyperrational is an argument not against individual freedom, but against state planning and social control.

[23]F.A. Hayek, "The Meaning of Competition," in idem, *Individualism and Economic Order* (Chicago: University of Chicago Press, 1948), pp. 92–106.

*taxis* for a consciously planned one.[24] Examples of a *cosmos* include the market system as a whole, money, the common law, and even language. A *taxis*, by contrast, is a designed or constructed organization, like a firm or bureau; these are the "islands of conscious power in [the] ocean of unconscious cooperation like lumps of butter coagulating in a pail of buttermilk."[25]

Most commentators view Hayek's work on knowledge, discovery, and competition as an outgrowth of his participation in the socialist calculation debate of the 1920s and 1930s. The socialists erred, in Hayek's view, in failing to see that the economy as a whole is necessarily a spontaneous order and can never be deliberately made over in the way that the operators of a planned order can exercise control over their organization. This is because planned orders can handle only problems of strictly limited complexity. Spontaneous orders, by contrast, tend to evolve through a process of natural selection, and therefore do not need to be designed or even understood by a single mind.

## HAYEK AND AUSTRIAN ECONOMICS

Clearly, the Austrian revival owes much to Hayek. But are Hayek's writings really "Austrian economics"—part of a separate, recognizable tradition—or should we regard them, instead, as an original, deeply personal, contribution?[26] Some observers charge that Hayek's later work, particularly after he began to turn away from technical economics, shows more influence of Karl Popper than of Menger or Mises: one critic speaks of "Hayek I" and "Hayek II"; another writes on "Hayek's Transformation."[27]

---

[24]F.A. Hayek, "The Confusion of Language in Political Thought," in idem, *New Studies in Philosophy, Politics, and Economics*, pp. 71–97. Earlier, Hayek had used "organism" and "organization," borrowed from Mises, to distinguish the two; this is the distinction cited by Ronald Coase in his famous 1937 article, "The Nature of the Firm," *Economica* N.S., 4 (1937): 386–405. See F.A. Hayek, "The Trend of Economic Thinking," in idem, *The Trend of Economic Thinking*, vol. 3, *The Collected Works of F.A. Hayek*, W.W. Bartley, III, and Stephen Kresge, eds. (Chicago: University of Chicago Press, 1991), pp. 17–34.

[25]D.H. Robertson, quoted in Coase, "The Nature of the Firm," p. 35.

[26]Wieser's have generally been considered a personal contribution, by Hayek himself and others.

[27]For Hayeks I and II, see T.W. Hutchison, "Austrians on Philosophy and Method (since Menger)," in idem, *The Politics and Philosophy of Economics: Marxians, Keynesians, and Austrians* (New York and London: New York University Press, 1984), pp. 203–32; for the "transformation," see Bruce J. Caldwell, "Hayek's Transformation," *History of Political Economy* 20 (Winter 1988): 513–41.

It is true that Popper had a significant impact on Hayek's mature thought. Of greater interest is the precise nature of Hayek's relationship with Mises. Undoubtedly, no economist had a greater impact on Hayek's thinking than Mises—not even Wieser, from whom Hayek learned his craft, but who died in 1927 when Hayek was still a young man. In addition, Mises clearly considered Hayek the brightest of his generation.[28] Yet, as Hayek noted, he was from the beginning always something less than a pure follower:

> Although I do owe [Mises] a decisive stimulus at a crucial point of my intellectual development, and continuous inspiration through a decade, I have perhaps most profited from his teaching because I was not initially his student at the university, an innocent young man who took his word for gospel, but came to him as a trained economist, versed in a parallel branch of Austrian economics [the Wieser branch] from which he gradually, but never completely, won me over.[29]

Much has been written on Hayek's and Mises's views on the socialist calculation debate.[30] The issue is whether a socialist economy is "impossible," as Mises charged in 1920, or simply less efficient or more difficult to implement. Hayek maintained later that Mises's "central thesis was not, as it is sometimes misleadingly put, that socialism is impossible, but that it cannot achieve an efficient utilization of resources."[31] That interpretation is itself subject to dispute. Hayek is arguing here against the standard view on economic calculation, found for instance in Schumpeter.[32] This view holds that Mises's original statement of the impossibility of economic calculation under socialism was refuted by Oskar Lange, Fred Taylor, and Abba Lerner, and that later modifications by Hayek and Robbins amounted to an admission that a socialist economy is possible in theory but difficult in practice because knowledge is decentralized and incentives are weak. Hayek's response in the cited text, that Mises's actual position has been exaggerated, receives support

---

[28]Margit von Mises, in *My Years with Ludwig von Mises*, 2nd enlarged ed. (Cedar Falls, Iowa: Center for Futures Education, 1984), p. 133, recalls of her husband's seminar in New York that "Lu met every new student hopeful that one of them might develop into a second Hayek."

[29]F.A. Hayek, "Coping with Ignorance," *Imprimis* 7, no. 7 (July 1978): 1–6.

[30]Hayek's writings on socialist economic calculation are collected in F.A. Hayek, *Socialism and War: Essays, Documents, Reviews*, vol. 10, *The Collected Works of F.A. Hayek*, Bruce Caldwell, ed. (Chicago: University of Chicago Press, 1997).

[31]Hayek, *The Fortunes of Liberalism*, p. 127.

[32]Joseph A. Schumpeter, *Capitalism, Socialism, and Democracy* (New York: Harper and Row, 1942), pp. 172–86.

from the primary revisionist historian of the calculation debate, Don Lavoie, who states that the

> central arguments advanced by Hayek and Robbins did not constitute a "retreat" from Mises, but rather a clarification directing the challenge to the later versions of central planning. . . . Although comments by both Hayek and Robbins about computational difficulties of the [later approaches] were responsible for misleading interpretations of their arguments, in fact their main contributions were fully consistent with Mises's challenge.[33]

Israel Kirzner similarly contends that Mises's and Hayek's positions should be viewed together as an early attempt to elaborate the Austrian "entrepreneurial-discovery" view of the market process.[34] Joseph Salerno argues, by contrast, in favor of the traditional view—that Mises's original calculation problem is different from the discovery-process problem emphasized by Lavoie and Kirzner.[35]

Furthermore, Hayek's later emphasis on group selection and spontaneous order is not shared by Mises, although there are elements of this line of thought in Menger. A clue to this difference is in Hayek's statement that "Mises himself was still much more a child of the rationalist tradition of the Enlightenment and of continental, rather than of English, liberalism . . . than I am myself."[36] This is a reference to the "two types of liberalism" to which Hayek frequently refers: the continental rationalist or utilitarian tradition, which emphasizes reason and man's ability to shape his surroundings, and the English common-law tradition, which stresses the limits to reason and the "spontaneous" forces of evolution.[37]

Recently, the relationship between Mises and Hayek has become a full-fledged "dehomogenization" debate, with some seeing Hayek's emphasis on knowledge and discovery as substantially different from Mises's emphasis on purposeful human action. Indeed, it has been argued that there are two strands of modern Austrian economics, both

---

[33]Don Lavoie, *Rivalry and Central Planning: The Socialist Calculation Debate Reconsidered* (Cambridge: Cambridge University Press, 1985), p. 20.

[34]Israel M. Kirzner, "The Socialist Calculation Debate: Lessons for Austrians," *Review of Austrian Economics* 2 (1988): 1–18.

[35]Joseph T. Salerno, "Ludwig von Mises as Social Rationalist," *Review of Austrian Economics* 4 (1990): 26–54.

[36]Hayek, "Coping with Ignorance."

[37]For more on the complex and subtle Mises–Hayek relationship, see Peter G. Klein, "Introduction" to Hayek, *The Fortunes of Liberalism*.

descended from Menger. One, the Wieser–Hayek strand, focuses on dispersed knowledge and the price system as a device for communicating knowledge. Another, the Böhm-Bawerk–Mises strand, focuses on monetary calculation (or "appraisal," meaning anticipation of future prices) based on existing money prices. Thus, the dispute is whether the differences between Hayek and Mises are primarily matters of emphasis and language or matters of substance.[38]

Regardless, there is widespread agreement that Hayek ranks among the greatest members of the Austrian School, and among the leading economists of the twentieth century. His work continues to be influential in business-cycle theory, comparative economic systems, political and social philosophy, legal theory, and even cognitive psychology. Hayek's writings are not always easy to follow—he describes himself as "puzzler" or "muddler" rather than a "master of his subject"—and this may have contributed to the variety of interpretations his work has aroused.[39] Partly for this reason, Hayek remains one of the most intriguing intellectual figures of our time.

---

[38]See, for example, Joseph T. Salerno, "Mises and Hayek Dehomogenized," *Review of Austrian Economics* 6, no. 2 (1993): 113–46; and Leland B. Yeager, "Mises and Hayek on Calculation and Knowledge," *Review of Austrian Economics* 7, no. 2 (1994): 93–109. Rothbard identifies three distinctive and often clashing paradigms within Austrian economics:

> Misesian praxeology, the Hayek–Kirzner emphasis on the market as transmission of knowledge and coordination of plans—rather than the Misesian emphasis on continuing coordination of prices, and the ultra-subjectivism of [Ludwig] Lachmann.

Review of Bruce Caldwell and Stephan Boehm, eds., "Austrian Economics: Tensions and New Directions," *Southern Economic Journal* 61, no. 2 (October 1994): 559–60. For a contrary view, see Kirzner's review of Jack Birner and Rudy Van Zijp, "Hayek, Co-ordination, and Evolution," *Southern Economic Journal* 61, no. 4 (April 1995): 1243–44:

> To fail to see the common economic understanding shared by Mises and Hayek, is to have been needlessly misled by superficial differences in exposition and emphasis. To compound this failure by perceiving a clash, among modern Austrians, of "Hayekians" versus "Misesians," is to convert an interpretive failure into a *dogmengeschictliche* nightmare.

[39]Along with himself, Hayek named Wieser and Frank Knight as representative puzzlers, and Böhm-Bawerk, Joseph Schumpeter, and Jacob Viner as representative masters of their subjects. As Hayek recalled,

> I owed whatever worthwhile new ideas I ever had to not being able to remember what every competent specialist is supposed to have at his fingertips. Whenever I saw a new light on something, it was as the result of a painful effort to reconstruct an argument which most competent economists would effortlessly and instantly reproduce.

SELECTED READINGS

Blaug, Mark. 1993. "Hayek Revisited." *Critical Review* 7, no. 1:51–60.

Caldwell, Bruce J. 1988. "Hayek's Transformation." *History of Political Economy* 20 (Winter): 513–41.

——. 1997. "Hayek and Socialism." *Journal of Economic Literature* 35, no. 4 (December): 1856–90.

Craver, Earlene. 1986. "The Emigration of the Austrian Economists." *History of Political Economy* 18, no. 1:1–32.

Garrison, Roger W. 1978. "Austrian Macroeconomics: A Diagrammatical Exposition." In *New Directions in Austrian Economics.* Louis M. Spadaro, ed. Kansas City: Sheed Andrews and McMeel. Pp. 167–204.

Garrison, Roger W., and Israel M. Kirzner. 1987. "Hayek, Friedrich August von." In *The New Palgrave Dictionary of Economics.* Vol. 2. John Eatwell, Murray Milgate, and Peter Newman, eds. London: Macmillan. Pp. 609–14.

Gray, John. 1986. *Hayek on Liberty.* 2nd Rev. Ed. Oxford: Basil Blackwell.

Hayek, F. A. 1997. *Socialism and War: Essays, Documents, Reviews.* Vol. 10. *The Collected Works of F.A. Hayek.* Bruce Caldwell, ed. Chicago: University of Chicago Press, and London: Routledge.

——. 1995. *Contra Keynes and Cambridge: Essays, Correspondence.* Vol. 9. *The Collected Works of F.A. Hayek.* Bruce Caldwell, ed. Chicago: University of Chicago Press, and London: Routledge.

——. 1994. *Hayek on Hayek: An Autobiographical Dialogue.* Stephen Kresge and Leif Wenar, eds. Chicago: University of Chicago Press, and London: Routledge.

——. 1992. *The Fortunes of Liberalism.* Vol. 4. *The Collected Works of F.A. Hayek.* Peter G. Klein, ed. Chicago: University of Chicago Press, and London: Routledge.

——. 1948. *Individualism and Economic Order.* Chicago: University of Chicago Press.

——. 1944. *The Road to Serfdom.* Chicago: University of Chicago Press.

——. 1941. *The Pure Theory of Capital.* Chicago: University of Chicago Press.

——. 1933. *Monetary Theory and the Trade Cycle.* London: Jonathan Cape.

——. 1935. *Prices and Production.* 2nd Rev. Ed. London: Routledge and Kegan Paul.

Hutchison, T.W. 1984. "Austrians on Philosophy and Method (since Menger)." In idem, *The Politics and Philosophy of Economics: Marxians, Keynesians, and Austrians.* New York: New York University Press. Pp. 203–32.

Kirzner, Israel M. 1988. "The Socialist Calculation Debate: Lessons for Austrians." *Review of Austrian Economics* 2:1–18.

Lavoie, Don. 1985. *Rivalry and Central Planning: The Socialist Calculation Debate Reconsidered.* Cambridge: Cambridge University Press.

O'Driscoll, Gerald P., Jr. 1977. *Economics as a Coordination Problem: The Contribution of Friedrich A. Hayek.* Kansas City: Sheed Andrews and McMeel.

Rothbard, Murray N. 1997. "The Present State of Austrian Economics." In idem, *The Logic of Action.* Cheltenham, U.K.: Edward Elgar. Vol. 1. Pp. 111–72.

Salerno, Joseph T. 1993. "Mises and Hayek Dehomogenized." *Review of Austrian Economics* 6, no. 2: 113–46.

Vanberg, Viktor J. 1994. "Spontaneous Market Order and Social Rules: A Critical Examination of F.A. Hayek's Theory of Cultural Evolution." In idem, *Rules and Choice in Economics*. London and New York: Routledge. Pp. 75–94.

# 13
# WILLIAM H. HUTT: THE "CLASSICAL" AUSTRIAN

JOHN B. EGGER

*William Harold Hutt*
*1899–1988*

THE AUSTRIAN SCHOOL'S defining precepts, concisely specified by Carl Menger in 1871, were consistent with important doctrines like rivalrous competition that had characterized economics from its earliest days. Though more true of Continental than of British writers hampered by an objective concept of value, Menger's insights could be folded into an evolutionary tradition that continued to develop—with a few backsliders like Marshall and Pareto—until the 1930s. This decade saw the Austro–Continental–Classical blend torn apart by the domination of microeconomics by mathematics and perfect competition, and by the wholesale overthrow of monetary theory by Keynes's macroeconomics. The economists whose method and philosophy best qualified them to resist these detours, and to continue the pre-1930s development of economic theory, were those closest to the Austrian tradition. In this sense, it was the mainstream's descent into mathematical microeconomics and Keynesian macroeconomics that made the Austrian School distinct.

This is the world in which William Harold Hutt found himself at the early stages of his academic career, but understanding his relationship to the Austrian School requires a more detailed look at his formative years. Born in London to working-class parents, Hutt earned a Bachelor of Commerce degree from the London School of Economics (LSE) in 1924. He was favorably impressed by some of his teachers: Lillian Knowles on economic history, H.C. Gutteridge on law, T.E. Gregory and

Herbert Foxwell on money and finance, and Edwin Cannan.[1] Hutt described Cannan, who taught him elementary economics and then money after Foxwell's retirement, as "the leading influence to which I was subjected during my first three years at L.S.E. . . . a remarkably wise and independent thinker."[2]

From 1924 until 1928, Hutt worked for publisher Sir Ernest Benn, whom he very much respected. Benn was so impressed with Hutt's first published article—"The Factory System of the Early Nineteenth Century," written in 1925—that he promoted Hutt to manage The Individualist Bookshop, Ltd. But Hutt continued to take courses informally at LSE, and when his friend from their undergraduate days, Arnold Plant, advertised for a Senior Lecturer for the University of Cape Town, Hutt applied. With strong support from Benn and Professor Cannan, he obtained the post, and arrived in South Africa in March 1928. (John R. Hicks, headed for a temporary post at Witwatersrand, was aboard the same ship.) Two years later, Plant received a professorship at LSE, and Hutt was appointed Chair of Commerce (later Dean of the Faculty of Commerce).

This background suggests much about Hutt's approach to economics. Austrian by neither birth nor residence, he could know nothing of Mises's *Privatseminars* in Vienna. He apparently did not read German, and Mises's *The Theory of Money and Credit* was not translated until 1934. Hutt and Hayek were contemporaries, in fact precisely the same age, but differed in country, culture, and language, and while Hayek's earliest works dated from about the time of Hutt's "Factory System," they were not widely known in the English-speaking world until years later. One might hope that Hutt had learned something at LSE of Menger and Böhm-Bawerk, but a strong Jevons and Marshall influence (especially from Foxwell) was more likely, and Hayek discovered in 1930 that Böhm-Bawerk was not well-known at LSE.

In short, until the early 1930s, when *The Theory of Money and Credit* was translated and Hayek began his flurry of activity at LSE, Hutt had no significant exposure to works that we now identify with the Austrian School. By then, though, Hutt was in Cape Town with heavy responsibilities as the Chair of the Faculty of Commerce. He was always a creative and independent scholar, as even his first article suggests, but his early- and

---

[1]See Edwin Cannan, *The Paper Pound of 1797–1821* (London: King, 1921); and idem, *A History of the Theories of Production and Distribution in English Political Economy from 1776 to 1848* (London: Percival, 1917). Also Alan Ebenstein, *Collected Works of Edwin Cannan*, 8 vols. (London: Routledge/Thoemmes Press, 1999).

[2]W.H. Hutt, unpublished memoirs, ca. 1984, p. 39.

mid-1920s training at LSE help to explain why he later identified himself as a *classical* economist.

Although Hutt and other critics of the Keynesian Revolution—including Arthur Marget and Henry Hazlitt—considered their work to be in the classical tradition, as the revolution's stunning popularity through the 1940s and 1950s pushed economists' memory of earlier monetary theory further into the background, Hutt and Hazlitt (Marget had left academic economics after the World War II and died in 1962) found themselves increasingly sharing perspectives with the School that had most firmly and consistently upheld pre-Keynesian monetary theory: the Austrians. Neither seems to have been attracted much to the aggregative, positivist method of the Chicago School's monetarism, a reaction to Keynesianism that to some extent shared its method. Hutt considered the Austrians to be the true heirs of the classical tradition with which, understandably, he preferred to be identified.

"The Factory System of the Early Nineteenth Century" was published in *Economica* (1926) and became more widely known when Hayek included it in *Capitalism and the Historians* (1954). Hutt's career change and the duties of shaping a satisfactory business curriculum in Cape Town explain a five-year hiatus, but his return to publishing on academic economics was a blockbuster: *The Theory of Collective Bargaining*.[3] Perhaps partly because his father had been a journeyman printer of modest income, the use of economic theory to understand the wages and employment of labor was one of Hutt's lifelong primary concerns. This short book—re-issued in 1975 and 1980 with addenda but its 1930 text unchanged—disputed prevailing beliefs that labor was at a "disadvantage" and that the labor market was inherently one of bilateral monopoly that left the wage rate "indeterminate." Peppered with quotations from British and American economists from Adam Smith onward, Hutt sought to correct others' views of the classical tradition, to contribute to it, and to offer practical advice on governments' labor policies. Though he circulated the book widely, its message was out of step with politically powerful doctrines, and it was largely ignored.

When he returned to this theme with *The Strike-Threat System* in 1973, his more thorough analysis of the impoverishing effect of labor unions and pro-union legislation could draw on four decades of Austrian scholarship unavailable in 1930.[4] It enabled him to reinforce his

---

[3]W. H. Hutt, *The Theory of Collective Bargaining* (London: P.S. King, 1930).

[4]W.H. Hutt, *The Strike-Threat System: The Economic Consequences of Collective Bargaining* (New Rochelle, N.Y.: Arlington House, 1973). When asked to review this

argument that unions gain at the expense of other labor, not capital, and that the transfer reduces total output. The book makes many references to Böhm-Bawerk, Mises, and Hayek. Hutt identified the principal improvement between 1930 and the 1970s as "the emphasis I now place on the *composition* of the assets stock and the composition of the stock of complementary assimilated knowledge and skills,"[5] an insight attributable to the Austrian School's focus on the complementarities among capital goods and labor skills within particular plans.

Hutt's perception of the ability of powerful groups—including, but not limited to, labor unions—to use the political process for private gain, despite general impoverishment, led him to the second of his three principal interests in economics, now known as public choice. His first South African article—and his second article on economics—was "Economic Aspects of the Report of the Poor White Commission," in 1933. (His best known work on the South African sociopolitical system, *The Economics of the Color Bar,* identified apartheid as a device by which white unions enlisted the force of government to prohibit non-white laborers from competing with them.[6]) His next few years were productive, especially considering his deanship, with nine articles on competition and monopoly, predatory pricing, and economic legislation.[7]

But it was his second book that has drawn much praise. *Economists and the Public* was published in the same year as Keynes's *General Theory*, and many economists have wished that Hutt's thoughtful work had

---

book, Ludwig von Mises said, "Professor Hutt's rank among the outstanding economists of our age is not contested by any competent critic."

[5]W.H. Hutt, *The Theory of Collective Bargaining, 1930–1975* (San Francisco: Cato Institute, 1980), p. xviii.

[6]W.H. Hutt, *The Economics of the Color Bar* (London: Andre Deutsch for The Institute of Economic Affairs, 1964).

[7]Hutt's published articles in these subjects are: "The Significance of State Interference With Interest Rates," *South African Journal of Economics* 1 (September 1933): 365–68; "Economic Aspects of the Report of the Poor White Commission," *South African Journal of Economics* 1 (September 1933): 281–90; "Economic Method and the Concept of Competition," *South African Journal of Economics* 2 (March 1934): 1–23; "Co-ordination and the Size of the Firm," *South African Journal of Economics* 2 (December 1934): 383–402; "The Nature of Aggressive Selling," *Economica* 2 (August 1935): 298–320; "Logical Issues in the Study of Industrial Legislation," *South African Journal of Economics* 3 (March 1935): 26–42; "Natural and Contrived Scarcities," *South African Journal of Economics* 3 (September 1935): 345–53; "Discriminating Monopoly and the Consumer," *Economic Journal* 46 (March 1936): 61–79; "The Price Mechanism and Economic Immobility," *South African Journal of Economics* 4 (September 1936): 319–30.

received the greater attention.[8] James Buchanan, a Nobel laureate for his own work in public choice who brought Hutt to the University of Virginia after Hutt's retirement in 1965, called it "one of Hutt's best works," and Arthur Seldon wrote that only Hutt's concern about Keynesianism kept him from being recognized as a public-choice pioneer. Hutt again considered the book a contribution to the British classical tradition, and included many references to it, particularly to John Stuart Mill, whose utilitarianism Hutt found appealing. The work's principal theme was that economists served the public best by taking a long view, focusing on policies that promoted the wealth-creating competitive market and ignoring whether they were politically feasible at the moment. (He reiterated this in *Politically Impossible. . . ?*[9]) He feared that concern with political feasibility would, inevitably, draw economists into the advocacy of politically attractive policies that served special interests to the detriment of society. Perhaps he sensed the need for such counsel during the Great Depression, but Keynes's work, which appeared in time for Hutt to acknowledge by squeezing in a last-minute paragraph, promoted precisely the destructive but politically irresistible short-run view against which Hutt warned. Keynes's book shaped decades of policy and teaching; Hutt's must be swept free of dust from library shelves. No one acquainted with Austrian economics would dispute that we would all be wealthier and smarter if their fates had been reversed.

Some readers will not embrace all of Hutt's advice. His utilitarian philosophy, which the examples of Mises and Hazlitt show is not objectionable in itself, and his conviction that humanity was best served by competitive institutions with flexible wages and prices, led him to oppose not only government coercion but "economic coercion and private monopoly." As early as his 1934 "aggressive selling" (predatory pricing) article and at least as late as 1977, Hutt argued for strong antitrust enforcement against private collusion, whether among laborers or producers, because it produced impoverishing and anti-social "contrived scarcities" hindering the market's ability to address "natural scarcities" (these terms are the title of a 1935 article).[10] He coined the term "consumers' sovereignty,"[11] a valuable response to the economically illiterate

---

[8]Hutt, *Economists and the Public* (London: Jonathan Cape, 1936).

[9]Hutt, *Politically Impossible. . . ?* (London: Institute of Economic Affairs, 1971).

[10]Cf. Hutt, "The Nature of Aggressive Selling," pp. 298–320, and idem, "Natural and Contrived Scarcities," pp. 345–53.

[11]See W.H. Hutt, "The Concept of Consumers' Sovereignty," *Economic Journal* 50 (March 1940): 66–77.

who identify businessmen with feudal nobility, but fundamentally misleading: as Rothbard responded in 1962, there is only "individual" sovereignty.[12]

The year 1939 saw Hutt's publication of *The Theory of Idle Resources*, a brilliant and creative work motivated by a perceived gap in existing analyses of unemployment, the Depression, and the popularity of Keynes's *General Theory*.[13] It was reissued in 1977 with Hutt's extensive addenda. Rewarding reading over a half-century later, its principal point is that one cannot conclude that a resource is "idle"—in the sense of not performing its best economic function—simply by looking at it. One must examine the causal economic process to discern the economic function in which a seemingly idle resource is engaged; sometimes "idleness" is its best use. Job search, for example, is formally considered unemployment (emphatically, however, not by Hutt), but is often a more productive activity for a worker with specific skills than an instantly attainable job flipping hamburgers, and changes in demand expected to be temporary can make a machine's or factory's apparent idleness mere "pseudo-idleness," a more productive "use" than costly conversion to other temporary uses.

In *Idle Resources*, Hutt continued his criticism of both government and private coercion, envisioning a free market with only "natural," and no "contrived," scarcities. Private coercion consisted of service-restricting practices of both labor unions and producer cartels, and it produced forms of idleness that policy can and should address—though only by preventing the activities that created them. Hutt repeatedly warned that the public works and inflation policies advocated by Keynes and his followers, whether a response to coercive idleness best addressed by legislatively rooting out its causes or to a superficial failure to recognize productive "pseudo-idleness" like frictional unemployment, would divert resources away from the productive uses they would find most quickly in an unfettered market. He vigorously retained this theme, which he shared with Hayek and Mises, throughout his life.

By the mid-1950s, Hutt had published about three dozen articles on a wide variety of economic topics. His 1943 book *Plan for Reconstruction* has been lauded by James Buchanan, and his 1954 contribution to a *festschrift* to Mises, "The Yield from Money Held," has been praised by

[12]Murray N. Rothbard, *Man, Economy, and State* (Auburn, Ala.: Ludwig von Mises Institute, [1962] 1993), pp. 561–63.

[13]W.H. Hutt, *The Theory of Idle Resources: A Study in Definition* (Indianapolis, Ind.: Liberty Press, [1939] 1977).

distinguished monetary theorists like George Selgin.[14] (It was Hutt's first significant work in the third of his three economic interests, monetary theory.) By this time, the influence of Mises and Hayek on Hutt's thinking had become noticeable, though of course much of his earlier work was consistent with Austrian theory. In 1955, the Foundation for Economic Education invited him to a Pennsylvania seminar, his first trip to the United States. Hutt, journalist George Schwartz, and Ludwig von Mises were the three lecturers, and he credits the discussion with the impetus to write the book that is probably his best known: *Keynesianism—Retrospect and Prospect*.[15] His personal recollection of Mises is interesting:

> Mises had inspired me for many years before I first met him, through his impressive contributions in articles and books, but it was not until 1955 . . . that I could first greet him face to face. He was physically smaller than I had expected, but I was immediately struck by his really remarkable personality—a magnetism and tenacity created by his deep emotional attachment to a free economy and the institutions on which it had to rely. His lectures, like his writings, were austere, although his verbal expositions were by no means devoid of an informal, natural sense of humor. The warmth of our relations was sustained until his death. But his lectures in 1955 were a powerful inspiration which influenced my own subsequent work.[16]

Almost inevitably, Hutt's attention returned to Keynes. Two other economists born in 1899, Hayek and Marget, had devoted much of their productive thirties to attempts to restore pre-Keynesian sanity to the economics profession; neither achieved the slightest short-run success, and each moved on to other things. Hazlitt, a few years older, apparently felt the same pressures as Hutt; virtually contemporaneously, Hazlitt published his *The Failure of the "New Economics."*[17] Hutt's *Keynesianism* and Hazlitt's *Failure* are very different in style, but they shared (with the almost universally ignored Marget's two-volume [1938 and 1942] *The*

---

[14]W.H. Hutt, *Plan for Reconstruction* (London: Kegan Paul, 1943); idem, "The Yield from Money Held," in *On Freedom and Free Enterprise: Essays in Honor of Ludwig von Mises*, Mary Sennholz, ed. (Princeton, N.J.: Van Nostrand, 1956).

[15]W.H. Hutt, *Keynesianism—Retrospect and Prospect: A Critical Restatement of Basic Economic Principles* (Chicago: Henry Regnery, 1963).

[16]Hutt, "Memoirs," p. 93. Since Hutt had been involved in the formation of the Mont Pèlerin Society (1947) and had attended the second and many other of its subsequent general meetings, it is surprising that he did not meet Mises until 1955.

[17]Henry Hazlitt, *The Failure of the "New Economics": An Analysis of the Keynesian Fallacies* (New Rochelle, N. Y.: Arlington House, 1959).

*Theory of Prices*) the observation that, in Keynes's *General Theory*, "what is true is not new, and what is new is not true."

Published at the peak of Keynesian policy and academic influence, and somewhat hampered by Hutt's idiosyncratic terminology, the four-hundred-and-fifty page *Keynesianism* had no noticeable effect on the profession. Although its Preface thanks Ludwig Lachmann for valuable discussions, and Mises and Marget for their "courageous and independent work," the book contains few citations to Mises, and even fewer to Hayek. Nonetheless, younger economists now working in the Austrian tradition will find the book a delight. (*The Keynesian Episode*[18] should be considered its updated and Americanized second edition.) Subtitled "A Critical Restatement of Basic Economic Principles," it describes the Keynesian doctrine and its appeal, then analyzes the coordinating role of market prices and the natures of money, income, saving, and consumption. Hutt then specifically targets such standard Keynesian fare as "the multiplier," "the accelerator," and the liquidity-preference theory of interest.

Again, Hutt produced a magnificent work Austrians would love to claim as one of their own, but which he himself viewed as thoroughly classical in nature. Keynes considered the foundation of his own work his refutation of Say's Law, for which he coined the phrase "supply creates its own demand" to express; the central theme of Hutt's *Keynesianism* was to reassert the validity and relevance of Say's perceptiveness. Later, he focused precisely on this, with his provocative short study *A Rehabilitation of Say's Law*.[19] By then, he was delighted to find works by Clower, Leijonhufvud, and Yeager courageously advocating the use of forms of Say's Law.[20]

The theme of *Keynesianism* was one that those unacquainted with Hutt may have learned from Mises or Hayek, but which Hutt seems to have developed directly from Say: depressions and unemployment result from mispricing, not from any supposed deficiency of aggregate demand. Hutt found Keynes's structure of aggregated concepts so confusing that he declared it "hinders the perception of certain things as well as the saying of them,"[21] and he professed great admiration for the

---

[18]W.H. Hutt, *The Keynesian Episode: A Reassessment* (Indianapolis, Ind.: Liberty Press, 1979).

[19]W.H. Hutt, *A Rehabilitation of Say's Law* (Athens: Ohio University Press, 1974).

[20]Ibid., p. 48.

[21]Hutt, *Keynesianism-Retrospect and Prospect*, p. ix.

brilliant young macroeconomists of the 1970s and 1980s who produced valid insights despite being hobbled with these concepts and language. He viewed Keynes's theory as an apologia for the basest political goal of power, one that refused to address the institutions hindering price adjustments and instead advocated the use of monetary and fiscal policy. Using macroeconomic policy to resolve microeconomic problems, Hutt pointed out, inevitably conceals and exacerbates the problem by diverting resources into uses other than those which an unhampered market would have produced. Whatever they may do to measurable statistics, which he had noted in 1939 could not measure "idleness," these policies are impoverishing. By the 1970s, Hutt optimistically perceived the emergence of the economics profession from "the Keynesian episode" (which Leland Yeager, with greater descriptive accuracy, called "the Keynesian diversion"[22]), and its return to pre-Keynesian methods and truths.

Hutt was an enthusiastic member of the Mont Pèlerin Society, and enjoyed its meetings immensely. He was thrilled when Hayek won the Nobel Memorial Prize in Economics, and attended many Austrian and libertarian conferences into the final years of his life. Many younger Austrians remember him as a kind and courtly man, intellectually sharp and devoted to liberty. Those unfamiliar with his work have a real treat yet ahead. Of his principal works, I would begin with *Keynesianism* and *Idle Resources*, then *Collective Bargaining* and *Strike-Threat*, and finally *Economists*. One may wonder how much greater his effect on economics might have been if he had chosen a different career path. Nonetheless, the exciting rediscovery of the Austrian tradition foretells the day when economists widely know and appreciate the works of William Harold Hutt.

## SELECTED READINGS

Hutt, William Harold. 1980. *The Theory of Collective Bargaining 1930–1975*. San Francisco: Cato Institute.

——. 1979. *The Keynesian Episode: A Reassessment*. Indianapolis, Ind.: Liberty Press.

——. [1939] 1977. *The Theory of Idle Resources: A Study in Definition*. Indianapolis, Ind.: Liberty Press.

——. 1974. *A Rehabilitation of Say's Law*. Athens: Ohio University Press.

——. 1973. *The Strike-Threat System: The Economic Consequences of Collective Bargaining*. New Rochelle, N.Y.: Arlington House.

---

[22]Leland B. Yeager, "The Keynesian Diversion," *Western Economic Journal* 11, no. 2 (June 1973): 150–63.

——. 1963. *Keynesianism—Retrospect and Prospect: A Critical Restatement of Basic Economic Principles*. Chicago: Henry Regnery.

——. 1936. *Economists and the Public*. London: Jonathan Cape.

——. 1930. *The Theory of Collective Bargaining*. London: P.S. King.

# 14
# WILHELM RÖPKE: A HUMANE ECONOMIST

SHAWN RITENOUR

*Wilhem Röpke*
*1899–1966*

WILHELM RÖPKE DEVOTED his scholarly career to combating collectivism in economic, social, and political theory. As a student and proponent of the Austrian School, he contributed to its theoretical structure and political vision, warning of the dangers of political consolidation and underscoring the connection between culture and economic systems. More than any other Austrian of his time, he explored the ethical foundations of a market-based social order. He defended the free market from socialist cultural critics by pointing out that social crises and cultural decline are not the product of the free society; one needs to look to state control, political centralization, the welfare state, and inflation as primary sources of social decay. Röpke influenced the direction of postwar German economic reform, became a leading intellectual force in shaping the postwar American conservative movement, particularly its "fusionist" branch,[1] and has been compared with Mises as an archetype of the individualist thinker.[2]

Röpke was born on October 10, 1899, at Schwarmstedt in Hanover, Germany. He was the son of a physician who brought him up in the classical and Protestant Christian tradition. Serving in the German army

---

[1]George H. Nash, *The Conservative Intellectual Movement in America* (Wilmington, Del.: Intercollegiate Studies Institute, 1996), pp. 166–67.

[2]W.H. Hutt, *The Keynesian Episode: A Reassessment* (Indianapolis, Ind.: Liberty Press, 1979), p. 265.

during World War I, he was shocked by the sheer brutality of war, and it had a profound effect on his life. He became, in his words, "a fervent hater of war; of brutal and stupid national pride, of the greed for domination and of every collective outrage against ethics."[3]

Consistent with intellectual trends, Röpke initially blamed war on capitalist imperialism and was drawn toward socialism as its only alternative. But he had a change of mind after reading Ludwig von Mises's *Nation, State, and Economy*, published in 1919. That work was "in many ways the redeeming answer to the many questions tormenting a young man who had just come back from the trenches."[4] A socialist economy was, necessarily, a centrally-planned economy. Such a regime would seriously hinder international trade, which generates cooperation between nations and decreases the likelihood of war. The only form of socialism compatible with international trade, he concluded, is the national variety, which Röpke could not abide. He then recognized socialism for what it is: collectivism through empowerment of the state.

A drive to understand the causes and crisis of World War I led Röpke to pursue the study of economics and sociology. He studied economics at the University of Marburg, receiving his doctorate in 1921 and the *Habilitation* in 1922. The following year he married Eva Finke, and they raised three children. His first academic position was at Jena in 1924. Two years later, at the Vienna Convention of the German Association for Sociology, he met Ludwig von Mises.[5] Röpke moved to Graz in 1928 and became a full professor at his alma mater in Marburg in 1929.

Following the political victories of the Nazis in 1932, his uncompromising opposition to fascism earned him the honor of being one of the first professors to be forced out of his job. Röpke left Marburg for Frankfurt; and soon after giving a public address highly critical of the Nazis in early 1933,[6] he and his family left his homeland. Röpke then accepted an offer to become professor of economics at the University of Istanbul.

Röpke taught at Istanbul from 1933 to 1937, when he accepted a position at the Institute of International Studies in Geneva, Switzerland.

---

[3]Wilhelm Röpke, *International Order and Economic Integration* (Dordrecht, Holland: D. Reidel Publishing, 1959), p. 3.

[4]Quoted in Richard Ebeling, "Introduction" to Ludwig von Mises, *Money, Method, and the Market Process* (Norwell, Mass.: Kluwer, 1990), p. xxv.

[5]In Mises's personal memoir, he listed Röpke as one of a handful of German intellectuals "whose company enriched me greatly." See Ludwig von Mises, *Notes and Recollections* (Spring Mills, Penn.: Libertarian Press, 1978), pp. 104–05.

[6]Wilhelm Röpke,"End of an Era?" in idem, *Against the Tide* (Chicago: Regnery, 1969), pp. 79–97.

There he joined Ludwig von Mises, who had been a part of the Institute's faculty since 1934. Although Mises left Geneva for the United States in 1940 following the beginning of World War II, Röpke chose to stay and remained at the Institute until his death in 1966. To restore the broadest possible understanding of freedom, Röpke, along with Mises and F.A. Hayek, called an international meeting of historians, philosophers, economists, and journalists who shared his concern over the steady erosion of liberty; and in 1947 this group formed the Mont Pèlerin Society.

Through the Society, Röpke was able to meet with and influence the thinking of Ludwig Erhard, economics minister and Chancellor of West Germany. Erhard later revealed that during World War II he was able to illegally obtain Röpke's books, which he "devoured like life-giving water in the desert."[7] The product of Röpke's influence on Erhard has been tagged the post-World War II "German Economic Miracle," although Röpke pointed out that the economic success experienced by West Germany was not a miracle at all; it was the result of adopting correct social and legal institutions fostering the market economy. Looking back at the West German economic policies of the 1950s, he lamented that free-market reforms had not gone far enough.[8]

### FASCISM

Röpke's early work outlined themes that would recur throughout his career: the curses of collectivism and scientism and the central importance of moral and social institutions that sustain the free society. His 1931 analysis of fascist economics,[9] published under the pseudonym Ulrich Unfried, protested against anti-capitalist intellectuals who were using the world-wide depression to pave the way for national socialism. The "capitalism" that the anti-capitalists rail against, he wrote, was not free-market capitalism but state corporatism, characterized by sporadic interventions and government-business partnerships.

> And in order to refloat the economy whose functioning has been so largely impaired by past interventions, those same critics of capitalism clamor for more interventions, more planning, and hence a further emasculation of our economy. It is as though one poured sand into an engine and then hoped to start it up again by pouring in more sand.[10]

---

[7]Quoted in Gottfried Dietze,"Forward" to *Against the Tide*, p. ix.

[8]Wilhelm Röpke, *A Humane Economy* (Chicago: Henry Regnery, 1960), p. 28.

[9]Reprinted as "The Intellectuals and Capitalism" in Röpke, *Against the Tide*, pp. 25–44.

[10]Ibid., p. 31.

To avoid conflicting meanings, Röpke used the term "market economy" instead of "capitalism." He also rejected denoting socialism as a "planned economy"—every economy is planned, he said; the question is whether it is planned by entrepreneurs and free people, or by the state. Instead, he found it more accurate to refer to a collectivist system as an "office economy."[11]

Röpke recognized that as a social and economic system, fascism is not a third way between the free market and communism.[12] It is merely another form of totalitarianism that sought to "combine its general totalitarianism with the individualistic character of society."[13] Such a middle-of-the-road policy created an extreme interventionist state whose chief production agent was the government-created monopolist.

Fascism has a grave moral defect, Röpke argued: it fails to recognize the individual as the key social unit.[14] Correct economic reasoning, he said, begins not with the nation but with human action; and correct social policy begins with the recognition that society is made up of individual souls. Fascism, on the other hand, by ignoring the individual soul, is socialism's close cousin because it exults in the idolatry of the state.[15]

---

[11]Wilhelm Röpke, "The Problem of Economic Order," in *Two Essays by Wilhelm Röpke*, Johannes Overbeek, ed. (Lanham, Maryland: University Press of America, 1987), pp. 1–45.

[12]Wilhelm Röpke,"Fascist Economics," *Economica* (February 1935): 85–100. Röpke sums up his analysis: "Fascist Economics has nothing new to offer, whether in practice or in theory. The present position of our economic system is certainly untenable, but the alleged alternative which Fascist Economics seems to present is no real alternative at all." Also see Ludwig von Mises, *A Critique of Interventionism* (New Rochelle, N.Y.: Arlington House, 1977), pp. 107–38.

[13]Ibid., p. 91.

[14]Röpke, in *A Humane Economy*, p. 5, explains:

> [m]y picture of man is fashioned by the spiritual heritage of classical and Christian tradition. I see in man the likeness of God; I am profoundly convinced that it is an appalling sin to reduce man to a means (even in the name of high-sounding phrases) and that each man's soul is something unique, irreplaceable, priceless, in comparison with which all other things are as naught. I am attached to a humanism which is rooted in these convictions and which regards man as the child and image of God, but not as God himself, to be idolized as he is by the hubris of a false and atheist humanism. These, I believe, are the reasons why I so greatly distrust all forms of collectivism.

[15]Röpke, *Against the Tide*, pp. 93-94. In one of his last lectures delivered before his leaving Germany, he protested that "Men are gripped by a desire to be told what to do and to be ordered about, to the point almost of masochism. The state has become the subject of unparalleled idolatry."

## BUSINESS CYCLES

Much was written in the early 1930s regarding the depression, its causes, and remedies, and in 1936 Röpke gave the English-speaking world his own contribution, *Crises and Cycles*.[16] Using the monetary and capital theories of Böhm-Bawerk, Mises, Strigl, and Hayek, Röpke backed the view that the initial downturn was the result of prior credit expansion on the part of the central bank. He noted that "modern trade-cycle theory is indeed unanimous concerning the fundamental principle that the alternation of boom and depression is first and foremost an alteration in the volume of long-term investments and thus in the activity in the industries producing capital goods."[17] Röpke traced the existence of economic downturns to the existence of a complex division of labor, which makes possible the "roundaboutness" of production, combined with an overinvestment in higher-order goods spurred on by credit expansion.[18]

In his textbook, *The Economics of a Free Society*, first published in German in 1937, he further clarified his point. For such overinvestment to occur, he wrote, "some sort of compulsion will be required to loosen the bond which ties capital goods production to the voluntary savings of the population, and to raise the relative restriction of consumption above the point which the population itself is prepared to undergo via its savings."[19] In short, the boom of the boom-bust trade cycle will not occur on the free market; it is the result of state intervention in credit markets skewing investment decisions.[20]

---

[16]Wilhelm Röpke, *Crises and Cycles* (London: William Hodge, 1936). This is a revised and extended English translation of his work, *Krise und Konjunktur*, which was published in 1932, while Röpke was still in Germany.

[17]Röpke, *Crises and Cycles*, p. 25.

[18]Röpke summarizes his theory:

> The cause of a major disequilibrium of the economic process is an excess of real investments in fixed and working capital in the sense that the rate of investment has increased in a great volume and in a quicker tempo than is compatible with the preservation of economic equilibrium. The proportion in which the productive forces of the economic system are being devoted to the production of consumption goods or that of capital goods, i.e., the proportion between consumption and accumulation can vary, in magnitude and tempo, only within rather narrow limits without engendering disruption and lack of coordination.

"Socialism, Planning, and the Business Cycle," *Journal of Political Economy* (June 1936): 325.

[19]Wilhelm Röpke, *Economics of the Free Society* (Chicago: Henry Regnery, 1963), p. 213.

[20]For an application of the Röpkeian theory of the business cycle to modern finance, see James Grant, *The Trouble with Prosperity* (New York: Times Books, 1996), pp. 115–60.

A developed division of labor and capital overinvestment can also exist in a planned economy, he argued, so socialism would not be immune to economic downturns. In fact, such a system would be even more unstable. "In a socialistic society it [forced saving] may be replaced by open force exerted by the state, with the effect that the population would be driven, directly and authoritatively, to forego possibilities of consumption in favor of accumulation."[21] Additionally, a collectivist economy will not have a mechanism by which unwise investments are liquidated, causing economic disruptions to persist. "The economic disharmony which promises to become a chronic ailment of the socialist economy will be markedly different from the temporary disharmonies of the capitalist economy."[22]

To prevent business cycles, Röpke argued, requires a free market, a gold standard, and no government-created monetary inflation. At the same time, Röpke did not rule out credit expansion or reflation as possibly necessary to move the economy out of a depression,[23] a policy not unlike that advanced by later monetary disequilibrium theorists.[24] Demonstrating uncommon integrity, Röpke later recanted his early acceptance of this Keynesian-style policy.[25]

---

[21]Wilhelm Röpke, "Socialism, Planning, and the Business Cycle," *Journal of Political Economy* 44, no. 3 (June 1936): 328–29.

[22]Ibid., p. 321.

[23]Ibid., pp. 185–98. Röpke saw credit expansion during a severe crisis as a type of "conformable intervention." On pp. 196–97, he says:

> We must know that, whether we like it or not, we are dependent on the entrepreneurs and their optimistic mood, that we must not drive them to exasperation and at the same time be surprised that recovery will not come. . . . The issue between laissez-faire, a conformable trade-cycle policy [credit expansion during a crisis] and Planning [price and product controls] may be summed up as follows. In certain circumstances it is just as wrong to rely on the natural respiration of economic life resuming automatically as it is wrong to club it to death and then to make attempts at replacing the natural organism by an artificial one made of tin and wire. Both the uncompromising Liberal and the Planner—each is wrong where the other is right, and right where the other is wrong.

[24]Leland B. Yeager, *The Fluttering Veil: Essays on Monetary Disequalibrium* (Indianapolis, Ind.: Liberty Fund, 1997), pp. 15–17.

[25]Röpke, *A Humane Economy*, p. 295. In a footnote, Röpke writes,

> I am ashamed to say that I must take my share of the blame for creating this concept of "functional finance" (*Krise und Konjunktur* [1932] and my subsequent book *Crises and Cycles* [1936]), but I am forced to admit now that it has stood the test neither of counter-arguments nor of experience.

## CRITIQUE OF KEYNES

In the East, collectivism took the form of full-blown socialism. In Germany and Italy, fascism rose and fell. But the post-war West was not immune to the call of collectivism, and Röpke saw Keynesian economics as paving the way. He argued that the Keynesian program was destructive in both its economic and moral consequences.

In a 1952 critique of the *United Nations Report on National and International Measures for Full Employment*, Röpke warned that if governments keep interest rates perpetually low, as the "new economics" recommended, chronic inflation is the necessary consequence.[26] Röpke foresaw that a fully implemented "full-employment" policy would result in "stagflation," which the United States experienced in the 1970s. Additionally, chronic inflation creates political pressure for repressed inflation.

Having lived through Germany's hyperinflation, Röpke feared the consequences of an unrestrained monetary authority. He developed a theory of repressed inflation based on interventionism and the Austrian theory of economic calculation. The government monetary authorities first inflate the money supply and then impose price and other economic controls in order to mitigate the consequent rise in prices. This only makes things worse, for, as the Austrians demonstrated during the socialist calculation debate, market prices are crucial for rational economic planning on the part of entrepreneurs. The result is that official prices do not reflect actual economic values, and the economy is riddled with bottlenecks, sporadic unemployment, and general economic chaos.[27] This repressed inflation was a major feature of post-war European economies.

Röpke viewed inflation as a Keynesian means for transferring wealth. When a central bank inflates the money supply, the new money always enters the economy in the hands of particular individuals. They are the first ones to spend the new money, making their purchases at the original price levels, happy that their wealth has seemingly increased. As the new money works itself through the economy, however, increased demand for goods results in increased prices. Those who receive the new money later or not at all must pay the higher prices and incur a

---

[26]Wilhelm Röpke, "The Economics of Full Employment," in *The Critics of Keynesian Economics*, Henry Hazlitt, ed. (New Rochelle, N.Y.: Arlington House [1960] 1977), pp. 370–74.

[27]Wilhelm Röpke, "'Repressed Inflation': The Ailment of the Modern Economy," in Röpke, *Against the Tide*, pp. 111–31.

decrease in their real wealth. Explaining this Austrian insight within his moral framework, Röpke argued that this amounts to little more than legalized theft and redistribution.[28]

For Röpke, however, Keynes's positivistic–scientistic method was an even more damaging part of his legacy. In a critique of Keynes, included in the final 1963 edition of his revised text *The Economics of a Free Society*, Röpke pinpointed one of Keynes's most dangerous ideas. Keynes and his followers saw the economic system as part of a mathematical–mechanical universe, with economic activity being the product of quantifiable aggregates, such as consumption and investment, instead of a result of actions by individuals. Keynes took the human out of "human action" and reduced the economic system to a machine.[29] Man became a mere social unit, merely reacting to changed conditions according to economic instincts.[30]

Keynes's focus on the management of economic aggregates fed the hubris of modern economists by justifying their role as the keepers of the keys to the economic kingdom. Keynesian economists, making Gross National Product their highest end, were advocating an economic variant of scientism.[31] Such economism leads to collectivism, according to Röpke, because it banishes from consideration humane values such as liberty and peace, and justifies government coercion to tax funds from individuals in the name of "growing the economy."[32]

---

[28]Röpke, *A Humane Economy*, p. 191.

[29]Röpke, *The Economics of the Free Society*, p. 224. Elsewhere, Röpke writes concerning Keynesian economic policy, "economic policy would thus, indeed, attain the dignity of engineering, without regard to the fact that society can never be made into a machine nor can statistics succeed morality as a guide to behavior or policy." "The Economics of Full Employment," p. 369.

[30]F.A. Hayek, *The Counter-Revolution of Science* (Indianapolis, Ind.: Liberty*Press*, [1952] 1979).

[31]Regarding the connection between scientism and collectivism see Wilhelm Röpke, *Civitas Humana* (London: William Hodge, 1948), pp. 67–72. See also Hayek, *The Counter-Revolution of Science*, pp. 93–110.

[32]Regarding government capital formation, Röpke writes,

> We are at one of the great crossroads, where decisions of almost incalculable implications have to be made. It is here that we must make our stand if we are to succeed in stemming the sinister, trampling march of a proletarianized mass society with its mechanized, compulsory social welfare system and its ultimately inevitable goal of a totalitarian mammoth state. This demands, above all else, that the center of gravity in the responsibility for people's lives should be shifted from the state back to where it belongs by all standards of common sense and historical experience—to the individual

WELFARE, DOMESTIC AND INTERNATIONAL

After the war, the United States Congress and the Truman administration passed the Marshall Plan, which pledged the largest ever transfer of foreign aid to help rebuild war-torn Europe, a plan wholly embraced by intellectual and political establishments on both sides of the Atlantic. But Röpke dissented from this conventional view on grounds that European economic recovery would not be brought about by foreign aid but through a restoration of the market economy that had been hampered during the war. The problem of economic disorder, he said, is the result of repressed inflation, a "policy that created chaos in the name of planning, confusion in the name of guidance, retrogression and autarky in the name of progress, and mass poverty in the name of justice."[33] Regardless of U.S. aid,

> it will still be up to every beneficiary country in Europe whether or not to avail itself of this unique opportunity for liberating the economy from inflationary controls. Unless this is done, however, it is to be feared that the new American billions will trickle away just as the old ones did.[34]

What's more, Marshall Plan aid could have the deleterious effect of forestalling market reform. The aid would not likely be used to make a transition to the market possible, but rather to subsidize and entrench the current system. In the regions of Europe for which the U.S. government was responsible—for example the American-occupied zone of Germany—the U.S. had "for two-and-a-half years applied economic principles that cannot be described otherwise than as collectivist."[35] Röpke reminds his European readers that the American economy itself was in many ways planned, inflationary, and collectivistic. "A whole generation of American economists, after all, has been brought up to think of the permanent inflationary pressure implied in the 'full employment' policy as an ideal and indeed a necessity."[36]

In 1958, as Western economies began to replace outright planning and price control with wealth redistribution, Röpke wrote a blistering assault on the welfare state. He cited not only the costs of the welfare state,

---

surrounded by his family, to free organizations, to the broad masses of the people themselves. ("The Formation and Use of Capital," in *Against the Tide*, p. 162.)

[33]Wilhelm Röpke, "Marshall Plan and Economic Policy," in *Against the Tide*, p. 123.

[34]Ibid., p. 126.

[35]Ibid., p. 127.

[36]Ibid., p. 128.

which far exceed its supposed benefits, but also the social effects. Compulsory aid "paralyzes people's willingness to take care of their own needs," and its financial burden makes people depend more on the state and expect more from it. "To let someone else foot the bill" is the "very essence" of the welfare state; moreover, the people who pay are "forced to do so by order of the state"—the opposite of charity.

> In spite of its alluring name, the welfare state stands or falls by compulsion. It is compulsion imposed upon us with the state's power to punish noncompliance. Once this is clear, it is equally clear that the welfare state is an evil the same as each and every restriction of freedom.[37]

## MONOPOLY

Röpke was a relentless critic of the tendency towards bigness in economic and political life. And he was one of the earliest modern economists to point out that, like the business cycle, monopoly is not a product of the free market, but a result of government intervention.[38] As early as 1936, he documented that the free market was generating competition, not monopolies. In a later defense of the market economy, Röpke maintained that market capitalism is not bigness per se. Similarly, proper legal institutions are those that foster a truly free market, not "big business" in the name of efficiency.[39] He argued that monopolists were able to maintain their position in the market due to legal privileges, and he concluded that government regulation cannot work as a cure for economic concentration. On the contrary, it is the office economy that tends toward concentration. The collectivist economy leads to the politicization of all

---

[37]Wilhelm Röpke, "Robbing Peter to Pay Paul: On the Nature of the Welfare State," *Against the Tide* (Chicago: Regnery, 1969), p. 212.

[38]Röpke's position on this seems to have evolved over time. While he did maintain in some earlier writings that monopolists could maintain their position in a free market, and that antitrust laws were necessary (see *The Social Crisis of Our Time*, p. 179), he later came to the conclusion that perpetual monopoly was the product of government privilege. In his next-to-last book (*A Humane Economy*), pp. 241–42, he writes that

> it is of no avail to look to government for new compulsion and new legislation, which would only accelerate centrism elsewhere. . . . There is a lot more to be said about economic concentration, especially with respect to taxation and company law, than I said in my earlier works. . . . [T]he government itself, by means of its laws, its tax system, and its economic and social policies, continuously and injudiciously weights the scale in favor of industrial concentration. This has nothing to do with the frequently overstated technical and organization advantages of scale.

[39]Röpke, *Civitas Humana*, p. 30.

economic life, resulting in national monopolies and all economic decisions in the hands of central planners.[40]

It is in this context that we must consider Röpke's remarks on the negative consequences of capitalism as it developed historically. Röpke occasionally used strident language to criticize how the rise of capitalism also fed forces of monopoly and urbanization. But these negative consequences are not, however, to be attributed to free-market capitalism, but should be seen instead as a holdover from the feudal system. Economic power was concentrated, not because the free market necessarily led to such concentration, but because pre-liberal property arrangements went largely unchanged after the free-market system developed. Feudal lords enjoyed certain social and legal privileges over the serfs, and these were not abolished with the rise of capitalism. Murray N. Rothbard has recognized a similar problem regarding desocialization in the former Soviet Union.[41] While opposing some aspects of industrialization, Röpke criticized by what he called "agricultural nationalism," the drive to keep industrialization at bay for the sake of protecting traditional ways of life at the expense of social progress.[42]

Röpke attacked all manner of interventionist policies not just those that stopped short of socialism. Intervention creates more problems than it solves. "The more stabilization, the less stability."[43] Like Mises, Röpke pointed out that pursuing an interventionist policy of price controls, trade quotas, and exchange controls starts "a chain of repercussions necessitating more radical acts of intervention until we finally

---

[40]Röpke, "The Problem of Economic Order," p. 21.

[41]In a discussion about granting ownership shares to factory workers, Rothbard writes, "A problem immediately arises in granting shares to workers in the factories. . . . Should the managing *nomenklatura* be cut in on the shares of ownership?" He goes on to add,

> A . . . commonly suggested route to privatization deserves to be rejected out of hand: that the government sell all its assets to the public at auction, to the highest bidder. . . . [W]hy does the government deserve to own the revenue from the sale of these assets? After all, one of the main reasons for desocialization is that the government does not deserve to own the productive assets of the country. But if it does not deserve o own the assets, why in the world does it deserve to own their monetary value?

Rothbard, Murray, "How and How Not to Desocialize," *Review of Austrian Economics* 6, no. 1 (1992): 74–75.

[42]Wilhelm Röpke, *International Economic Disintegration* (Philadelphia: Porcupine Press, [1942] 1978), pp. 150–61.

[43]Röpke, *Economics of the Free Society*, p. 219.

arrive at a Collectivist Economy pure and simple."[44] Furthermore, such measures are doomed to failure because "economic life is dependent on the psychological attitude of countless individuals."[45] Economic agents make free choices. They are not cogs in a giant national economic machine.

## POLITICAL THEORY

After World War II, Röpke turned his attention to promoting economic and political institutions that would prevent another world conflict. Building on his theory that centralization and decentralization are the two countervailing principles that determine all aspects of social and political life, he turned his energies to analyzing how these principles affect the international political order. Some type of international economic order is necessary. His colleague Mises had described the ideal of a classically liberal supranational state.[46] But Röpke, recognizing the impracticality of such a state, attacked all plans for political integration, particularly those that called for a European-wide regulatory power.

A supranational or multinational government is not likely to embrace the liberal ideal because a political regime insulates itself from the people it rules. It grows increasingly oppressive and corrupt, raising up welfare states and trampling on private property. For this reason, the centralization of decisionmaking power is incompatible with free-market economies. As the alternative, Röpke embraced the nineteenth-century "universalist-liberal" solution to the problem of an international order: vibrant commerce between politically autonomous small states.[47] In order to allow for international trade to take place, a truly international monetary system is necessary. Instead of a worldwide currency, national currencies backed by a non-political gold standard should serve as the arbiter of exchange.

Röpke agreed with other economists in the Austrian tradition regarding the importance of international trade to peaceful cooperation between nations. Protectionism undermines the division of labor, inhibits productivity, and reduces income, and, if carried far enough, transforms a nation's economy into a type of giant firm, with all of its monopolistic

---

[44]Ibid., p. 195.

[45]Röpke, *International Economic Disintegration*, p. 176.

[46]Ludwig von Mises, *Omnipotent Government: The Rise of the Total State and Total War* (Spring Mills, Penn.: Libertarian Press, [1944] 1985), pp. 265–71; *Liberalism* (Irvington-on-Hudson, N.Y.: Foundation for Economic Education, 1996), p. 148.

[47]Röpke, *International Order and Economic Integration*, p. 74.

drawbacks. Moreover, Röpke distinguished between international trade and international political intervention. Free trade and imperialism are not linked but are opposed to one another. It is possible to sacrifice economic liberty in the name of international trade or economic development. For example, pushing other countries to buy an exporting nation's goods is contrary to the Röpkeian ideal.[48] Government control of "investment," whether domestically or internationally, is never a wise path, especially not in underdeveloped countries. What these countries need is not capital or technology per se, but the cultural and social conditions allowing for development (i.e., private property rights enforced by a morally just legal system).

The decentralization of the political process, Röpke argued, is incompatible with mass democracy. Under democracy, politicians are prone to be swayed by masses of privately interested voters, so that the economic system degenerates into a spoils system where the victors are the mass that can muster fifty-one percent of the vote.[49] Such a system only serves to bring about and legitimize centralized power. The only legitimate government is a government by rulers that are widely recognized as competent and socially beneficial.[50] If the political system is decentralized, those who are the most capable and are recognized as possessing the most integrity would be those who the various locales would allow to rule for any length of time.[51]

---

[48]In ibid., p. 84, Röpke says,

> [I]mperialism is not only not an essential component of capitalism, but, quite apart from all the economic links in the chain of cause and effect, is a concomitant which is foreign to, and even opposed to, the capitalistic system. A bellicose policy by no means furthers the interests of capitalism, but is directly opposed to them. An economic system which rests upon division of labor and exchange needs peace if it is to flourish.

[49]In *A Humane Economy*, p. 220, Röpke writes,

> Democracy . . . degenerates into arbitrariness, state omnipotence, and disintegration whenever the decisions of government, as determined by universal suffrage, are not contained by the ultimate limits of natural law, firm norms, and tradition. It is not enough that they should be laid down in constitutions; they must be so firmly lodged in the hearts and minds of men that they can withstand all onslaughts.

[50]Röpke, *Civitas Humana*, p. 86.

[51]This line of thought has been extended in the writings of Hans-Hermann Hoppe. See Hoppe, *Natural Elites, Intellectuals, and the State*, (Auburn, Ala.: Ludwig von Mises Institute, 1995); idem,"The Political Economy of Monarchy and Democracy, and the Idea of a Natural Order," *Journal of Libertarian Studies* 11, no. 2 (Summer 1995): 94–121.

## SOCIAL THEORY

During and following World War II, Röpke broadened his research interests beyond economic and political theory and into cultural and even religiously based analytics. His resulting critique of modern society developed out of his conviction that trends in the sciences and politics were undermining and even destroying the idea of the individual soul and replacing it with the concept of mass man. Röpke began to concentrate on this problem with more focus beginning in 1942 with the publication of the book that would later be translated into English as *The Social Crisis of Our Time*. He sought to trace the evolution of thought and action that led to the crisis of collectivism he saw, and sought to defend freedom in the face of statism of all stripes.

Röpke was also skeptical of the role of the economist as social engineer, whether in promoting "efficiency" or "social justice." He followed Mises's method in viewing the economic agent as *homo agens*, a humans who acts, rather than *homo oeconomicus*, an individual motivated by purely material motives. "The ordinary man is not such a *homo oeconomicus*," he writes, "just as he is neither hero nor saint. The motives that drive people toward economic success are as varied as the human soul itself."[52] Because life is indeed more than food, and the body more than raiment, one cannot look only to economics to provide a life worth living.

Röpke set out to defend liberty against leftist criticism by highlighting the fundamental social problem man has to face: how can conflicting interests in society be successfully harmonized? Individuals having different value scales are not immune to the temptation of taking advantage of others when they have the chance. Freedom and voluntary exchange are crucial if the conflicting interests of different parties are to be coordinated peacefully. Collectivism, on the other hand, necessarily means coercion and conflict between competing interests. But, for an individual to be truly free, he must have control over his economic will. For a society to take advantage of the division of labor, it is necessary to have an institutional framework that allows for a freely adjusting price mechanism and the private ownership of the tools of production and competition.[53] Such is the only modern economic system that maintains the integrity of the individual person.

A prime virtue of the free market is that it erects a wall of separation between politics and society. Businessmen need not rely on government

[52]Röpke, *A Humane Economy*, p. 121.

[53]Ibid., pp. 102–04.

privilege or a party's favor in order to enjoy financial security. The only way for even the most greedy entrepreneur to reap profits for any length of time is by rendering a valuable service to the consumer.[54] Röpke writes, "Freedom, immunity of the economic life from political infection, clean principles and peace—these are the non-materialist achievements of the pure market economy."[55] Röpke, like Mises, likened the individual's decisions to purchase or to refrain from purchasing as a daily ballot, electing the most successful entrepreneur. In fact, Röpke thought the market election more just and efficient than a political election, because the market is not a winner-take-all mechanism.[56]

Although Röpke was a critic of the ethics of materialism, he did not embrace intervention as a means to suppress displays of consumerism. For example, Röpke rejected the possibility of categorizing goods into "luxuries" and "needs" because the exercise

> presupposes that bureaucracy knows better than the consumers what is good and useful. . . . In other words, the government has the astonishing audacity to require of us that we should prefer its arbitrary list of priorities to our own.[57]

All market activity, international or otherwise, presupposes a moral, social, and institutional framework; and Röpke identified religious convictions and natural hierarchy as institutions that have historically served as effective bulwarks against state power. In order for individuals to retain their freedoms, continually expand the division of labor, and live full lives, they must own property, embrace family and community, participate in civic associations and churches, and enjoy the security of certain traditions. These points, he thought, were too often neglected in classically liberal literature. Röpke writes:

---

[54]Ibid., p. 105.

[55]Ibid., p. 108.

[56]Röpke, in *The Social Crises of Our Time*, p. 103, writes,

> The process of the market economy is, so to speak, a *plebiscite de tous les jours*, where every monetary unit spent by the consumer represents a ballot, and where the producers are endeavoring by their advertising to give "election publicity" to an infinite number of parties (i.e., goods). This democracy of consumers has the . . . great advantage of a perfect proportional system: there is no nullifying of the minorities' will by the majority, and every ballot carries its full weight. The result is a market democracy, which in its silent precision surpasses the most perfect political democracy.

See also Ludwig von Mises, "Profit and Loss," in *Planning for Freedom* (South Holland, Ill.: Libertarian Press, [1952] 1980), pp. 108–50.

[57]Röpke, *Against the Tide*, p. 145.

> The market economy, and with it social and political freedom, can thrive only as a part and under the protection of a bourgeois system. This implies the existence of a society in which certain fundamentals are respected and color the whole network of social relationships: individual effort and responsibility, absolute norms and values, independence based on ownership, prudence and daring, calculating and saving, responsibility for planning one's own life, proper coherence with the community, family feeling, a sense of tradition and the succession of generations combined with an open-minded view of the present and the future, proper tension between individual and community, firm moral discipline, respect for the value of money, the courage to grapple on one's own with life and its uncertainties, a sense of the natural order of things, and a firm scale of values.[58]

From his earliest years, Wilhelm Röpke fought collectivist and statist power in every way an intellectual could. His tools included not only economic theory but also a vision of moral goodness rooted in Christian faith. As Hayek said of Röpke: "let me at least emphasize a special gift for which we, his colleagues, admire him particularly—perhaps because it is so rare among scholars: his courage, his moral courage."[59] If we are concerned about fostering societies where people can live more humane lives, Röpke's advances in both Austrian economics and his vision of the good society deserve close attention.

SELECTED READINGS

Röpke, Wilhelm. 1987. "The Problem of Economic Order." In *Two Essays by Wilhelm Röpke*. Johannes Overbeek, ed. Lanham, Maryland: University Press of America. Pp. 1–45.

——. [1966] 1977. "The Economics of Full Employment." In *The Critics of Keynesian Economics*. Henry Hazlitt, ed. New Rochelle, N.Y.: Arlington House. Pp. 370–74.

——. 1969. *Against the Tide*. Chicago: Henry Regnery.

——. 1964. *Welfare, Freedom, and Inflation*. Tuscaloosa: University of Alabama Press.

——. 1963. *Economics of the Free Society*. Chicago: Henry Regnery.

——. 1960. *A Humane Economy*. Chicago: Henry Regnery.

——. [1942] 1978. *International Economic Disintegration*. Philadelphia: Porcupine Press.

---

[58]Röpke, *A Humane Economy*, p. 98.

[59]F.A. Hayek, *The Fortunes of Liberalism: Essays on Austrian Economics and the Ideal of Freedom*, vol. 4, *The Collected Works of F.A. Hayek*, Peter G. Klein, ed. (Chicago: University of Chicago Press, 1992), p. 197.

——. 1959. *International Order and Economic Integration*. Dordrecht, Holland: D. Reidel Publishing.

——. 1950. *The Social Crisis of Our Time.* Chicago: University of Chicago Press.

——. 1948. *Civitas Humana*. London: William Hodge.

——. 1947. "Repressed Inflation." *Kyklos* 1.

——. 1936. *Crises and Cycles.* London: William Hodge.

——. 1936. "Socialism, Planning, and the Business Cycle." *Journal of Political Economy* 44, no. 3 (June).

——. 1935. "Fascist Economics." *Economica* (February): 85–100.

# 15
# Murray N. Rothbard: Economics, Science, and Liberty

HANS-HERMANN HOPPE

*Murray N. Rothbard*
*1926–1995*

MURRAY N. ROTHBARD has come to occupy a position of unique influence within the intellectual tradition of Austrian economics for a combination of three central reasons.

First, Rothbard is the latest representative of the *mainstream* within Austrian economics.[1] As in other intellectual traditions, various interconnected branches can be identified within the Austrian School of economics. Rothbard is the latest exponent of the main rationalist branch of the Austrian School, starting with the School's founder Carl Menger, and continuing with Eugen von Böhm-Bawerk, and Ludwig von Mises. Like Menger, Böhm-Bawerk, and Mises, Rothbard is an outspoken rationalist and critic of all variants of social relativism: historicism, empiricism, positivism, falsificationism, and skepticism. Like his acknowledged

[1]Among academia in general, currently F.A. Hayek is by far the most prominent Austrian economist. It is worth emphasizing, then, that Hayek is not a representative of the rationalist mainstream of Austrian economics, nor does Hayek claim otherwise. Hayek stands in the intellectual tradition of British empiricism and skepticism, and is an explicit opponent of the continental rationalism espoused by Menger, Böhm-Bawerk, Mises, and Rothbard. On this topic see further Joseph T. Salerno, "Ludwig von Mises as Social Rationalist," *Review of Austrian Economics* 4 (1990): 26–54; Jeffrey M. Herbener, "Introduction," in *The Meaning of Ludwig von Mises*, Jeffrey M. Herbener, ed. (Boston: Kluwer Academic Publishers, 1993); Hans-Hermann Hoppe, "Einführung: Ludwig von Mises und der Liberalismus," in Ludwig von Mises, *Liberalismus* (St. Augustine: Academia Verlag, 1993); idem, "F.A. Hayek on

predecessors, Rothbard defends the view that economic laws not only exist, but more specifically that they are "exact" (Menger) or "aprioristic" (Mises) laws. In contrast to the propositions of the (empirical) natural sciences, which must be continually tested against ever new data, and thus can never attain more than hypothetical validity, the propositions of economics concern necessary, non-hypothetical relations and assume apodictic validity. According to the Austrian mainstream, all economic laws can be derived deductively from a few elementary facts of nature and man (Menger), or from a single axiom (Mises), i.e., the proposition "man acts," which one cannot dispute without running into a performative contradiction, and which is, thus, indisputably true, and a few empirical—and empirically testable—assumptions. Like his predecessors, Rothbard considers it neither necessary nor indeed possible to test economic propositions by studying data of experience. Experience can illustrate the validity of an economic theorem, but experience can never refute or falsify it, because ultimately its validity rests solely on the indisputable validity of the axiom of action, and on the validity (and correct exercise) of the rules of deductive reasoning and logical inference. Indeed, trying to "empirically test" an economic law involves a category mistake and is a sign of confusion. Further, like Menger, Böhm-Bawerk, and Mises before him, Rothbard adheres firmly to epistemological and methodological individualism. Only individuals act; consequently, all social phenomena must be explained—logically reconstructed—as the result of purposeful individual actions. Every "holistic" or "organicist" explanation must be categorically rejected as an unscientific pseudo-explanation. Likewise, every mechanistic explanation of social phenomena must be discarded as unscientific. Humans act under conditions of uncertainty. The idea of a social mechanical equilibrium is useful only insofar as it enables us to grasp what actions are *not*, and in what respect they are fundamentally different and categorically distinct from the operations of machines and automatons.

Second, Rothbard is the latest and most comprehensive system-builder within Austrian economics. Only among rationalists does a constant desire for system and completeness exist. While they contributed much to its foundation, neither Menger nor Böhm-Bawerk accomplished

---

Government and Social Evolution," *Review of Austrian Economics* 7, no. 1 (1994): 67–93; idem, "Die öesterreichische Schule und ihre Bedeutung für die moderne Wirtschaftswissenschaft," in Hans Hoppe, Kurt Leube, Christian Watrin, and Joseph Salerno, *Ludwig von Mises's 'Die Gemeinwirtschaft'* (Düsseldorf: Verlag Wirtschaft und Finanzen, 1996); Murray N. Rothbard, "The Present State of Austrian Economics," in idem, *The Logic of Action* (Cheltenham, U.K.: Edward Elgar, 1997), vol. 1.

this ultimate intellectual desideratum. This feat was accomplished only by Mises, with the publication of his monumental *Human Action*.[2] "Here at last," Rothbard wrote about *Human Action*, "was economics *whole* once more, once again an edifice. Not only that—here was a structure of economics with many of the components newly contributed by Professor Mises himself." Since then, only Rothbard has accomplished a similar achievement with the publication of *Man, Economy, and State* and its companion volume *Power and Market*.[3] Modeled after Mises's *magnum opus*, and even more comprehensive and complete, what Rothbard stated about Mises and *Human Action* can be said of himself and *Man, Economy, and State*. In fact, no less of an authority than Mises himself did so in reviewing the book for the *New Individualist Review*. Mises hailed Rothbard's treatise

> as an epochal contribution to the general science of human action, praxeology, and its practically most important and up-to-now best elaborated part, economics. Henceforth all essential studies in these branches of knowledge will have to take full account of the theories and criticisms expounded by Dr. Rothbard.[4]

Today Mises's *Human Action* and Rothbard's *Man, Economy, and State* are the two towering and defining achievements of the Austrian School. No one can be considered seriously today, whether as a student of Austrian economics or as its critic, who has not read and studied *Human Action* and *Man, Economy, and State*.

Third, Rothbard is the latest and most systematically political Austrian economist. Just as rationalism implies the desire for system and completeness, so it implies political activism. To rationalists, human beings are above all *rational* animals. Their actions, and the course of human history, are determined by *ideas* (rather than by blind evolutionary forces of spontaneous evolution and natural selection). Ideas can be true or false, but only true ideas "work" and result in success and progress, while false ideas lead to failure and decline. As the discoverer of true ideas and eradicator of false ones, the scholar assumes a crucial role in human history. Human progress is the result of the discovery of truth and the proliferation of true ideas—enlightenment—and is thus entirely

---

[2]Ludwig von Mises, *Human Action*, 3rd rev. ed. (Auburn, Ala.: Ludwig von Mises Institute, [1949] 1966).

[3]Murray N. Rothbard, *Man, Economy, and State: A Treatise on Economic Principles* (Auburn, Ala.: Ludwig von Mises Institute, [1962] 1993); idem, *Power and Market* (Menlo Park, Calif.: Institute for Humane Studies, 1970).

[4]Ludwig von Mises,"A New Treatise on Economics," *The New Individualist Review* 2, no. 3 (1962): 39–42.

in the scholar's hands. The truth is inherently practical, and in recognizing an idea as true (or false), a scholar cannot but want it to be implemented (or eradicated) immediately. For this reason, in addition to pursuing his scholarly ambitions, Menger served as personal tutor to the Austrian Crown Prince Rudolf, and as an appointed life-member of the Austrian House of Lords (Herrenhaus). Similarly, Böhm-Bawerk served three times as Austrian minister of finance, and was a lifetime member of the *Herrenhaus*. Likewise, Mises was the nationally prominent chief economist of the Vienna Chamber of Commerce and advisor to many prominent figures during Austria's first Republic, and later, in the U.S., he served as advisor to the National Association of Manufacturers and numerous other organizations. Only Mises went even further. Just as he was the first economic system-builder, so was he the first to give the Austrian activism systematic expression by associating Austrian economics with radical-liberal-libertarian-political reform (as laid out in his *Liberalism* of 1927). Only Rothbard, who likewise served in many advisory functions and as founder and academic director of several educational organizations, accomplished something comparable. Proceeding systematically beyond even Mises, Rothbard accomplished —in his *Ethics of Liberty*[5]—an integration (*via* the concept of private property) of value-free Austrian economics and libertarian political philosophy (ethics) as two complementary branches of a grand unified social theory, thereby creating a radical—Austro-libertarian—philosophical movement.

In the area of theoretical economics, Rothbard contributed two major advances beyond the standards set by Mises's *Human Action*. First, Rothbard provided systematic clarification of the theory of marginal utility, and then advanced a new reconstruction of welfare economics and, entirely absent in Mises's system, an economic theory of the state.

Building on the foundations of a strictly ordinalist interpretation of marginal utility laid out by Mises as early as 1912 in his *Theory of Money and Credit*,[6] Rothbard explained that the word "marginal" in marginal utility does not refer to increments of utility (which would imply measurability), but rather to the utility of increments of goods (and thus has nothing to do with measurability). The good to which utility is attached, and the increments in its size, can be described in physical terms. The

[5]Murray N. Rothbard, *The Ethics of Liberty* (Atlantic Highlands, N.J.: Humanities Press, 1982).

[6]Ludwig von Mises, *The Theory of Money and Credit*, H.E. Batson, trans. (Indianapolis, Ind.: Liberty Fund, [1912] 1980).

good and its increment extend in space, and thus can be measured and counted in unitary quantitative addition. In distinct contrast, the utility attached to a physical good and its unitary physical increments is a purely intensive magnitude. It does not extend in space, and hence is immeasurable and intractable by unitary counting and the rules of arithmetic. All attempts to construct a cardinal measure of utility are in vain. *Qua* intensive magnitude, utility can be treated only ordinally; that is, as a rank order on a one-dimensional individual preference scale (and every economic phenomenon, in particular monetary calculation and "objective" cost accounting, must ultimately be reducible to and explained as the simple outcome of ordinal individual rank order judgments). Apart from their placement on one-dimensional individual preference scales, no quantitative relationship between different goods and different quantities of the same good exists. In particular, no such thing as total utility—conceived of as the addition or integration of marginal utilities—exists. Rather, "total" utility is the marginal utility of a larger-sized quantity of a good, and, Rothbard explained,

> [t]here are, then two laws of utility, both following from the apodictic conditions of human action: first, that *given the size of a unit of a good, the (marginal) utility of each unit decreases as the supply of units increases*; second, *that the (marginal) utility of a larger-sized unit is greater than the (marginal) utility of a smaller-sized unit*. The first is the law of diminishing marginal utility. The second has been called the law of increasing total utility. The relationship between the two laws and between the items considered in both is purely one of rank, i.e., ordinal.[7]

Graphically, Rothbard illustrated, the relationship can be represented thus[8]:

Ranks in Value

- 3 eggs
- 2 eggs
- 1 egg
- 2nd egg
- 3rd egg

The higher the ranking on this individual value scale for eggs, the higher the value. By the second law, 3 eggs are valued more highly then 2 eggs and 2 eggs more highly than one. By the first law, the 2nd egg will be ranked below the first on the value scale, and the 3rd below the 2nd.

---

[7]Rothbard, *Man, Economy, and State*, pp. 270–71; emphasis in the original.

[8]Rothbard, *The Logic of Action*, vol. 1, p. 222.

No mathematical relationship exists between, for instance, the marginal utility of 3 eggs and the marginal utility of the 3rd egg except that the former is greater than the latter.

As Lionel Robbins, influenced by Wicksteed and Mises, had first brought home to mainstream economics, from the ordinal character of utility it follows logically that every interpersonal as well as intrapersonal comparison of utility must be regarded as impossible (unscientific), and hence every social welfare proposal involving any such comparison is arbitrary.[9] While mainstream welfare economics was thrown into disarray upon full realization of this conclusion, Rothbard provided a radically new strictly ordinalist reconstruction of welfare economics based on the twin concepts of individual self-ownership and demonstrated preference.[10]

Self-ownership simply means this: every individual owns (controls) his own physical human body. "Man's nature," explained Rothbard, "is a fusion of 'spirit' and matter."[11] Every living human body is appropriated and controlled by a single independent (autonomous) conscious mind and will —a self or ego. Accordingly, as long as it is alive, we refer to a human body as a *persona* (rather than a *corpus*). (Mainstream welfare economics also accepts the concept of self-ownership, even if only implicitly, by virtue of the fact that it speaks of separate *individual* utility maximizers.) The concept of demonstrated preference is implied in that of self-ownership. It simply means "that actual choice reveals, or demonstrates, a

---

[9]See Lionel Robbins, *The Nature and Significance of Economic Science* (London: Macmillan, 1932), chap. 6. The impossibility of inter- and intra-personal utility comparisons does not imply that two individuals or time periods cannot be compared objectively, of course. In fact, every individual can determine objectively whether his quantitative supply of any particular good has increased, decreased, or remained the same. And if his supply of one good has increased (decreased) while the supply of his other goods has remained the same, surely it can be said objectively that this individual is better (worse) off and has attained a higher (lower) rank on his individual value scale. Likewise, every individual participating in a monetary economy can determine objectively whether the monetary value of his assets has increased, decreased, or remained constant.

[10]Rothbard's contributions to welfare economics are strewn throughout his entire body of work. They begin with his 1956 essay "Toward a Reconstruction of Utility and Welfare Economics," and reach their completion in 1982 with his *Ethics of Liberty*. See also Hans-Hermann Hoppe, "Book Review of *Man, Economy, and Liberty*," *Review of Austrian Economics* 4 (1990): 257–58; idem, *The Economics and Ethics of Private Property* (Boston: Kluwer, 1993), pp. 232–33; Jeffrey M. Herbener, "The Pareto Rule and Welfare Economics," *Review of Austrian Economics* 10, no. 1 (1997): 79–106.

[11]Rothbard, *The Ethics of Liberty*, p. 31.

man's preferences; that is, that his preferences are deducible from what he has chosen in action."[12] Every action involves a man's purposeful use of his physical body, and thus demonstrates that he values this body as a *good*. Furthermore, in using it in one way rather than another, he simultaneously demonstrates with every action what he considers the most highly valued use of this good at the time of his acting. In accordance with the ordinal character of utility, actions reveal only the *existential fact* of preference orders and ranks. They do not reveal anything about the "differences" or "distances" of ranks or the "intensity" of preference, nor do they ever demonstrate "indifference." Indeed, both "differences" of rank and "indifference," i.e., value-*equality*, presuppose cardinal utility.

Based on the concepts of self-ownership and demonstrated preference, and in accordance with Pareto's strictures concerning the possibility of meaningful ordinalist welfare statements, Rothbard deduced the following set of propositions: If a man uses his body ("labor") to extend his control over (appropriate) other nature-given things (unowned "land"), as he must if only in order to stand, this action demonstrates that such things are also goods for him. Hence, he must have gained in utility by appropriating them. At the same time, his action does not make anyone else worse off, because in appropriating previously unowned resources nothing is taken away from others. Others could have appropriated these resources, too, if they had considered them valuable. Yet, they demonstrably did not do so. Indeed, their failure to appropriate them demonstrates their preference for *not* appropriating them. Hence, they cannot possibly be said to have lost any utility on account of another's appropriation. Proceeding from the basis of acts of original appropriation, any further act, whether of production or consumption, is equally Pareto-superior on demonstrated preference grounds, provided only that it does not affect the physical integrity of the resources appropriated or produced with appropriated means by others. The producer-consumer is better off, while everyone else is left in control of the same quantity of goods as before. As a result, no one can be said to be worse off. Finally, every voluntary exchange of goods proceeding from this basis is a Pareto-superior change as well, because it can only take place if both exchange parties expect to benefit from it, while the supply of goods controlled in action (owned) by others remains unchanged.

Based on these propositions, Rothbard proceeded to advance an entirely new Austrian theory of the state. While every act of original appropriation, production-consumption, and exchange (the free market)

---

[12] Rothbard, *The Logic of Action*, vol. 1, p. 212.

always and necessarily increases social utility, no act of expropriation (the non-consensual-unilateral-taking of goods from their original appropriator and producer-consumer) can possibly do so. Obviously, this is true of all acts typically considered criminal, such as physical aggression, invasion, robbery, theft, and fraud. While the criminal controls a larger quantity of goods and is thus better off, his victim controls a correspondingly smaller quantity of goods and is made worse off; hence, no criminal act fulfills the Paretian strictures and can ever be said to increase *social* utility. While criminal acts are typically considered illegal and man is permitted to defend himself against them, the same conclusion about utility is true of all acts of government agents: "*no act of government whatever can increase social utility.*"[13] Yet, they are considered legal and one is not permitted to defend oneself against them.

Rothbard's conclusion concerning the rejection of the institution of government on welfare-economic grounds is based on the standard and non-controversial definition of the state

> as that organization which possesses either or both (in actual fact, almost always both) of the following characteristics: (a) it acquires its revenue by physical coercion (taxation); and (b) it achieves a compulsory monopoly of force and of ultimate decisionmaking power over a given territorial area.[14]

As for its first pillar, it is clear that government agents benefit from acts of taxation; otherwise, they would abstain from them. Just as clearly, the subjects of taxation—the original appropriators-producers of the goods taxed—cannot be said to benefit from such acts; otherwise, they would pay the same quantity of goods voluntarily and no compulsion would be necessary.

Similarly, it is clear that government agents gain in utility by achieving a territorial monopoly of ultimate decisionmaking (jurisdiction). Most importantly, in doing so the question of whether taxes are justified or not becomes moot and is decided from the outset in favor of government. However, just as clearly, every subject of government's ultimate decisionmaking power is thereby made worse off. By virtue of his acts of original appropriation and production, a man demonstrates his preference for exercising exclusive control (jurisdiction) over the appropriated and produced goods. Unless he abandons, sells, or voluntarily surrenders them to someone else (in which case this person would demonstrate *his* preference for gaining exclusive control over them), he cannot

[13]Ibid., p. 243.

[14]Rothbard, *The Ethics of Liberty*, p. 171.

possibly be said to have changed this evaluation. If, contrary to his demonstrated preference for *not* giving up his privately appropriated and produced goods, the state attains a territorial monopoly of ultimate decisionmaking (jurisdiction), this is only possible as the result of an act of expropriation. If the government is the ultimate decisionmaker, then by implication no single man has exclusive control over his own appropriated and produced goods. In effect, the state has assumed ownership of all goods appropriated and produced by "its" residents, and has reduced them to the rank of tenants. Whereas the government's range of control is enlarged, every private owner's range of control regarding his own appropriations and products, and their value, is correspondingly reduced. Most importantly, as a tenant no one can exclude the government from access to his privately appropriated and produced goods; that is, everyone is left without means of physical defense *vis-à-vis* possible government intervention or invasion.

Consequently Rothbard concluded, if all government action rests on expropriation, and no expropriation can be said to increase social utility, then welfare economics must call for the abolition of the state. Scores of political philosophers and economists, from Thomas Hobbes to James Buchanan and the modern public-choice economists, have attempted to escape from this conclusion by portraying the state as the outcome of contracts, and hence, a voluntary and welfare-enhancing institution. In reply to such endeavors, Rothbard agreed with Joseph Schumpeter that "the theory which construes taxes on the analogy of club dues or of purchase of services of, say, a doctor only proves how far removed this part of the social sciences is from scientific habits of mind."[15] From Hobbes to Buchanan, statists had tried to overcome the apparent contradiction in the idea of a "voluntary" state equipped with compulsory judicial monopoly and the power to tax by recourse to the intellectual make-shift of "implicit" or "conceptual" agreements, contracts, or constitutions. Rothbard explained that all of these typically tortuous attempts ultimately only lead to the same inescapable conclusion: "implicit" and "conceptual" contracts are the very opposite of contracts, i.e., no contracts. Hence, it is impossible to derive a welfare-economic justification for the state. No one can possibly—demonstrably—agree to permanently surrender jurisdiction over his person and private property to someone else unless he had sold or otherwise given all of his current possessions away and subsequently committed suicide; likewise no one who is alive, can possibly—demonstrably—enter a contract that permits someone else—his protector—to determine forever

[15]Rothbard, *The Logic of Action*, vol. 1, p. 247.

unilaterally, without the continued consent of the protected, the tribute that the protected must pay for his protection.

In particular, Rothbard scorned the idea of a "limited" protective state as self-contradictory and incompatible with the promotion of social utility. Limited government always has the inherent tendency to become unlimited (totalitarian) government. Given the principle of government—judicial monopoly and the power to tax—any notion of restraining government power and safeguarding individual life and property is illusory. Under monopolistic auspices, the price of justice and protection will rise and the quality of justice and protection will fall. A tax-funded protection agency is a contradiction in terms—an expropriating property protector—and will lead to more taxes and less protection. Even if a government limited its activities exclusively to the protection of pre-existing property rights, the further question of *how much* security to produce would arise. Motivated (like everyone else) by self-interest and the disutility of labor, but with the unique power to tax, a government agent's answer will invariably be the same: to *maximize expenditures* on protection—and almost all of a nation's wealth can conceivably be consumed by the cost of protection—and at the same time to *minimize* the *production* of protection. Moreover, a judicial monopoly will lead to a deterioration in the quality of justice and protection. If one can only appeal to government for justice, justice and protection will be perverted in favor of government, constitutions and supreme courts notwithstanding. Constitutions and supreme courts are government constitutions and courts, and whatever limitations to government action they might contain or find is determined by agents of the very institution under consideration. Predictably, the definition of property and protection will be altered and the range of jurisdiction expanded to the government's advantage.

Instead, in accordance with the "one ethical judgment" that "even the most rigorously *wertfrei* economists have been willing to allow themselves . . . (of feeling) free to recommend any change or process that increases social utility under the Unanimity Rule,"[16] Rothbard reached the same anarchist conclusion as the French–Belgian economist Gustave de Molinari before him: defense, protection, and judicial services

> would therefore have to be supplied by people or firms who (a) gained their revenue voluntarily rather than by coercion and (b) did not— as the State does—arrogate to themselves a compulsory monopoly of police or judicial protection. . . . [D]efense firms would have to be as

[16]Ibid., p. 244.

> freely competitive and as noncoercive against noninvaders as are all other suppliers of goods and services on the free market. Defense services, like all other services, would be marketable and marketable only.[17]

Every private-property owner would be able to partake of the advantages of the division of labor, and to seek better protection of his property than that afforded by self-defense, through cooperation with other owners and their property. That is, anyone could buy from, sell to, or otherwise contract with anyone else concerning protective and judicial services, and he could at any time unilaterally discontinue any such cooperation with others and fall back on self-reliant defense or change his protective affiliations.

Rothbard's other major advance was in the theory of monopoly and competition. Here too, Rothbard recalled the French tradition of radical laissez-faire economics of Jean-Baptiste Say and his followers (to which Molinari belonged). Rothbard's positive doctrine of competition and monopoly is plain and simple (as a theory should be). Competition is defined as conduct within the framework of the described rules of Pareto-superior action: of original appropriation, production-consumption, and voluntary exchange and contract. More specifically applied to *entrepreneurial* action, competition means the existence of unrestricted "free entry." Every individual is at liberty to employ his own property in any way he sees fit, and to enter any line of production deemed profitable. As long as this free-entry condition is met, Rothbard concluded, all product prices and production costs tend to be minimum prices and minimum costs. In distinct contrast, monopoly and monopolistic competition are defined by the absence of free entry, i.e., as the presence of exclusive privilege. The state, defined as the compulsory territorial monopolist of jurisdiction and protection, is thus the prototype of a monopoly. Every individual—except the agents of the state—is prohibited from using his property for the production of self-defense and justice, and thus from competing with the state. All other monopolies go back to this originary state-monopoly of jurisdiction (legislation and regulation) as their ultimate source. Every other monopoly involves "a grant of special privilege by the State, reserving a certain area of production to one particular individual or group."[18] Entry into the area is legally restricted to other actual or potential producers, and this restriction is enforced by state police. As long as free entry is restricted or absent, concluded Rothbard, whether in the production of justice and security or that of any other

---

[17]Rothbard, *Power and Market*, p. 2.

[18]Rothbard, *Man, Economy, and State*, p. 591.

good or service, product prices and production costs will be higher than otherwise, i.e., too high. (Thus, to Rothbard the notion of government anti-monopoly or antitrust policy was a *contradictio in adjecto*. Competition required instead the abolition of the state's very own territorial monopoly of jurisdiction.)

Moreover, Rothbard refuted every alternative theory as nonsense, nonoperational, or false. It is nonsense, for instance, to define a monopolist as someone who has control over his price (a "price-searcher"). Every businessman has perfect control over his price (and no control at all over the quantity bought at that price by consumers). Hence, under this definition, no one exists who is *not* a monopolist. Likewise, it is nonsense to define a monopolist as "the only seller of any given good," for in an objective sense, every seller of every product is always the only seller of his own unique product (brand). Thus, everyone is a monopolist with a one-hundred-percent market share of one's own product. Yet, this circumstance does not affect in the slightest that each entrepreneur must compete at all times with every other entrepreneur for consumer spending, regardless how unique or different one's goods may be. On the other hand, in a subjective sense, no seller of anything can ever be established definitely as a monopolist. According to this interpretation, the term "given good" means "a good as defined by *consumers*." Thus, the determination of whether or not the seller of something is its only seller, or of how large his market-share is, depends on the consumers' definition of what this good is; that is, on their classification of particular *physical objects* into various groups of *homogeneous goods*. Not only can such classifications continually change, but different consumers can classify the same physical objects differently. Hence, in this sense the term monopolist becomes practically useless and non-operational, and all attempts to measure a product's market-share must be considered futile.

Finally, Mises's theory of monopoly price is untenable. Mises had argued that

> [m]onopoly is a prerequisite for the emergence of monopoly prices, but it is not the only prerequisite. There is a further condition required, namely a certain shape of the demand curve. The mere existence of monopoly does not mean anything in this regard.... Not every price at which a monopolist sells a monopolized commodity is a monopoly price. Monopoly prices are only prices at which it is more advantageous for the monopolist to restrict the total amount to be sold than to expand his sales to the limit which a competitive market would allow.[19]

---

[19]Mises, *Human Action*, p. 359.

As Rothbard explained, this argument is fallacious. First off, it will have to be noted that every restrictive action must, by definition, have a complementary expansionary aspect. The factors of production which the monopolist releases from employment in some production line A do not simply disappear. Rather, they must be used otherwise: either for the production of another exchange good B, or for an expansion in the production of the consumer good of leisure for its owner. Thus, even if monopoly prices existed, this would have no negative welfare-social utility-implications. From the monopolist's act of not-selling, it follows that he must believe himself to be better off keeping rather than selling his goods, and no one else is made worse off because of his act (because everyone else still controls the same quantity of goods as before). Consequently, Mises's monopoly price and the shape of the demand curve facing a monopolist cannot be operationally or conceptually distinguished from any other price and demand curve facing any other seller.

Production, explained Rothbard, *precedes* the sale of final products, and production costs must be incurred *before* consumers can demonstrate their preference for one's products. Hence, it is nonsense, for instance, to define a monopoly price as a price above marginal cost (or of marginal revenue higher than marginal cost) because the cost curves on the one hand and the demand and revenue curves on the other do not exist simultaneously. The only curves that exist simultaneously with cost curves are entrepreneurially estimated *future* demand and revenue curves. However, in deciding on the quantity of goods to be produced, every producer will always set his output so as to maximize his expected money earnings, *ceteris paribus*. That is, in the monetary calculations leading to his output-decision, expected price and marginal revenue are never *equal* to marginal cost. No one will produce anything unless he expects its price to *exceed* its cost; and no one will expand his output, unless he expects marginal revenue to be *higher* than marginal cost. Thus, every entrepreneur assumes in his calculations that in the future he will be facing a downward sloping demand curve, with elastic and inelastic stretches. Likewise, at the subsequent point of sale when all costs have been incurred by the producer and the only relevant demand is that of consumers for existing stocks of produced products, every entrepreneur will assume a downward sloping demand curve. That is, every entrepreneur will set his price at such a height that any price higher than the actually chosen one will encounter an elastic demand, and thus lead to lower sales revenues.

If the actually chosen sale price coincides with the original estimation, and if the market clears at this price, the entrepreneurial forecast has been correct. On the other hand, the actual demand can differ from the initial projection, and one or another type of entrepreneurial forecasting error may be revealed. At the point of sale, the entrepreneur can come to the conclusion that he mistakenly produced either "too little" or "too much." In the first case, actual demand (prices and revenue) is higher than expected, yet profits could have been still greater if production had been further expanded. The entrepreneur originally estimated demand beyond a specific output-point to be inelastic (such that a larger output would lead to lower total revenue), while it is now revealed as being elastic beyond this point. In the second case, the actual demand (prices and revenue) is lower than expected. Losses could have been avoided if less had been produced. The entrepreneur estimated demand beyond a certain output-point to be elastic, such that a larger quantity could be sold for a higher total revenue, while it is now revealed as inelastic.

In any case, whether or not his original forecast was correct, every entrepreneur must subsequently make a new output decision. Under the assumption that they regard their past experience (present demand) as indicative of their future experience (demand), three possible decisions exist. Entrepreneurs whose initial forecasts had been correct will produce the same quantity as before. Entrepreneurs who had initially produced "too little" will now produce a larger quantity, and entrepreneurs who had previously produced "too much" will restrict current sales and future production. How, asked Rothbard, can this latter entrepreneurial response to earlier overproduction be distinguished from Mises's alleged "monopoly price" situation? He answered that in fact it could not.

> Is the higher price to be gained from such a cutback necessarily a "monopoly price"? Why could it not just as well be a movement from a *subcompetitive* price to a competitive price? In the real world, a demand curve is not simply "given" to a producer, but must be estimated and discovered. If a producer has produced too much in one period and, in order to earn more income, produces less in the next period, *this is all that can be said about the action.* . . . Thus, we cannot use "restriction of production" as the test of monopoly vs. competitive price. A movement from a subcompetitive to a competitive price also involves a "restriction" of production of this good, coupled, of course, with an expansion of production in other lines by the released factors. *There is no way whatever to distinguish such a "restriction" and corollary expansion from the alleged "monopoly-price" situation.* . . . But if a concept has no possible grounding in reality, then it is an empty and illusory, and not a meaningful, concept. On the free market, there is no way of distinguishing a "monopoly price" from a "competitive price" or a "subcompetitive price" or of establishing any changes as movements from one

to the other. No criteria can be found for making such distinctions. The concept of monopoly price as distinguished from competitive price is therefore untenable. We can only speak of the *free-market price*.[20]

In addition to these major innovations, Rothbard contributed many new theoretical insights. Two examples will have to suffice here. For one, Rothbard utilized the well-known Misesian argument concerning the impossibility of economic calculation (cost-accounting) under socialism in order to demonstrate, even more generally, the impossibility of one big cartel on the free market.[21]

> T]he free market placed definite limits on the size of the firm, i.e., the limits of *calculability* on the market. In order to calculate the profits and losses of each branch, a firm must be able to refer its internal operations to *external markets* for *each* of the various factors and intermediate products. When any of these external markets disappears, because all are absorbed *within* the province of a single firm, calculability disappears, and there is no way for the firm rationally to allocate factors to that specific area. The more these limits are encroached upon, the greater and greater will be the sphere of irrationality, and the more difficult it will be to avoid losses. One big cartel would not be able rationally to allocate producers' goods at all and hence could not avoid severe losses. Consequently, it could never really be established, and, if tried, would quickly break asunder.[22]

The second example, likewise inspired by Mises, is from the area of monetary theory. Mises, stimulated in turn by Menger's work, had demonstrated that money *qua* medium of exchange must originate as a *commodity* money (such as gold). Rothbard complemented Mises's theory of the origin of money—his famous "regression theorem"—with a theory of the destruction or devolution of money by government, or what might be termed a "progression theorem." He demonstrated, most succinctly in his *What Has Government Done to Our Money?*,[23] the praxeologically necessary sequence of actions taken by government in order to achieve—as its ultimate goal—complete money counterfeiting autonomy. Having of necessity to begin with a market-provided commodity money such as gold, a government will first monopolize the minting; next, it will monopolize the issue of money substitutes (titles to money, ready redeemable banknotes); subsequently, it will engage in fractional

---

[20]Rothbard, *Man, Economy, and State*, pp. 607, 614; emphasis in the original.

[21]Ibid., pp. 544–50.

[22]Ibid., p. 585.

[23]Murray N. Rothbard, *What Has Government Done to Our Money?* (Auburn, Ala.: Ludwig von Mises Institute, 1990).

reserve banking and issue money substitutes in excess of actual money; and finally, as the inevitable result of the bank crisis (bank run) brought about by fractional-reserve banking, it will suspend the redeemability of its notes, cut the tie between paper (title) and money (gold), confiscate all privately owned money, and institute a pure fiat money.

Yet, Rothbard's achievements go far beyond his innovations in economic theory. They go far beyond even his accomplishment of integrating these innovations into a grand, comprehensive and unified system of Austrian economics. Although an economist by profession, Rothbard's work encompasses also political philosophy (ethics) and history.

Unlike the utilitarian Mises, who denied the possibility of rational ethics, Rothbard recognized the need for an ethical system to complement value-free economics so as to make the case for the free market truly watertight. Drawing on the theory of natural rights, in particular on the work of John Locke, and on the genuinely American tradition of anarchistic thought of Lysander Spooner and Benjamin Tucker, Rothbard developed a system of ethics based on the principles of self-ownership and the original appropriation of unowned natural resources through homesteading. Any other proposal, he demonstrated, either does not qualify as an ethical system applicable to everyone *qua* human being, or it is not viable, for following it would literally imply death while it requires a surviving proponent, and thus leads to performative contradictions. The former is the case with all proposals which imply granting A ownership over B and resources homesteaded by B, but not giving B the same right with respect to A. The latter is the case with all proposals advocating universal (communal) co-ownership of everyone and everything by all, for then no one would be allowed to do anything with anything before he had everyone else's consent to do whatever he wanted to do. And how could anyone consent to anything if he were not the exclusive (private) owner of his body? In *The Ethics of Liberty*, his second *magnum opus*, Rothbard deduced the entire corpus of liberal-libertarian law—from the law of contracts to the theory of punishment—from these first axiomatic principles; and in his *For A New Liberty*,[24] he applied this ethical system to a diagnosis of the present age and the proposal, and economic analysis, of the political reforms necessary to achieve a free and prosperous commonwealth.

Furthermore, although first and foremost a theoretician, Rothbard was also an accomplished historian, and his writing contains a wealth of

[24]Murray N. Rothbard, *For A New Liberty* (New York: Macmillan, 1973).

empirical information rarely matched by any empiricist or historicist. In fact, it is Rothbard's recognition of economics and political philosophy (ethics) as pure aprioristic theory, and of theoretical reasoning as logically anteceding and constraining every historical investigation, which makes his empirical scholarship superior to that of most orthodox historians, and has established him as one of the outstanding "revisionist" historians. Particularly noteworthy in the area of economic history is his book *America's Great Depression,*[25] which applies the Mises–Hayek business-cycle theory to explain the 1929 stock-market crash and the ensuing economic depression. In political history, there is his four-volume history of colonial America, *Conceived in Liberty,*[26] and in the field of intellectual history there is his posthumously published monumental if uncompleted two-volume history of economic, social, and political thought, *Economic Thought Before Adam Smith* and *Classical Economics.*[27] In these and other books and countless articles, Rothbard provided integrated economic-sociological-political analyses of almost every critical episode in American history: from the panic of 1819, the Jacksonian period, the War for Southern Independence, the Progressive era, World War I and Wilsonianism, Hoover, FDR and World War II, to Reaganomics and Clintonianism. With an eye for the minutest detail of history's byways, time and again Rothbard challenged common wisdom and historical orthodoxy and provided his readers with a vision of the process of history as a permanent struggle of good against evil: between truth and falsehood, and between forces of liberty and power elites exploiting and enriching themselves at the expense of others and covering their tracks through lies and deceptions.

These amazing scholarly achievements notwithstanding, Rothbard's academic career, much like Mises's, was hardly a success by conventional standards. The twentieth century has been the age of socialism and interventionism. Schools and universities are government-funded and government-controlled institutions; hence, the most eminent appointments go either to socialists or interventionists, while "intransigent," "dogmatic," or "extremist" proponents of laissez-faire capitalism are excluded or relegated to the fringes of academia. Rothbard had no illusion in this regard, and never complained or appeared to be bitter

---

[25]Murray N. Rothbard, *America's Great Depression* (New York: Richardson and Snyder, 1983).

[26]Murray N. Rothbard, *Conceived in Liberty,* 4 vols. (New Rochelle, N.Y.: Arlington House, 1975).

[27]Murray N. Rothbard, *An Austrian Perspective on the History of Economic Thought,* 2 vols. (Cheltenham, U.K.: Edward Elgar, 1995).

about his academic fate. His influence did not rest on institutional powers, but solely on the power of his ideas and the force of logic.

Murray Rothbard was born and raised in New York City as the only child of immigrant parents. His father, a chemist, came from Poland and his mother from Russia. Upon winning a scholarship, Rothbard attended private schools and went on to study economics at Columbia University, where, in 1956, he received his Ph.D. with a dissertation written under the economic historian Joseph Dorfman. For more than a decade beginning in 1949, Rothbard also participated in Mises's private seminar at New York University. After working several years for various foundations, most notably the William Volker Fund, Rothbard taught at the Brooklyn Polytechnic Institute, an engineering school, from 1966 until 1986. From 1986 until his death, he was the S.J. Hall Distinguished Professor of Economics at the University of Nevada, Las Vegas. As one of two economics professors at Brooklyn Polytechnic, Rothbard was a member of the social science department, which fulfilled only a subservient function within the university. In Las Vegas, the department of economics, housed in the university's Business College, did not offer a doctoral program. Thus, throughout his academic career Rothbard was prevented from claiming a single doctoral student as his own.

Rothbard's fringe existence in academia did not prevent him from exerting intellectual influence or attracting students and disciples, however. Through the sheer flood of his publications and the unrivaled clarity of his writing, modeled after that of H.L. Mencken, Rothbard became the creator and one of the principal agents of the contemporary libertarian movement, which in the course of three decades has grown from a handful of proponents into a genuine mass movement (including but extending far beyond a party of this name, the Libertarian Party, to a wide and complex network of groups and associations on into the U.S. Congress and many state legislatures). Naturally, in the course of this development, Rothbard and his theoretical position did not remain unchallenged or undisputed. There were ups and downs in institutional alignments, coalitions, breaks, and realignments in his career. However, in association with the Center for Libertarian Studies, under Burton S. Blumert, and the Ludwig von Mises Institute, under Llewellyn H. Rockwell, Jr., and as founder-editor of their scholarly flagships, *The Journal of Libertarian Studies* (1977) and *The Review of Austrian Economics* (1987),[28] Rothbard has remained beyond his death without

[28]In 1998 the journal that Rothbard founded became the *Quarterly Journal of Austrian Economics*, published by Transaction Publishers..

doubt the most important and highly respected intellectual authority within the entire libertarian movement, and to this day his rationalist-axiomatic- deductive-Austro-libertarianism provides the intellectual benchmark in reference to which not only everyone and everything *within* libertarianism is defined, but increasingly everyone and everything in American politics.

SELECTED READINGS

Block, Walter, and Llewellyn H. Rockwell, Jr. eds. 1988. *Man, Economy, and Liberty: Essays in Honor of Murray N. Rothbard*. Auburn, Ala.: Ludwig von Mises Institute.

Rothbard, Murray N. [1982] 1998. *The Ethics of Liberty*. New York: New York University Press.

——. 1997. *The Logic of Action*. 2 vols. Cheltenham, U.K.: Edward Elgar.

——. 1995. *Economics Before Adam Smith*. Vol. 1 *An Austrian Perspective on the History of Economic Thought*. Cheltenham, U.K.: Edward Elgar.

——. 1995. *Classical Economics*. Vol. 2. *An Austrian Perspective on the History of Economic Thought*. Cheltenham, U.K.: Edward Elgar.

——. 1995. *Making Economic Sense*. Auburn, Ala.: Ludwig von Mises Institute.

——. 1990 [1963]. *What Has Government Done to Our Money?* Auburn, Ala.: Ludwig von Mises Institute.

——.1983. *America's Great Depression*. New York: Richardson and Snyder.

——. 1973. *For a New Liberty*. New York: Macmillan.

——. 1975. *Conceived in Liberty*. 4 vols. New Rochelle, N.Y.: Arlington House.

——. 1970. *Power and Market*. Menlo Park, Calif.: Institute for Humane Studies.

——. 1962. *Man, Economy, and State: A Treatise on Economics*. Princeton, N.J.: D. Van Nostrand; reprinted in 1993 by the Ludwig von Mises Institute, Auburn, Ala.

INDEX

Compiled by Richard Perry


Action
    cause and effect, 81–82
    and choice, 228–29
    expectations as key to, 35
    general theory of, 73, 129–30
    praxeology, 63, 71, 81, 84, 95, 158, 163
    purposive behavior, 84, 94, 99, 108–09
Anderson, Benjamin M., Jr., 154, 162n, 169, 177n
    *The Value of Money*, 154, 169
Aquinas, Saint Thomas, 8
Aristotelian, 16
Associations
    American Economic Association, 140
    American Philosophical Society, 140
    Center for Libertarian Studies, 240
    French Free-Trade Association, 61
Austrian School
    business-cycle theory, 40, 119–20, 124, 133–35, 152–53, 185–87, 209–10, 238
    calculation debate, 190–91
    as derisive attack, 75
    discovery procedure, 65, 187–91
    edifice of correct theory, 163
    goods theory, 20, 51–52, 82–85
    influence, v–xii
    marginal utility, 10, 33, 54–55, 72, 79, 85, 87–88, 90, 94, 99, 107, 115–16, 130–31, 146, 226–28
    methodology, logical, 17–18, 128
    price theory, 19, 80–81, 94–99, 107
    property, 40, 84, 91, 93
    and Spanish Scholastics, 9
    time preference, 9, 40, 54, 116, 123–24, 132–33
    value
        and price, 9, 34, 54–55, 76, 80–82, 88–89, 94–100, 108
        paradox of, 10, 19, 33, 78, 87–88,
        as subjective, 4, 33, 62–63, 72, 85–90, 96, 125–27, 130
        theory, 85–90, 115–16
        as uniform theory, 33, 126
Axiomatic-deductive theory, 224
Azpilcueta Navarrus, Martín de, 6, 8, 11

Baird, A.C., 169n
Balmes, Jaime, 10, 11
Bank of England, 26
Bartley W.W., III, 14n, 27, 185n, 189n
Bastiat, Frédéric, 32, 59–69, 81n, 82n, 172n, 173
    background, 59–61
    British Anti-Corn Law League, 61
    "Broken Window Fallacy," 173
    "The Candlemaker's Petition," 67
    capital
        and entrepreneurship as captains of economic ship, 62
        and wages, 62
    *Economic Sophisms*, 61
    *Economic Harmonies*, 61
    economics
        from consumer viewpoint, 62
        as economic harmony, 59, 63
        as the theory of exchange, 63
    entrepreneur
        dynamic rivalrous process, 59–60
        discovery, 65
    free trade
        trade barriers and war, 65, 67
        harm when lacking, 65
    free market, plan-coordination function of, 59
    French Academy of Science, 61
    French Free-Trade Association, 61
    influence, 68
    international monetary relations, 67
    intervention, government
        tariffs, abolished, 60
        state used to plunder citizens, 62, 64–65
        "The Influence of English and French Tariffs," 61
    laissez-faire, 68
    law of comparative advantage, 67
    *Le Libre-Exchange* (newspaper), 61
    natural rights, 66
    opportunity costs, 63
    praxeology, 63
    pre-Austrian, 61
    property
        customs duties as rights violations, 66
        as function of government, 66
        private, essential for freedom, 66
    rent, land, 64
    subjective value, 62–63
    "The Tax and the Vine," 61
    "What is Seen and What is Not Seen," 62

Batson, H.E., 226
Beltrán, Lucas, 3n
Benn, Sir Ernest, 196
Berlin Wall, xi
Biddle, Clement C., 46
Birner, Jack, 192
Black, R.D. Collison, 80
Blaug, Mark, 183n, 193
Block, Walter, 241
Blumert, Burton S., 240
Boehm, Stephan, 192n
Böhm-Bawerk, Eugen von, 13, 36, 40, 42, 76, 95, 97–99n, 101–02, 105n, 113–24, 128, 146–50n, 153–54, 160, 163, 182–83, 186, 192, 196, 198, 209, 223–24, 226
  Austrian Minister of Finance, 114
  background, 113–14
  *Capital and Interest*, 42, 43, 114, 163
    Vol. I *History and Critique of Interest Theories*, 114
    Vol. II *Positive Theory of Capital*, 115–17
    Vol. III *Further Essays on Capital and Interest*, 115
  capital
    bull's-eye figure, 117–19
    and entrepreneurship, 116
    and interest theory, 116–19
    and saving, 118–19
  criticisms of, 120–21
  entrepreneur, 116, 119
  exploitation theory embraced by Karl Marx, critique of, 114–16
  influence, 120–21
  interest
    return on investment, 116
    theory, 116
    time, 115–16
  *Karl Marx and the Close of His System*, 114, 128
  macrocosm, 117
  marginal utility, 115–16
  methodology, 115
  production and time, 115–16
  "The Positive Theory of Capital and Its Critics," 121
  research agenda, excluded areas, 120
  time preference, 116
  University of Innsbruck, 114
  University of Vienna, 113–14
  value, theory of, 115–16
  wages, 116
Bolingbroke, Lord, 16
Bonds, government, as use of savings, 39
Bordo, Michael D., 21, 23n, 26
Boulding, Kenneth, 183
Bovadilla, Jeronimo Castillo de, 5
Boyers, W. Hayden, 82
Bretton Woods, 173
Brewer, Anthony, 14n, 17n, 22n, 24n, 26
British Classical School, 10, 36
British Anti-Corn Law League, 61
British Navigation Acts of, 1581, 1651, and 1660, 55
Brown, J. Douglas, 140
Bruno, Leoni, 11
Buchanan, James M., 107, 111, 199, 231
Burns, Arthur F., 177n
Business cycle, viii, 41, 119–20, 124, 133–35, 152–53, 186–87, 209–10, 238

Cabanis, Pierre Jean Georges, 45n
Caldwell, Bruce J., 73n, 100, 121, 183n, 189n, 190n, 192–93
  *The Collected Works of F.A. Hayek*, 190n
Camacho, Francisco Gómez, 5n
Cannan, Edwin, 196
Cantillion, Richard, 10, 13–28, 36, 46, 59, 68, 79
  background, 13–15
  costs, 21
  entrepreneur, 15, 18–19
  *Essai sur la Nature du Commerce en Général*, 13, 15–16
    economy, analysis of, 15
    entrepreneur, 15
    first treaty on economics, 13
    government as inefficient/corrupt, 16
    mercantilism, critique of, 17
    monetary economy, analysis of, 16
  founding father of modern economics, 14
  influence, 14
  interest
    theory, 24
    usury laws, 24
  market prices, 19–20
  mercantilist
    mistakenly labeled as, 22, 25
    thinking, breaking out of, 14
    as short run policy, 24
  methodology
    logical–deductive theorizing, 17
    *ceteris paribus* assumption, 18
  money
    bimetallism, 25

government failure to micromanage, 25
national banks, warning against, 25
theory, 23–24
"Observations on the Trade and Luxury of Both Nations," 16
opportunity costs, 20–21
physiocrats, 14, 21
population theory, 21
production determined by demand, 18
spatial economics, 23
value, 20
wages, 23
Capital
as capitalization, 40, 132–33
and entrepreneurship, 36–42, 52–54, 62, 116, 134–35
and interest theory, 36–42, 52–54, 116–19, 133–34
malinvestment of, 135, 186–87
and saving, 36–42, 51, 118–19, 133
time, 131–32
and wages, 62, 116
Cassel, Gustav, 115
Chafuen, Alejandro, 2, 11, 79n
Charles V, Emperor/King of Spain, 9
Chase, Stuart, 171n
Chicago School, v
Clark, John B., 119, 121, 127–28, 140n
Classical School, 14, 76–79
Clintonianism, 239
Clower, R.W., 202
Coats, A.W., 80n
Cobden, Richard, 61
Command society, 8
Commons, John R., 139
Competition
dynamic, 5, 188
as free entry, 233–34
labor, 131
and profit and loss, 77
Comte, Charles, 59, 68
Condillac, Abbé Etienne Bonnot de, 45n
Conrad, Johannes, 124
Cortney, Philip, 177n
Costs
opportunity, 21
of production theory, 5, 85
subjectivism of, 106–07
Coudroy, Felix, 60
Covarrubias y Leiva, Diego de, 4, 5
Crane, Stephen, 169n
Craver, Earlene, 144n, 154, 184n, 193
Credit expansion, 7, 124, 135, 152–53, 186–87, 209–10
Croome, H.M., 186n
Crusoe economics, 33–34, 99
Čuhel, Franz, 149, 150n
Currency School, 146, 148, 153
Cycle theory, *See* Business cycle

Davanzaty, Bernardo, 6
Davidson, Audrey, 13n
Davidson, Eugene, 162, 164
De Gaulle, Charles, 164
Decker, Matthew, 16
Dempsey, Father Bernard W., 8
Dewey, John, 171n
Dietz, Gottfried, 207
DiLorenzo, Thomas J., 59–69
Dingwall, James, 48n, 100
Director, Aaron, 184
Dolan, Edwin, 1n, 12, 79n, 151n, 184
Dorfman, Joseph, 128, 240
Doren, Mark van, 169n

Eatwell, John, 103, 112, 122
Ebeling, Richard, 206
Ebenstein, Alan, 196n
Earned Income Tax Credit, 178
Economics
as allocation of scarce resources, 33
consumer viewpoint, 62
discovery procedure, 188
edifice, systematic, 224–25
and ethics, 226, 238
goods, 20, 51–52, 82–85
harmony, 59, 63
ideas, search for true, 225
macrocosm, 117
marginal utility, 10, 33, 54–55, 72, 79, 85, 87–88, 90, 94, 99, 107, 115–16, 130–31, 146, 226–28
political activism and, 225–26
price theory, 19, 80–81, 88–90, 94–99, 107
scope of, 108–09
socialist calculation debate, 189
spontaneous order, 188–89
time, 110
theory of exchange, 63
universality and immutability of laws, 80
wants
ranking of, 84, 86
satisfaction of, 83, 94–95
welfare, 226–31

Edgeworth, F.Y., 36n
Edwards, James Rolph, 151n
Egger, John B., 195–204
Einaudi, Luigi, 164
Ekelund, Robert, 13n
Elgar, Edward, 222
Entrepreneur
  bull's-eye, 117–19
  and competition, 233–34
  discovery process, ix, 65, 236
  foresight, 52–53, 91
  knowledge, 30–31, 90–93
  as risk bearer, 15
  as rivalry, 5, 59–60
  theory, 36–42, 90–93, 135–36
  uncertainty, 18–19, 37, 53, 90, 93, 107, 135, 235–36
Equilibrium, vii–ix
Erhard, Ludwig, 164, 207
Exchange, 34
Exploitation theory, socialist, 133

Ferdinand I, King of Austria, 9
Ferguson, Adam, 188
Fetter, Frank A., 43, 46, 123–41, 163
  action, 129–30
  American Economic Association, 140
  *American Economic Review*, 140
  American Philosophical Society, 140
  background, 124–25
  business cycle, 124, 133–35
  capital
    capitalization of, 132–33
    and entrepreneurship, 134–35
    and interest theory, 133–34
    malinvestment of, 135
    and saving, 133
  *Encyclopedia of the Social Sciences*, 140
  entrepreneur
    theory, 135–36
    uncertainty, 135
  influence, 139–41
  interest, 132–33
  *Journal of Political Economy*, 140
  marginal utility, 130
  methodology, 123, 128–29
  money, theory of, 133–34
  *Principles of Economics*, 123
  *The Quarterly Journal of Economics*, 126, 140
  rent, 123, 130–33
  time, 131–32
  time preference, 132–33
  value, subjective, 125–27, 130
  wages, 127–32, 136–37
  wants, 129
  welfare
    intervention, 138
    economists as enlightened advisors, 138
Fischer, Louis, 169
Fisher, Irving, 46, 146, 148
Foundation for Economic Education (FEE), 201
Foxwell, Herbert, 196
Free market, plan-coordination function of, 59
Free trade
  harm inflicted on citizens when lacking, 65
  trade barriers and war, 65, 67
French Academy of Science, 61
Friedman, Milton, v, 46, 178, 184
Frisch, Ragnar, 117

Galiani, Abbé Ferdinando, 6
Garrett, Garet, 177n
Garrison, Roger, 113–22, 167n, 193
  "Austrian Capital Theory: The Early Controversies," 121
George, Henry, 104, 124, 128
  *Progress and Poverty*, 104, 124
Gilbert, Milton, 151
Goodwin, Craufurd D.W., 80
Gossen, Hermann Heinrich, 95n
Gournay, Jacques Claude Marie Vincent, 30
Grant, James, 209
  *The Trouble with Prosperity*, 209n
Grattan, Clinton Hartley, 169n
Gray, Alexander, 50–51, 57
Gray, John, 193
Great Depression, ix
  *see also* Rothbard; Business Cycle
Greaves, Bettina Bien, 171n
Gregory, T.E., 183, 195
Gresham's Law, 49
Grice-Hutchinson, Marjorie, 2, 11
Groenewegen, Peter D., 43
Grünberg, Karl, 144, 154
Gutteridge, H.C., 195

Haberler, Gottfried von, 159, 184
Hahn, L. Albert, 177n
Hayek, F.A., 1n, 14n, 17–20, 23, 26n–27, 38, 66, 72–74n, 82n, 91n, 98n, 100, 102n, 106, 111, 118–23, 139, 152, 154–56, 159, 165, 172, 177n, 181–94, 196–98, 201–03, 207, 209, 212n, 220, 223n, 239

background, 181–85
business cycle, v–xii
credit expansion, 186–87
theory, 185–87
*Capitalism and the Historians*, 197
*The Constitution of Liberty*, 165, 187n
*Counter-Revolution of Science*, 165
*Denationalization of Money: An Analysis of the Theory and Practice of Concurrent Currencies*, 183, 187n
economics
discovery procedure, 188
spontaneous order, 188–89
calculation debate, 189
*The Fatal Conceit*, 185
*Hayek on Hayek*, 193
Hayekian triangles, 185
*Individualism and Economic Order*, 193
influence, 189–92
malinvestments, 186–87
*Monetary Theory and the Trade Cycle*, 186, 193
Nobel Memorial Prize in Economics, xi, 181, 184, 203
*Prices and Production*, 185, 186, 193
*The Pure Theory of Capital*, 183, 186, 193
*The Road to Serfdom*, 139, 172, 185, 193
time, 186
Hayekian, 31, 65
Hayekian triangles, 185
Hazlitt, Henry, 63, 68, 69, 162, 167–79, 197, 201, 211
*The Anatomy of Criticism: A Trialogue*, 170, 179
attacking the New Deal, 170
background, 167–68
Bretton Woods agreement, 173
business cycle, 169
*The Conquest of Poverty*, 178, 179
*The Critics of Keynesian Economics*, 177n,
Earned Income Tax Credit, 178
*Economics in One Lesson*, 63, 172, 179
as editorialist and book reviewer, 171
*The Failure of the "New Economics": An Analysis of the Keynesian Fallacies*, 176, 179, 201
*The Foundations of Morality*, 179
*The Free Man's Library*, 176
identified with free market causes, 173
*From Bretton Woods to World Inflation: A Study of the Causes and Consequences*, 173n
*The Great Idea*, 176n, 179
*The Illusions of Point Four*, 175
influence, 178–79
*Instead of Dictatorship*, 170
labor union privileges , 175
magazines and newspapers involved with
*American Mercury*, 172
*The Freeman*, 178
*Human Events*, 178
*Los Angeles Times*, 178
*Man vs. The Welfare State*, 178–79
*The Nation*, 168
*National Review*, 178
*Newsweek*, 174
*New York Evening Mail*, 168
*New York Evening Post*, 168
*New York Sun*, 168
*New York Times*, 171
*The Review of Austrian Economics*, 178
*Times Book Review*, 168
*Wall Street Journal*, 168
National Industrial Recovery Administration, 171
*A New Constitution Now*, 170, 179
postwar issues, 174–76
*Thinking as a Science*, 168, 179
*The Way to Will Power*, 168
*Will Dollars Save the World?*, 175
*The Wisdom of Henry Hazlitt*, 179
*The Wisdom of the Stoics: Selections from Seneca, Epictetus, and Marcus Aurelius*, 177n
Hearn, William E., 81n
Hébert, Robert F., 13n, 15n, 21n, 23n, 26n, 27
Heinz, Grete, 14n
Helfferich, Karl, 146
Hennings, Klaus, 113n, 116n, 117n, 118n, 120n, 121
Henry III, King, 3
Henry IV, King, 3
Henry of Navarre, *See* Henry IV,
Herbener, Jeffrey M., 123–41, 223, 228
"Introduction" in *The Meaning of Ludwig von Mises*, ed., 223n
"The Pareto Rule and Welfare Economics," 228n
Herford, C.H., 101n, 103n, 104n, 111
Hicks, Sir John, 181, 183, 196
Higgs, Henry, 13n, 18n, 27
Historian, revisionist, 239

Historical School
"Austrian" as derisive attack on Menger, 75
examination of history, 157
German, 144
*Methodenstreit* (methodological debate), 63
Hobbes, Thomas, 231
Holcombe, Randall G. (Introduction), v–xii
Homesteading, 229
Hone, Joseph, 27
Hoover, Herbert, viii–ix, 239
Hoppe, Hans-Hermann, 84n, 162n, 217n, 223–41
"Book Review of *Man, Economy, and Liberty*," *228n*
*The Economics and Ethics of Private Property*, 228n
*Natural Elites, Intellectuals, and the State*, 219n
Hoselitz, Bert F., 37, 48n, 100n
Howard, Stanley E., 140
Howey, Richard S., 80n
Hoxie, Robert F., 126, 129, 141
Huncke, George, 98, 114, 121
Huszar, George B. de, 82n
Hutchison, T.W., 189n, 193
Hülsmann, Jörg Guido, 13n, 20n, 27, 93n
"Cantillon as a Proto-Austrian: Further Evidence," 20, 27
"Knowledge, Judgment, and the Use of Property," 93n
Hume, David, 24, 41, 76, 153
Hutt, William H., x, 177n, 195–204, 205
articles on competition and monopoly, 198
background, 195–96
*"The Factory System of the Early Nineteenth Century,"* 197
*The Economics of the Color Bar*, 198
*Economists and the Public*, 198
intervention, 198–200
full employment measures, 200
*The Keynesian Episode: A Reassessment*, 202, 205n
*Keynesianism–Retrospect and Prospect*, 200
labor policies, 197–98
observation on Keynes, 201–03
*Plan for Reconstruction*, 200
*Politically Impossible. . .?*, 199
*A Rehabilitation of Say's Law*, 202
*The Strike-Threat System*, 197
*The Theory of Collective Bargaining*, 197
The *Theory of Idle Resources*, 200

Individual
liberty, 218–20, 224, 228–29
not mechanistic aggregates, 150
mechanistic view unscientific, 224
Inflation, 6, 149, 152, 210–11
Interest
as property right, 40
and quantity of money relationship, 41
return on investment, 38, 53, 116
risk premium, 53–54
and state, 53
as supply and demand relationship, 41
theory, 24, 38–41, 43, 116, 132–33
time, 38–40, 53–54, 115–16, 132
as usury, 39–40,
*See also* Capital
Intervention, 8, 16, 60, 62, 64–65, 144, 155–57, 198–200, 214–16, 227–31
International relations, 67, 213, 216–17

Jaffé, William, 80n, 100
James, William, 168
Jefferson, Thomas, 45
Jenks, Jeremiah W., 124
Jesuits (Society of Jesus), 1, 8
Jevons, William Stanley, vii, 13, 17, 72n, 80n, 101–05n, 108, 111, 115, 126, 127n, 149, 196
Journals and Newspapers
*American Economic Association Publications*, 125n, 141
*American Economic Review*, 124, 127n, 138n–41, 187n
*American Mercury*, 172
*Annals of the American Academy of Political and Social Science*, 125n
*Atlantic Economic Journal*, 22n, 28
*Austrian Economics Newsletter*, 174n, 177n
*Critical Review*, 183n, 193
*Economic Inquiry*, 100
*Economic Journal*, 27, 104, 107, 155, 183, 198n, 199n
*Economica*, 23n, 187n, 198n, 208n
*Encyclopedia of the Social Sciences*, 140
*The Free Market*, 167n
*The Freeman*, 114n, 122, 178
*History of Political Economy*, 100, 144, 184n
*Human Events*, 171n, 178
*Journal des Economistes*, 61
*Journal des Economistes et Etudes Humaines*, 99n

*Journal of Economic Literature*, 193
*Journal of Economic Perspectives*, 117
*Journal of Libertarian Studies*, 17n, 27, 28, 61, 217n
*Journal of Monetary Economics*, 21n
*Journal of Political Economy*, 21n, 28, 127n, 128n, 140, 209n, 210, 221
*Journal of Political Economics*, 138n
*Le Libre-Exchange* (newspaper), 61
*Los Angeles Times*, 178
*The Nation*, 168
*National Review*, 178
*New Individualist Review*, 225
*The New Republic*, 174n
*New York Evening Mail*, 168
*New York Evening Post*, 168
*New York Sun*, 168
*New York Times*, 171
*Newsweek*, 174
*Quarterly Journal of Economics*, 27, 126, 119, 121, 126n, 139–41
*Reader's Digest*, 172
*Reason*, 168n, 174n
*The Review of Austrian Economics*, 93n, 178, 191n, 192n, 193, 194, 215n
*South African Journal of Economics*, 198n
*Southern Economic Journal*, 192
*Times Book Review*, 168
*Wall Street Journal*, 168
*Wiener Tagblatt* (newspaper), 74
*Wiener Zeitung* (official newspaper), 73
*Yale Review*, 119

Kahane, J., 73n
Kaldor, N., 186n
Kauder, Emil, 80, 100
Kelley, David, 47n, 57
Kelley, John L., 167n
Kemmerer, E.W., 140
Keynes, John Maynard, viii, 46, 121, 181, 195
*The General Theory*, vii, 117, 168, 176, 183, 198, 200
observations of
Hayek, F.A., 183
Hazlitt, Henry, 176–77
Hutt, W.H., 201–03
Röpke, Wilhelm, 211–12
*Treatise on Money*, 155, 183
Kirzner, Israel M., x–xi, 101–12, 119n, 122, 184, 191, 193
*Classics in Austrian Economics: A Sampling in the History of a Tradition*, ed., 102, 111
*Essays on Capital and Interest: An Austrian Perspective*, 119n
*Market Theory and the Price System*, 103, 111
Klein, Peter G., 72n, 100, 181–94, 220n
*The Fortunes of Liberalism*. Vol. 4. *The Collected Works of F.A. Hayek*, ed., 72n, 100, 193, 220n
Knapp, George Friedrich, 144
Knies, Karl, 113n, 114n
Knight, Frank, 119, 121, 177n, 184, 192n
Knowles, Lillian, 195
Kresge, Stephen, 14n, 27, 185n, 189n

Labor, policies, 197–98
Laissez-faire, 31–32, 56, 66, 68, 80
Lachmann, Ludwig M., 184, 202
Lange, Oskar, 156, 190
Lavoie, Don, 191, 193
Law, John, 14, 17, 26
Law of diminishing returns, 35–36
Law of markets, *See* Say's Law
Lawrence, Joseph Stagg, 177n
Leijonhufvud, Axel, 202
Lerner, Abba P., 156, 183, 190
Lessines, Giles, 8
Libertarian, 2–3
Liggio, Leonard P., 14n, 27
Lindahl, Erik, 117
Link, Edith Murr, 144n
Locke, John, 236
London School of Economics (LSE), 107, 183, 195
Long, Breckinridge, 172
Luebe, Kurt, 224
Lugo, Cardinal Juan de, 5, 8
Luhnow, Harold, 162

Machlup, Fritz, 154, 159, 184
Machovec, Frank M., 110n, 111
Macy, Jon Albert, 169
Madison, James, 45
Malthus, Reverend Thomas R., 22
Mangoldt, Hans von, 93n
Mantoux, Etienne, 177n
Marget, Arthur, 197, 201,
*Theory of Prices*, 202
Marginal utility, 10, 33, 54–55, 72, 79, 85, 87–88, 90, 94, 99, 107, 115–16, 130–31, 226–28
Marginalist Revolution, 126
Mariana, Juan de, 1–12
Austrian School, 9

background, 1–2
central control, lack of knowledge, 8
credit expansion as robbery, 7
*De monetae mutatione* (On the alteration of money), 3
*De rege et regis institutione* (On the King and the royal institution), 2
*Discurso de las enfermedades de la Compañía* (A discourse on the sicknesses of the Jesuit order), 8, 11
influence, 9
inflation, prevention of, 7
Jesuit, 2
laws, too many cause loss of respect for, 9
libertarian, 2
money
debasement, 4, 7
quantity theory of, 6
scarcity, 4
natural law as superior to might of state, 3
price
controls, 4
equilibrium, 5
property, private, King not owner, 3
summary, 9–11
taxation
inflation as, 6
consent of people needed, 3
state and, 4
tyrannicide, defender of, 2
tyrant, 3
value
and price, 4
subjective, 4
Market self-regulation, 51
Marmontel, Jean François, 30
Marshall, Alfred, 43, 46, 105, 106, 148n, 195, 196
Marshall Plan, 213
Marx, Karl, 50n, 62, 114, 127
*Das Kapital*, 62
Marxian, 154, 169
Marxism, 128, 144
Mayer, Hans, 102n, 111, 154
McCloughry, Roy, 102
McCormick, Brian J., 183n
McDonald, Alice, 121
Mencken, H.L., 170, 240
Menger, Carl, 2, 6, 10–13, 26n, 34, 46, 48, 54, 57, 68, 71–102, 105, 113–16, 123, 126–27n, 139, 144, 146, 149, 160, 184, 189, 191–92, 195–96, 223–26, 237
action
cause and effect, 81–82
general theory, 73
man as beginning and end , 81
praxeology, 71, 81, 84, 95
purposive behavior, 84, 94, 99
background, 71–76
Classical School
calculable action only, 77
destruction of mercantilists, 72
distribution, 79
Crusoe economics, 99
economics
theory of goods, 82–85
imputed price, 88–90
universality and immutability of economic law, 80
economizing involves ranking wants, 84, 86
want satisfaction, 83, 94–95
entrepreneur
foresight, 91
knowledge, 90, 93
theory, 90–93
uncertainty, 90, 93
*Geld* (Money), 76
Historical School
"Austrian" as derisive attack on Menger, 75
*Methodenstreit* (methodological debate), 75
influence, 98–100
*Irrthumer des Historismus in der deutschen Nationalökonomie* (The errors of historicism in German economics), 75
laissez-faire, 80
marginal utility, 72, 79, 85, 87–88, 90, 94, 99
*Principles of Economics*, vii, 6, 13, 15, 71–100, 113, 115, 144
production and distribution theory
as pseudo-explanation, 85
price, 98
time, 90
property, 84
Scholastics, 79
University of Vienna, 73
*Untersuchungen uber die Methode der Sozialwissenschaften und der politischen Okonomie insbesondere* (Investigations into the method of the social sciences with special reference to economics), 75
value
and price, 76, 80–82, 88–89, 94–100

paradox, 78, 87–88
subjective, 72, 86, 96
theory, vii, 85–90
*Wiener Tagblatt* (newspaper), 74
*Wiener Zeitung* (official newspaper), 73
*Zur Theorie des Kapitals*, 76
Mercado, Tomás de, 8
Mercantilism, 14, 17, 24
Methodology, 17–18, 47–48, 123, 128–29, 149–51, 158, 224
Milgate, Murray, 103, 112, 122
Mill, John Stuart, 43, 46, 128, 177n, 199
Mises, Ludwig von, v–xii, 26n, 38, 41, 46, 50, 57, 62, 68–75n, 81–84, 93n, 95, 98n, 102, 105–11, 114, 119–25, 128n–29n, 137n, 139, 143–65, 171, 172n, 177, 181–83, 186, 189–92, 196, 198, 200–02, 205–09, 216n, 219, 223–28, 234–39
action
edifice of correct economic theory, 163
real action of individuals not mechanistic aggregates, 150
praxeology, 158, 163
background, 143–146
*Bureaucracy*, 139, 162
business cycle, 152–153
Currency School, 146, 148
*Die Gemeinwirtschaft* (Socialism), 156, 182
*Die Wirtschaftsrechnung in sozialistischen Gemeinwesen* ("Economic Calculation in the Socialist Commonwealth"), 155
*Economic Journal*, 155
German Historical School, 144
*Grundprobleme der Nationalökonomie* (Epistemological problems of economics), 158, 164
Historical School, 157
*Human Action: A Treatise on Economics*, x, 62, 137n, 156, 162–63, 177n, 223, 224
influence, 159–65
intervention
economic calculation, impossibility of, 155
ineffective and counterproductive, 144, 157
unstable, 157
*Kritik des Interventionismus*, 157
laissez-faire, 157
*Liberalism*, 216
*Liberalismus* (The free and prosperous commonwealth), 120, 226
methodology, 149–51, 158
migration, vi
money
Austrian circle, 146–47
balance-of-payments deficits, 147
as commodity, 151
inflation favors government, 149
marginal utility of, 146
not government created, 151
optimal money supply, 149
process analysis of individual action, 148
reserves and free banking, 152
theory, 146–55
*Nation, Statt, und Wirtschaft* (Nation, state, and economy), 153, 206
National Bureau of Economic Research, 161
*Nationalökonomie* (Economics), 160
*Nationalökonomisch Gesellschaft* (Economic Society), 155
New York University Graduate School of Business, 162
*Notes and Recollections*, 160
*Omnipotent Government: The Rise of the Total State and Total War*, 159, 216n
*On the Manipulation of Money and Credit*, 165
Peel's Act of 1844, 152
*Privatseminar*, 159, 182, 196
"Profit and Loss" (in *Planning for Freedom*), 163, 219n
scholar and creator, 155–65
*Socialism*, 156, 163, 171, 182
*Theories des Geldes and der Umlaufsmittel* (The theory of money and credit), 148
*Theory and History*, 164
*The Theory of Money and Credit*, 120, 152, 154–55, 163, 185, 196, 226
*The Ultimate Foundation of Economic Science: An Essay on Method*, 164
University of Geneva, professor of International Economic Relations at the Graduate Institute of International Studies, 159
University of Vienna, 143, 159
Vienna Chamber of Commerce, 145
William Volker Fund, 162n
Mises, Margit von, 145n, 155n, 163n–65, 171, 172, 190n,
*My Years with Ludwig von Mises*, 145n, 155n, 163n–65, 172, 190n

Mississippi System, 14, 17
Modigliani, Franco, 177n9
Molina, Luis de, 5, 8
Molinari, Gustave de, 232
Money
  Austrian circle, 146–47
  bimetallism, 25, 42, 49
  counterfeiting autonomy, 237
  debasement, 4, 7
  as demand deposit, 7–8
  inflation favors government, 149
  and marginal utility, 146
  not created by government, 151
  optimal supply of, 50, 149
  and process analysis, 16, 148
  quantity theory of, 6, 49
  regression theorem, 235
  reserves, 7, 8, 49, 152
  scarcity of, 4,
  theory, 7–8, 42, 48–50, 133–34, 146–55
Monopoly, 233–37
Mont Pèlerin Society, 163n, 164, 201n, 203, 207
Morgenstern, Oskar, 159, 184
Moss, Laurence, 2, 11
Müller-Armack, Alfred, 164
Murphy, Antoin E., 15n, 16n, 27
Myrdal, Gunnar, 181

National banks, 25
National Bureau of Economic Research, viii
National Industrial Recovery Administration, 171
Natural law, 3
Natural rights, 66
Nash, George H., 167n, 205
Neumann, Franz, 161
New Deal, 170
Newman, Peter, 103, 112, 122
Newspapers, *See* Journals and Newspapers
Nobel Memorial Prize in Economics (Hayek), 181, 184, 203
Nock, Francis J., 75n, 100

Ohlin, Bertil, 182
O'Driscoll, Gerald P., Jr., 194
O'Mahony, David, 27
Opportunity costs, 20–21, 34, 40, 63, 107
Overbeek, Johannes, 208

Palmer, R.R., 45n, 57
Palyi, Melchior, 177n
Paradox of value, 10
Pareto, 110, 195, 233
  rule, 137
  strictures, 229–30
Patinkin, Don, 151
Peel's Act of 1844, 152
Pennington, James , 7
Perry, Arthur Latham, 81n
Philip II, King of Spain, 4
Philippovich, Eugene von, 144, 154
Physiocracy, 14, 21, 32, 35, 37–39
Pigou, Arthur Cecil, 148
Plant, Arnold, 183, 196
Popescu, Oreste, 5n
Popper, Karl, 159, 165, 189, 190
Population theory and Cantillion, 21
Prendergast, Renee, 19n, 27
Pre-Austrian, 61
Prinsep, C.R., 46
Price
  fixing, 4
  theory, 4, 19–20
Private property, *See* Property
Production
  as demand, 18
  and distribution theory, 35–36, 38, 85, 90, 98
  as pseudo-explanation, 85
  theory of pricing, 4
  time, 35, 110, 115–16, 186
Property, 40, 84, 91, 93

Quantity theory of money, *See* Money
Quesnay, Françiois, 59, 68

Rand, Ayn, 177
Raico, Ralph, 164n
Reaganomics, 237
Reisman, George, 50n, 57, 72, 112, 164n
Rent, 64, 123, 130–33
Ricardo, David, 46, 54, 76, 117, 127, 146, 148, 153
Ricardian, 32, 123, 128
Ricardian Currency School, 152
Ripley, William Z., 139n
Ritenour, Shawn, 205–21
Robbins, Lionel, 101–05, 109–12, 182, 183, 191, 228
Robertson, Dennis Holme, 148, 183, 189n
Rockwell, Llewellyn H., Jr., 76n, 167n, 240–41
  *Man, Economy, and Liberty: Essays in Honor of Murray N Rothbard*, ed., 202
Roll, Eric, 46n, 57
Roosevelt, Franklin D., 239
Roover, Raymond de, 5, 8

Röpke, Wilhelm, 164, 177n, 182, 205–21
*Against the Tide*, 202
background, 205–07
business cycle
credit expansion, 209
malinvestment, 209–10
*Civitas Humana*, 202
*Crises and Cycles*, 209
democracy, problems of, 217
*The Economics of the Free Society*, 209, 212
economists as planners, 212, 218
on Fascism, 207–08
*A Humane Economy*, 202
individual liberty, 218–20
inflation, 210–11
influence, 207, 220
Institute of International Studies in Geneva, 206
*International Economic Disintegration*, 216n
*International Order and Economic Integration*, 215n
international relations, 213, 216–17
Keynes
critique of, 211–12
inflation and repressed inflation, 210–11
mechanistic system, 212
monopoly as government intervention, 214–16
political theory, 216–17
redistribution of wealth, 211–13
*The Social Crisis of Our Time*, 218
social theory, 218–20
welfare, 213–14
*Welfare, Freedom, and Inflation*, 220
Rosenberg, Wilhelm, 161
Rothbard, Murray N., x–xi, 1n, 2n, 3n, 4n, 5n, 8, 11, 13n, 14, 15n, 17, 26n, 27, 29–44, 46, 49, 51n, 52, 53n, 55n, 57, 63, 64, 66, 68, 69, 79n, 89n, 103n, 112, 130n–33, 143–65, 167n, 170, 171n, 176–77, 184, 192n, 194, 200, 215, 223–41
action
choice, 228–29
individuals, 224
mechanistic view unscientific, 224
*America's Great Depression*, 239, 241
Austrian School, vin
background, 240
Center for Libertarian Studies, 240
*Classical Economics*, 239, 241
*Conceived in Liberty*, 239, 241
*Economic Thought Before Adam Smith*, 239, 241
economics
and ethics, 226, 238
ideas, search for true, 225
political activism and, 225–26
as systematic edifice, 224–25
welfare, 226–31
entrepreneur
as discovery, 236
uncertainty, 235–36
*Ethics of Liberty*, 226
*For A New Liberty*, 238, 241
historian, revisionist, 239
homesteading, 229
individualism, 224, 228–29
influence, 239–41
*Journal of Libertarian Studies, 240*
Libertarian Party, 240
liberty, 238
*The Logic of Action*, 241
*Making Economic Sense*, 241
*Man, Economy, and State*, 225, 241
marginal utility
comparison of unscientific, 228
law of diminishing, 227
law of increasing total, 227
ordinal only, 227
methodology
aprioristic, 224
axiomatic-deductive, 224
money, 237–39
counterfeiting autonomy, 237
fiat, 238
regression theorem, 237
Monopoly
antitrust, 234
cartel
calculation problem, 237
size limitation of, 237
competition and, 233
control, lack of, 234
term
as non-operational, 234
as empty and illusory, 236
Pareto strictures, 229–30
*Power and Market*, 225, 241
*The Review of Austrian Economics*, 240
self-ownership, 228
State
citizen as tenants, 231

impossibility of justification, 231
and liberty, 239
limited state as self-contradictory, 232
physical coercion, 230
power, monopoly decisionmaking, 230
property rights diminished, 232
protection
distortion of, 232
private firms, 233
social utility, no action increases, 230
taxation, 232
theory of, 229–33
*What Has Govenment Done to Our Money?*, 237, 241
Rousseau, Jean Jacques, 60
Rudolf, Crown Prince of Austria, 75, 160, 226
Rueff, Jacques, 164, 177n
Russell, Bertrand, 169n, 171n
Russell, Dean, 60n, 62n, 64n, 67n, 69
Ryan, Christopher, 2, 11

Saint-Peravy, Guerineau de, 35, 37
Salas, Juan de, 5
Salerno, Joseph T., 14n, 27, 71–100, 167n, 191–94, 223–24
"Comment on the French Liberal School," 14n, 28
"The Influence of Cantillon's *Essai* on the Methodology of J.B. Say," 14n, 27
"Ludwig von Mises as Social Rationalist," 191n
"Mises and Hayek Dehomogenized," 192n, 194
"The Neglect of the French Liberal School in Anglo-American Economics: A Critique of Received Explanations," 79, 82
Samuelson, Paul, x–xi, 117, 184
*Foundations*, 184
San Bernardino de Siena, 5
Santayana, George, 171n
Saravia de la Calle, Louis, 4, 7, 8
Say, Jean-Baptiste, 10, 14, 45–58, 59, 68, 79, 177n, 233
background, 45–47
British Navigation Acts of, 1581, 1651 and 1660, repeal of, 55
capital
and entrepreneurship, 52–54
and interest theory, 52–54
and saving, 51
Chair of Political Economy
*Conservatoire des Arts et Métiers*, 45
*Collège de France*, 45
*Cours Complet d'Économie Politique Pratique*, 45
editor of *La Décade Philosophique*, 45
entrepreneur, 52–54
influence, 46, 57
interest
return on investment, 53
risk premium, 53–54
and state, 53
time, 53–54
laissez-faire, 56
law of markets, 50–52
*Letters to Mr. Malthus*, 45
market self-regulation, 51
methodology, 47–48
money
any nominal supply as optimal, 50
bimetallism, 49
coins marked as mass of gold or silver, 48
as integral part of rise of modern civilization, 50
quantity theory, 49
reserves, 49
theory, 48–50
Say's Law (of markets)
essential to defense of free markets, 50
declining prices beneficial to society, 52
money ultimately used for purchase of some kind, 51
price of goods and production, 52
rising prices attract additional investment, 51
under/overproduction as maladjustment by some violent means, 51
taxation
absurdity of enriching nation, 56
as unproductive consumption, 56
state and
interference as superfluous, 55
engenders internal abuse and tyranny, 56
time preference, 54
*A Treatise on Political Economy: or the Production, Distribution and Consumption of Wealth*, 45, 46
utility theory, 54–55
value
ability to create, 54
expectations, 54
labor theory of, 54

mutually beneficial, 55
theory, 54–55
zero-sum game, 55
Say's Law (of markets), 38, 50–52, 202
Schäffle, Albert, 113n
Schmoller, Gustav, 75, 139
Schneider, Louis, 75n, 100
Scholastics, 1, 39, 79
*See also* Spanish Scholastics
School of Salamanca, 1
Schumpeter, Joseph, 13–14, 17, 26n, 28, 36n, 43–44, 71, 99, 100–01n, 104, 112–16, 120–22, 190, 192n, 231
Schwartz, George, 201
Sechrest, Larry J., 45–58
Seldon, Arthur, 199
Selgin, George, 201
Senior, Nassau, 46
Sennholz, Hans F., 76n, 100, 114, 121
Sennholz, Mary, 201
Sereny, Gitta, 172
Shackle, George, 183
Sickle, John Van, 161
Smart, William, 105n
Smith, Adam, 10, 15, 22, 36, 46–47, 52, 54, 59, 76, 80n, 94, 127, 136
*Wealth of Nations*, 14, 46–47, 80n
Socialism, xi
*See also* Mises, Hayek
Society of Jesus, *See* Jesuits
Soto, Jesús Huerta de, 1–12
"New Light on the Prehistory of the Theory of Banking and the School of Salamanca," 7, 12
Soule, George, 174
South Sea Bubble, 14, 17
South Sea Company, 26
Sowell, Thomas, 50n, 57
Spanish Scholastics
competition as dynamic concept of rivalry among entrepreneurs, 5
costs of production theory, 5
pre-Austrian, 9
*See also* Mariana, Juan de, 1–12; School of Salamanca; Scholastics
Spann, Othmar, 154, 182
Spatial economics, 23
Spencer, Herbert, 168
Spengler, Joseph J., 21n, 28
Spooner, Lysander, 238
Sraffa, Piero, 184
Stigler, George J., 105n, 112, 184
Stiglitz, Joseph, 188n
Streissler, Erich W., 73n, 75n, 80, 82n, 100
Streissler, Monika, 73n, 75n, 100
Strigl, Richard von, 209
Súilleabháin, Micheál Ó., 17n

Tarascio, Vincent J., 22n, 28
Taussig, Frank W., 163
Taxation
inflation as, 6,
state and, 3, 32, 55–56
state monopolies as, 4
Taylor, Fred, 190
Thompson, Dorothy, 169n
Thornton, Mark, 13–28
Time preference, 9, 40–41, 54, 116, 123–24, 132–33
Tinbergen, Jan, 117
Tooke, Thomas, 8
Tracy, Destutt de, 45n, 59, 68
Trade cycle, *See* Business cycle
Tucker, Benjamin, 238
Tucker, Jeffrey, 13n, 167–79
*Henry Hazlitt: A Giant of Liberty*, comp., 173n, 179
Turgot, A.R.J., 10, 14, 19n, 29–44, 46, 59, 68, 79
action, expectations as key, 35
background, 29–30
business cycle, 41
capital
capitalization, 40
and entrepreneurship, 36–42
and interest theory, 36–42
and saving, 36–42
government bonds unproductive use of savings, 39
Crusoe economics, 33–34
economics as allocation of scarce resources, 33
*Elegy to Gournay*, 30
entrepreneur
particular knowledge, 30–31
theory, 36–42
uncertainty, 37
influence, 42–43
interest
property right of lender, 40
and quantity of money, 41
return on investment, 38
supply and demand, 41
theory, 38–41, 43
time, 38–40

time, 38–40
usury, 39, 40
laissez-faire, 31–32
law of returns, 35–36
*Letter to the Abbé Terray on the Duty of Iron*, 32
marginal utility, 33
money
bimetallism, 42
business cycle, 41
theory, 42
*Observations on a Paper by Saint-Peravy*, 35
opportunity costs, 34, 40
*Paper on Lending at Interest*, 40
physiocrats, 32, 35, 37–39
*Plan for a Paper on Taxation in General*, 32
production/distribution theory, 35–36, 38
*Reflections on the Formation and Distribution of Wealth*, 30, 35
Royal Agricultural Society of Limoges contest, 35
single tax, 32, 35
taxation, 32
time preference, 40–41
two-person exchange, 34
University of Paris, 29
value
and price, 34
paradox, 33
subjective, 33
*Value and Money*, 32, 42
Tyrannicide, 2
Tyrant, 2, 3,
University of Geneva, 159
University of Salamanca, *See* School of Salamanca
University of Vienna, 73, 113, 114, 144, 159, 182
Usury, 39, 40

Value
and costs, 4
and price, 9, 34, 54–55, 76, 80–82, 88–89, 94–100, 108
paradox of, 10, 19, 33, 78, 87–88,
subjective, 4, 33, 62–63, 72, 85–90, 96, 125–27, 130
theory, 85–90, 115–16
as uniform theory, 33, 126
*See also* Costs; Labor
Vanberg, Viktor J., 194
Vaughn, Karen I., vin
Viner, Jacob, 192n
Virgil, 161
Vitoria, Francisco de, 3

Waddell, D.A.G., 28
Wages, 23, 37, 116, 127–32, 136–37
Walker, Amasa, 81n
Walras, Léon, 80n, 115, 126, 149
War of Spanish Succession, 16
Wasson, R. Gordon, 177n
Watrin, Christian, 224
Weber, Max, 160
Wells, H.G., 171n
Wenar, Leif, 185n
Wicksell, Knut, 120, 153, 182, 186
Wicksteed, Philip, 101–12, 172n, 228
background, 101–04
*The Common Sense of Political Economy*, 104, 108
costs, subjectivism of, 106–07
economics, scope of, 108–09
entrepreneur, 107
*An Essay on the Co-ordination of the Laws of Distribution*, 104
opportunity costs, 107
purposefulness of action, 108–09
"The Scope and Method of Political Economy in the Light of the 'Marginal' Theory of Value and Distribution," 104
time, 110
value
marginal, 107
and price, 108
Wieser, Friedrich von, 76, 87n, 101, 105n, 113–14, 120, 123, 127n–28, 154, 182, 190, 192,
*Natural Value*, 113, 128
William Volker Fund, 162n, 184n, 240
Williams, John H., 177n
Wilson, Louis Round, 169n
Wilsonianism, 239
Wittgenstein, Ludwig, 182
Wright, David McCord, 177n

Yagi, Kiichiro, 73n, 74n, 81n, 82n, 83n, 85n, 100
Yeager, Leland B., vin, 10, 177n, 192n, 202, 203, 210n

Zijp, Rudy Van, 192n

# About the Contributors to this Volume

THOMAS J. DILORENZO is professor of economics at Loyola College.

JOHN B. EGGER is professor of economics at Towson State University.

ROGER W. GARRISON is professor of economics at Auburn University.

JEFFREY M. HERBENER is professor of economics and head of the economics program at Grove City College.

RANDALL G. HOLCOMBE is DeVoe Moore professor of economics at Florida State University.

HANS-HERMANN HOPPE is professor of economics at the University of Nevada, Las Vegas and co-editor of *The Quarterly Journal of Austrian Economics*.

ISRAEL M. KIRZNER is professor of economics at New York University.

PETER G. KLEIN is associate professor of economics at the University of Georgia.

SHAWN RITENOUR is Roderique assistant professor of economics at Southwest Missouri Baptist University.

MURRAY N. ROTHBARD (1921–1995), dean of the Austrian School, was the S.J. Hall distinguished professor of economics at the University of Nevada, Las Vegas, and academic vice president of the Ludwig von Mises Institute.

JOSEPH T. SALERNO is professor of economics at Pace University and co-editor of *The Quarterly Journal of Austrian Economics*.

LARRY J. SECHREST is professor of economics at Sul Ross University.

JESÚS HUERTA DE SOTO is Titular professor of economics at the Complutense University of Madrid.

MARK THORNTON holder of the O.P. Alford III chair at the Mises Institute, is associate professor of economics at Columbus State University.

JEFFREY TUCKER is research director of the Ludwig von Mises Institute.